The Law of Vibration

The Revelation of
William D. Gann

T0322952

Tony Plummer

HARRIMAN HOUSE LTD

3A Penns Road
Petersfield
Hampshire
GU32 2EW
GREAT BRITAIN

Tel: +44 (0)1730 233870
Email: enquiries@harriman-house.com
Website: www.harriman-house.com

First edition published in Great Britain in 2013

978-0-85719-259-2

British Library Cataloguing in Publication Data

A CIP catalogue record for this book can be obtained from the British Library.

Printed in the UK by Lightning Source.

 Harriman House

*For the global community of
independently-minded technical
analysts and economists*

Contents

About the author

Tony Plummer is the director of Helmsman Economics Ltd. He is a former director of Hambros Bank Ltd, of Hambros Fund Management PLC, and of Rhombus Research Ltd. He is a Fellow of the Society of Technical Analysts in the UK and was, until November 2011, a Visiting Professorial Fellow in the Department of Economics at Queen Mary, University of London. He is the author of *Forecasting Financial Markets*, which describes the influence of crowd psychology on economic activity and financial market price behaviour.

Tony has worked and traded in financial markets since 1976, concentrating primarily on bonds and currencies. He now specialises in long-term economic and financial market analysis, and writes and lectures on group behaviour and trading competencies.

He has a Masters degree in economics from the London School of Economics and an Honours degree in economics from the University of Kent. He has had four years of training in Core Process Psychotherapy and is a qualified NLP practitioner.

Acknowledgements

My thanks go very specifically to: first, my wife Glenys who has made so much possible; second, my former Executive Director and mentor at Hambros Bank Ltd, David Tapper, without whom my deep interest in financial markets would never have been catalysed; and, third, my clients at Helmsman Economics Ltd, whose desire to stay one step ahead of the consensus has persistently energised my research into the patterns of collective human behaviour.

Preface

I have for many years been fascinated by the *hidden* aspects of Nature: by the order underlying the apparent chaos; by the limited set of mathematical ratios that appear to reflect that order; and by our personal involvement in that order. It is my strong belief that individual decisions are almost always contaminated by collective beliefs and shared moods, and that therefore we have far less control over our affairs than is supposed. The result, however, is a form of systemic coherence that is not yet accepted by conventional economic theory.

This book is about a critical aspect of this systemic coherence. It is about a very distinctive pattern that emerges in the presence of natural cyclical behaviour. Astonishingly, the pattern was hidden almost 2000 years ago in a small piece of text in the Greek version of the Christian Gospel of St. Matthew. The pattern was unearthed, and then buried again, by the famous financial market speculator William D. Gann. And the same pattern was alluded to, but also hidden, by the great mindfulness exponent George I. Gurdjieff. The lineage of the cycle pattern suggests that it represents a genuine revelation. It has taken me more than 20 years to unravel the code that has hidden this revelation, and I feel very privileged to have been able to do it.

This book, then, is about a *law of vibration* that is alleged to permeate the cosmos. There is strong evidence that this law influences financial market fluctuations and economic cycles. But the exciting possibility is that signs of the law of vibration can be found in a whole range of research disciplines – from cosmology at one end to quantum physics at the other. It may be that William Gann was an important link in a chain of transmission that – at a minimum – can be dated back almost two millennia.

Introduction

THE ROLE OF SHOCKS

It is a great truth that real change only ever comes out of crisis. This is the way of evolution, which impacts all living organisms, at all levels of being and understanding. A new item of information – a shock – sends fluctuations deep into a system and the subsequent feedback becomes increasingly destabilising until the system flips into a different state. Unfortunately, the crisis is inevitably painful for all concerned. This is the path of change that involves such diverse events as wars, revolutions, stock market crashes, mental breakdowns and physical diseases.

In my opinion, the 2008 financial panic and subsequent recession was just such a shock. It will undoubtedly lead to changes – both to the economy and in our understandings about how it operates – for some years to come. We could just let it all happen, and come out at the other end much older and a little wiser, but a more productive approach would be to try to understand the real causes of the problem and then adjust ourselves as quickly as possible. In that way, we might be slightly less vulnerable to what Shakespeare called "outrageous fortune".[1]

THE CHALLENGE TO ECONOMIC THEORY

As a start, it is worth considering why economic theory was not able to anticipate the events of the last few years – that is, the explosion and collapse in various asset prices, and the associated economic boom and bust. A large part of the answer can be found in three areas of debate:

1. The supposedly simplifying assumptions that are used in theoretical analysis;

2. The re-balancing mechanisms that are thought to operate in an economy; and

3. The effectiveness or otherwise of government in influencing those mechanisms.

---

[1] William Shakespeare, *Hamlet*, Act 3, Scene 1.

When we make decisions, we have to take account of the fact that the future may not turn out as we expect. The starting point for economics, therefore, is to consider exactly how uncertain that future is. The so-called Keynesian (i.e. fiscalist, and usually socialist) view is that the future is so uncertain – and people so naturally cautious – that the economy will not spontaneously gravitate towards full employment equilibrium.[2] In addition, it is believed that the economy is likely to over-respond to negative exogenous shocks.

The neo-classical (i.e. monetarist, and usually conservative) view is that risk can be quantified in terms of probabilities and therefore priced by the relevant market.[3] Providing that markets are efficient, information is perfect and participants adhere to rational expectations, the economy will therefore be drawn towards its *natural* rate of unemployment. Quite obviously, a believer in Keynesian subjective uncertainty will conclude that government intervention is essential, while a believer in neo-classical objective risk will want government intrusion to be minimal.

SIMPLIFYING ASSUMPTIONS

So who's right? Unfortunately, as the situation stands, the answer is neither. And it is not just a question of whether the cynical Keynesian assumption about people's ability to deal with the future is more sensible than the unrealistic and unattainable neo-classical one. The fundamental flaw in both arguments is the presumption that people *normally* make their decisions independently of one another. They do not. Neuroscience confirms that we are Janus-faced: we are self-assertive, but we also integrate into larger wholes.[4]

First, we depend on the observed behaviour of others to provide information that we cannot access directly ourselves.[5] This modulates, and then offsets, the subjective uncertainty of Keynesian economics. Second, we absorb, and are stimulated by, the beliefs and emotions generated by others. This neutralises, and then destabilises, the objective risk presumed by neo-classical economists. Dependence on others' behaviour still allows *rational* individual decisions, but

[2] Robert Skidelsky, 'The Relevance of Keynes', *Cambridge Journal of Economics* (January 2011) and John M. Keynes, 'The General Theory of Employment', *Quarterly Journal of Economics* (February 1937).

[3] John F. Muth, 'Rational Expectations and the Theory of Price Movements', *Econometrica* (July 1961) and Robert Lucas, *Models of Business Cycles* (Basil Blackwell, Oxford, 1987).

[4] See, for example, Alexander Easton (Ed.) and Nathan Emery (Ed.), *The Cognitive Neuroscience of Social Behaviour* (Psychology Press, London, 2005).

[5] The idea of information *cascading* through a crowd, as a result of individuals responding to local perturbations in conditions, has become well established in Behavioural Finance. The missing element, however, is a clear recognition (and acceptance) that human beings are programmed – like animals in herds – to take note of the behaviour of others. No individual has all the information necessary for his/her survival. Research by John Dyer has found that it takes only 5% of people to have a decisive influence on the direction that a crowd of people would take; the rest simply follow. See John Dyer, et al, 'Consensus decision making in human crowds', *Animal Behaviour* 75:2 (February 2008).

the absorption of others' beliefs and moods means that these decisions are nevertheless formed within a *non-rational* environment.

It follows from this that government spending can be a powerful influence on individual decisions and on collective beliefs. However, this is not the same as saying that government is truly an independent agency – let alone a gifted one. The weakness in interventionist policies is that policy-makers themselves are affected by the general mood. This has been all too apparent in recent years where politicians have tried to buy votes by increasing spending during boom conditions *because it can be afforded*, only to find themselves having to raise taxes during difficult times *to share the burden*. The point is that, unless government intervention is genuinely contra-cyclical, the feedback between government activity and collective psychology can be profoundly de-stabilising. Government activity is a source of potential risk within the economic system.

ENERGY GAPS AND REBALANCING MECHANISMS

The 2008 financial implosion and the associated economic recession arose from the *correlated* decisions of people whose mood was influenced by rapidly-rising government spending and lax credit policies. It was a reaction to excesses and was not caused by a random, externally-generated, shock. The downswing was, in fact, an *energy gap* within the economic system and, as such, it reversed that system's polarity from growth to contraction.

I have dealt with this phenomenon in detail elsewhere,[6] but the purpose of such a gap is to initiate a process that will cleanse the system of excesses. Once the process starts, it will continue until it is naturally complete. Of course, since economic theory does not properly recognise the influence of collective behaviour, nor recognise the adjustment mechanisms created by system excesses, it cannot define the originating causes or suggest the appropriate solutions (if, indeed, there are any). And, since economic policy decisions are dependent on economic theory, the political result is disbelief, confusion and helplessness.

This sorry state of affairs exists despite the vast sums of private and public money that are devoted to research and teaching in the field of economics. New ideas obviously need to be recognised and adopted so that our understanding of reality can evolve. In my opinion, one essential change will be to include the concept of collective behaviour, not just as an occasional blemish on the otherwise smooth functioning of a rational system, but as a constant influence. And, fortunately, there are signs that the process of reconsideration and revision has started.[7]

---

[6] Tony Plummer, *Forecasting Financial Markets (6th Ed.)* (Kogan Page, London, 2010).
[7] See, for example, George A. Akerlof and Robert J. Shiller, *Animal Spirits: How Human Psychology Drives the Economy, and Why it Matters for Global Capitalism* (Princeton University Press, 2009).

AN ALTERNATIVE VIEW

Nevertheless, it is not certain that making alterations – however necessary – to the general equilibrium models of economic theory will actually make it any easier to deal with oscillations in economic activity. The primary reason is that such changes are unlikely to address the automatic presumption that economic and financial oscillations are the result either of people making poor decisions or of unforeseen shocks. So, almost by definition, it is assumed that the resulting perturbations are *errors* in the system, which can only be identified and dealt with after they have materialised.

But what if such assumptions were incorrect? What if fluctuations in economic activity and financial market prices were essentially a *non*-random consequence of collective behaviour? And what if a significant part of such fluctuations could, in fact, be anticipated?

The purpose of this book is to demonstrate that this alternative view was fundamental to the success of one of the greatest stock market traders of all time – William D. Gann. He believed – and traded upon – the idea that collective human behaviour exhibits a specific recurring pattern that unfolds through time. If Mr. Gann's financial success is a yardstick for genuine wisdom, then economic theory still has a significant paradigm shift to negotiate.

There are three aspects to the idea of non-random collective behaviour that need to be registered straightaway. First, it implies that there are forces at work about which we have very little conception and over which we (therefore) have very little control. Second, it implies that collective behaviour is not only non-random but is the outer signature of an inner system process that actively organises the behaviour of participating individuals.[8] And third, it implies that when individuals lose themselves to group behaviour – i.e. let their psychic structure be invaded and overrun by group demands[9] – their energies are in a sense sacrificed to group purposes. This deeply disturbing notion helps to explain the madness of financial market crowds, the blindness of religious and nationalist fervour, and the destructive power of a rioting mob.

The main point is that the phenomenon of collective behaviour involves two specific forces: directing people's energies towards objectives other than their own; and placing limitations on people's willingness to use their energies for alternative, non-group, purposes. The result, in effect, is an organism with its own simplistic psychological process. Moreover, this organism is characterised by energy fluctuations that are both rhythmic and patterned.

---

[8] Tony Plummer, *Forecasting Financial Markets*.
[9] Erich Neumann, *Depth Psychology and a New Ethic* (Shambhala, Boston (Ma.), 1990).

OLD AND ANCIENT TEXTS

Mr. Gann was quite explicit in claiming that the foundation of his knowledge was a small piece of text in one of the Christian Gospels.[10] The text had been written by St. Matthew (or by individuals who wrote under that name) and gave great significance to "the sign of the prophet Jonas". It seems that Mr. Gann had deduced that *the sign* was a reference to a universal law relating to cycles. My early inference was that, if Mr Gann's claims were in any sense correct, then some form of *gematria* was likely to be involved. Gematria is the technique of allocating numbers to letters in a text in order to convey extra information, and it was widely used by writers of ancient scripture to transmit esoteric understandings. This, in turn, suggested that the appropriate text to be used in St. Matthew's case was the original Greek version.

This turned out to be the case and, by mid-1990s, I had found some extraordinary geometric figures hidden within St. Matthew's text. However, Mr. Gann's central claim – that "the sign of the prophet Jonas" specifically provided a revelation about cycles – continued to elude me. Then, in late 2011, I chanced upon a research thesis by Sophia Wellbeloved referencing the struggle by the celebrated mindfulness exponent George I. Gurdjieff to produce a series of books that would preserve his teachings.[11] It alerted me to the possibility that St. Matthew's text may have incorporated a transmission methodology that extended beyond gematria. And this, amazingly, also turned out to be the case.

The results are literally *extra*-ordinary. They will be analysed in some detail in the following chapters in terms of the common themes and transmission techniques incorporated into three texts: W.D. Gann's *The Tunnel Thru The Air* (hereafter *Tunnel*),[12] G.I. Gurdjieff's *Beelzebub's Tales to His Grandson* (hereafter *Beelzebub's Tales*),[13] and St. Matthew's Gospel.[14]

William Delbert Gann died in 1955. He left behind a thought-provoking combination of very little money in his estate and a reputation of being one of the greatest stock market traders of all time. George Ivanovitch Gurdjieff died in 1949. He left behind a reputation for being exploitative and difficult to be with, but also a unique set of complex and deeply spiritual teachings that have the power to change people's lives for the better. St. Matthew probably died in the first century AD. Very little is known about him, but he left behind a record of the teachings of a man called Joshua ben Joseph, who is now referred to as Jesus. Those teachings had a profound effect on the course of history.

---

[10] William D. Gann, *The Tunnel Thru The Air* (Financial Guardian Publishing, New York, 1927).
[11] Sophia Wellbeloved, *Gurdjieff, Astrology & Beelzebub's Tales* (Abintra Books, Aurora (Or.), 2002).
[12] Gann, *Tunnel*.
[13] George I. Gurdjieff, *All and Everything: An Objectively Impartial Criticism of the Life of Man, or Beelzebub's Tales to His Grandson* (Routledge & Kegan Paul, London, 1950).
[14] Kurt Aland et al., *Greek-English New Testament* (Deutsche Bibelgesellschaft, Stuttgart, 1981).

The thread that links each of these writers in the context of this book is that they included secret/sacred geometries within the structure of their original written works.[15] These hidden geometries point to a fundamental pattern of vibration that is alleged to pervade the cosmos and that interacts with humanity on a personal and collective level. Mr. Gann called this pattern the "law of vibration".

The pattern is said to emerge as a result of discontinuities in the perpetual processes of expansion and contraction within the cosmos. According to Mr. Gurdjieff, the discontinuities are a function of the *Law of Seven*, and the forces of expansion and contraction are a function of the *Law of Three*. Amazingly, and compellingly, the writings of St. Matthew confirm that the pattern was known about almost 2000 years ago.

---

[15] It cannot be emphasised enough that, once the original texts have been revised and/or translated, the hidden information becomes inaccessible.

CHAPTER 1

THE ENIGMA OF
WILLIAM D. GANN

"'The Tunnel Thru The Air' is mysterious and contains a valuable secret, clothed in a veiled language."

W. D. Gann

A SECRET TRADING METHODOLOGY

William D. Gann was – by reputation – one of the most successful commodity and stock traders who ever lived. He operated in the United States during the early part of the twentieth century, was able to forecast the 1929 Wall Street Crash,[1] and is reputed to have amassed tens of millions of dollars through short-term speculation.[2] He is also reputed to have had access to a unique trading methodology whose central feature was a secret. He died in 1955, leaving behind a great deal of confusion as to whether or not he had actually revealed this secret.

It is known – partly through Mr. Gann's own admission – that the secret belonged to a hidden order of understanding.[3] This fact, more than anything else, has hampered open-minded research into his techniques: either his work has been associated with an irreligious view of the world or it has been regarded as being non-scientific hocus-pocus.

---

[1] William D. Gann, *Supply and Demand Letter: 1929 Annual Stock Forecast* (W. D. Gann Scientific Service Inc, New York, 23 November 1928).
[2] This was at a time when the average annual wage of a non-farm worker was about $1,500. See Stanley Lebergott, 'Wages and Working Conditions', *The Concise Encyclopedia of Economics* (Library of Economics and Liberty, Indianapolis (In.), 1993).
[3] Gann, *Tunnel*.

More recently, however, with the questioning of conventional religious beliefs, and with the growing realisation that the accuracy of scientific research is dependent on the contextual assumptions that are being used, an increasing number of people have been prepared to look more closely at Mr. Gann's ideas. This has probably been particularly easy for financial market traders insofar as the primary test for truth is profitability rather than religious or scientific nicety.

To date, the most important line of research has been in the area of astrology. Mr. Gann is known to have been particularly interested in the relationship between planetary alignments and human psychology,[4] and researchers have – with some justification – followed his lead. The findings need to be taken seriously because they confirm that correlations do exist between price movements and the positions of the planets.[5] More broadly, there is a growing body of evidence that correlations exist between mass human psychology and extra-terrestrial cycles.[6]

Nevertheless, astrology was not the only element of Mr. Gann's trading rules. A given astrological aspect might constitute a potential turning point, but there is always a degree of uncertainty as to whether a price reversal will actually occur; and uncertainty does not appear to be one of Mr. Gann's characteristics. He undoubtedly had access to other techniques that supplemented (or even supplanted) his astrological findings.

THE LAW OF VIBRATION

As anyone who has had contact with his work will know, the dominant (and unusual) feature of Mr. Gann's ideas was the use of mathematics and geometry. What is not clear from the available literature, however, is the actual source of (or originating authority for) these particular analytical tools. In his early years of trading, Mr. Gann was quite clear in stating that he had access to special knowledge. In 1909, he had indicated that he knew a secret law of vibration.[7] In 1927, he further emphasised the point that there was a "hidden secret" that others could learn.[8]

Moreover, there was a degree of commitment to his research on the law of vibration that suggests that it wasn't just a loosely conceptualised idea. In 1909, Mr. Gann maintained that he had spent ten years doing exhaustive research, including "nine months, working night and day in the Astor Library of New

---

[4] *Ibid.*
[5] In this context, mention needs to be made of the exceptional work done by Bradley F. Cowan. See, for example, his *Pentagonal Time Cycle Theory* (Private publication, USA, 2009).
[6] See especially Richard Tarnas, *Cosmos and Psyche: Intimations of a New World View* (Plume, New York, 2007).
[7] Interview with William D. Gann, *The Ticker and Investment Digest* 5:2 (December 1909).
[8] Gann, *Tunnel.*

York and in the British Museum of London".[9] Since Mr. Gann was born in 1878, this means that he started his research no later than the age of 21. Furthermore, a journey to London in the early 1900s would have been both time consuming and expensive.

Given his persistent reference to his knowledge as being *secret*, it seems probable that Mr. Gann had access to an understanding about the nature of life that was different to the understandings held by the contemporaneous religious and scientific communities.[10] If this is correct, it does not take a significant leap of imagination to suppose that the knowledge was genuinely esoteric and that Mr. Gann was using the ancient science of sacred geometry. This is certainly consistent with the reverential attitude to spiritual matters that he openly expressed in his 1950 book, *The Magic Word*.[11] Even so, there is an important point about this that is almost always missed. This is that sacred geometry cannot be applied to a mundane data series without a prior knowledge of the energetic forces that are driving that series. The analyst has to know what he or she is looking for. In other words, there is still something missing from extant knowledge about Mr. Gann's techniques.

It is, therefore, very relevant that two elements are missing from what we know about Mr. Gann's knowledge. First, no one has yet revealed, or been able to explain with any precision, how Mr. Gann's law of vibration is supposed to operate in financial markets. Second, as far as I know, nowhere does Mr. Gann explicitly mention the Golden Measure[12] or its related number series, the Fibonacci Sequence.[13] These omissions seem to me to be more significant than Mr. Gann's commission of geometry (and astrology). As this book will argue, not only do the law of vibration and the Golden Measure co-arise in all natural phenomena, but both were important parts of Mr. Gann's understandings about financial market behaviour. Indeed, he preserved them in a hidden form in his strange 1927 novel, *Tunnel*.[14]

THE TUNNEL THRU THE AIR

As anyone who has tried to read *Tunnel* will attest, it is hardly a work of literary genius in the conventional sense of the word. Indeed, the word *dreadful* would

---

[9] *The Ticker and Investment Digest* (December 1909).
[10] Gann, *Tunnel*. In the story, Robert Gordon – Mr. Gann's alter ego – says that "The general public is not yet ready for it (i.e. the secret) and probably would not understand or believe it if I explained it."
[11] William D. Gann, *The Magic Word* (Library of Gann Publishing Co, Pomeroy (Wa.), 1950).
[12] The late Robert Krausz mentioned this in a lecture that he gave at a Computrac conference in 1992. The Golden Measure is a number (0.618), a ratio (0.618:1) and a continuous proportion between three numbers (0.382, 0.618, and 1). See Chapters 2 and 3.
[13] The Fibonacci Sequence is the number series 0, 1, 1, 1, 2, 3, 5, 8, 13, 21, 34, 55,... etc. where the ratio of each number divided by its successor tends towards the Golden Ratio, 0.618:1.
[14] Gann, *Tunnel*.

be a very charitable appellation. Mr. Gann's injunction is to read the book three times: firstly, as an ordinary novel; secondly, to discern some of the hidden meanings; and thirdly, to find the hidden secret.[15] In other words, the reader has to look within the text for something far more important than the book's improbable love and war story.[16]

Throughout most of the book, Mr Gann uses the unusual device of having the relationship between the hero, Robert Gordon, and his future wife, Marie Stanton, conducted by the continuous exchange of letters. He also includes – sometimes within letters, but often separately – extensive quotations from the Bible, and a number of poems. The first point is that the procedure, in effect, pads out the story. More specifically, the addition of unnecessary material to a chapter can be used as a device to control the number of pages in that chapter. As we shall see, this turns out to be very important.

Second, the interchange of letters themselves may be taken as a metaphor for the oscillation between the generative and receptive polarities within Nature. This interpretation is strengthened by the regular intervention in the exchange of letters by a third party – namely, Mr. Walter Kennelworth. Technically, a *third force* is always necessary to balance and direct the exchange between the active (male) and passive (female) polarities. Indeed, Mr. Gann allows Robert Gordon to state that "In every law of nature there is… a positive, a negative and a neutral".[17]

The three forces, taken together, constitute an ancient spiritual law, called the *Law of Three*.

The Law of Three

The traditional symbol for the *Law of Three* was either an equilateral or isosceles triangle[18] and the traditional mathematical representation of the law was the Golden Ratio, 0.618:1 or 0.382:0.618. It is therefore relevant that the original dust jacket of *Tunnel* contains at least three references to the *Law of Three*. The first reference is a tiny equilateral triangle just inside the lower margin (which contains the infrastructure of a city). The second is an isosceles triangle on the top of a spire that projects itself out of that lower margin. The important point is that the positions of both triangles in relation to the width of the book are then defined by the Golden Ratio: the distance from the left-hand side of the book is 38.2% of the width of the book for the equilateral triangle and 61.8%

---

[15] *Ibid.*

[16] It is not my intention to provide a comprehensive analysis of *The Tunnel Thru The Air* – mainly because, for the purposes of this book, it is not necessary to do so. Nevertheless, this should not be taken to mean that all Mr. Gann's secrets are described in what follows.

[17] Gann, *Tunnel*. It is the reference to a *neutral* force that establishes Mr. Gann's credibility. The existence of this force was largely unknown at the time that Mr. Gann was writing *Tunnel*.

[18] An equilateral triangle has three sides of equal length. An isosceles triangle has two sides of equal length.

for the isosceles triangle; and the distance from the right-hand side of the book is 61.8% of the width of the book for the equilateral triangle and 38.2% for the isosceles triangle. Moreover, the measurements are exact. See Figure 1-1.

The third reference to the *Law of Three* is easy to miss. The author's name is centred under the title of the book, but the title itself is offset from centre. This is also shown in Figure 1-1. The consequence is that the trailing edge of the first letter of the author's name is located precisely over the equilateral triangle in the lower margin. Hence, the distance from the left-hand side of the book to the start of the author's name is 38.2% of the width of the book, and the author's name, W. D. Gann, is then contained within the remaining 61.8% of the width of the book.[19]

These three oblique references to the *Law of Three* are unlikely to have been an accident. Indeed, once a reader starts looking at *Tunnel* with the prior knowledge that it contains evidence of the *Law of Three*, it becomes increasingly obvious that the whole book was carefully designed to resonate with it. Each page is 4-7/8 inches wide and 7-3/16 inches high. The ratio between the two measurements approximates 0.666:1 which – as we shall see – is closely linked to the Biblical presentation of the Golden Ratio.

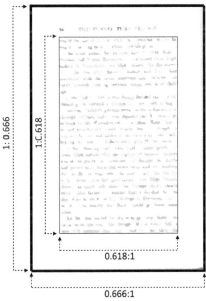

FIGURE 1-1: SCHEMATICS OF MR. GANN'S ORIGINAL BOOK JACKET AND PAGE LAYOUT

---

[19] The references on the dust jacket to the Golden Ratio have, of course, been lost in subsequent redesigned editions of *Tunnel*.

Meanwhile, the text on each page is presented in an area that measures 3-5/16 inches across and 5-3/8 inches down. The ratio of the width to the height is therefore 0.618:1. Each page, therefore, consists of a 0.666 x 1 *biblical* rectangle containing a 0.618 x 1 'Golden' Rectangle.[20] Again, see Figure 1-1.

The *Law of Three* will be analysed in more detail in Chapter 3. It is, however, only one element of the information that was hidden in *Tunnel*. Mr. Gann allows Robert Gordon to speak of an immutable "law of vibration", which is mathematically precise and which repeats itself as a series of cycles within cycles.

Gordon is also shown to be critically aware of the importance of the number 7. The climax of activity in *Tunnel*, for example, is called "Robert Gordon's Seven Days" where Gordon puts people to sleep for seven days and, during that time, destroys those of their buildings that are associated with religion, government, and business. He starts the task at 07.00 hrs on the 21st (3 x 7) day of the 7th month (July), and returns 7 days later.[21]

This placement of the number 7 in the context of cyclical time references a second ancient spiritual law, called the *Law of Seven*.

The Law of Seven

The *Law of Seven* **is** the law of vibration. It defines the *pattern* of rhythmic time cycles and identifies the *critical points* in these cycles where evolutionary change can occur. At its simplest level, the *Law of Seven* is inherent in, and defined by, the conventional Tonic Sol-Fa musical scale.[22] In its more complex form, the Law describes the patterns of oscillation in collective human behaviour. The *Law of Seven* will be analysed in more detail in Chapter 7.

The central proposal contained in *Tunnel*, therefore, is that economic activity and financial market speculation are both driven by two great cosmic laws: the *Law of Three* and the *Law of Seven*. The laws have a long history but, by tradition, knowledge about them has only been transmitted orally – and then only in the context of psycho-spiritual development. So how did Mr. Gann know about their existence, possibly even as early as 1898? In *Tunnel*, Mr. Gann (in the guise of Robert Gordon) states that he has "gained a great deal of knowledge by following the Bible".[23] This suggests that the two laws (or something very similar) are somehow hidden within the Bible.

---

[20] Artists have long known that the average person finds the Golden Rectangle attractive. See, for example, Mario Livio, *The Golden Ratio* (Review, London, 2002).

[21] "Robert Gordon's Seven Days" is the title of Chapter 39 (written XXXIX). Chapter 39 nevertheless lies between Chapters 33 and 35. This is unlikely to have been an accident, although its meaning is unclear. First, it may be an echo of, or an acknowledgement of, an earlier reference in *Tunnel* to Ezekiel, Chapter 39, which references a burning of the weapons of war over a period of seven years. This correlates with Robert Gordon's destruction of various cities in seven days. Second, it may be an allusion to a relationship between verse 39 in St. Matthew's Gospel and the *Law of Seven*. Verse 39 is the starting point for a series of calculations that reveals the presence of the *Law of Seven*.

[22] It has, therefore, also been referred to as the "Law of Octaves".

[23] Gann, *Tunnel*.

BIBLE SECRETS

It is an important fact that the Bible – like all ancient, and genuinely sacred, scripture – has two dimensions: the *exoteric* dimension, which deals primarily with external laws; and an *esoteric* (secret/sacred) dimension, which deals with inner (spiritual) laws. The latter dimension can only be accessed under the right circumstances – not the least of which is that it is accepted as existing in the first place. It follows, therefore, that if Mr. Gann was able to unlock the Bible's innermost secrets then he must also have had access to the necessary keys.

Unfortunately, and until relatively recently, Christian authorities have tended to deny the existence of an esoteric dimension to the Bible. Consequently, many practising Christians have viewed the assertion of its existence as being in some way *evil*, because it was occult. This point would not have been lost on Mr. Gann, and would undoubtedly have contributed to his circumspection in revealing the details of his knowledge. We shall be dealing with one of the relevant insights in Chapters 2 and 3. In the meantime, what is the proof that Mr. Gann had the necessary keys to access the hidden inner dimensions of the Bible?

In *Tunnel*, Mr. Gann refers directly to "the sign of the prophet Jonas", which is the subject of Chapter 12 of St. Matthew's Gospel.[24] Robert Gordon is made to say that "I believe that a man who understands the meaning of that [sign] has all the power under heaven and earth… I believe that that is the key to the interpretation of the future. I am sure I have found it and know how to apply it."

The analysis of St. Matthew's text is complicated and requires a prior knowledge of the ancient science of numbers. Nevertheless, once the correct tools are applied, the text reveals the presence of very meaningful mathematical and geometrical constructs. As Mr. Gann claimed, these do indeed include direct references to a law of vibration. We shall explore St Matthew's text in Chapters 4 and 5, and then look at some of the implications in Chapter 12.[25]

The anomaly in terms of Mr. Gann's claims, however, is that "the sign of the prophet" itself does not reveal either how the laws actually work or how they should be applied. In other words, it is still necessary to know about the existence – and operation – of the *Law of Three* and the *Law of Seven* prior to interpreting St. Matthew's text. It is thus difficult to get away from the conclusion that the Bible may not have been the only source of Mr. Gann's insights. He almost certainly obtained the initial knowledge from somewhere else.

---

[24] St. Matthew: Chapter 12, verses 38-40: "Then certain of the scribes and Pharisees answered, saying, Master, we would see a sign from thee. But he answered and said unto them: "An evil and adulterous generation seeketh after a sign; and there shall no sign be given it, but the sign of the prophet Jonas: For as Jonas was three days and nights in the whale's belly; so shall the Son of man be three days and three nights in the heart of the earth."

[25] Some of its implications remain beyond the understanding of this author.

BEELZEBUB'S TALES

It is a fact that *Tunnel* has some remarkable parallels with a book, written by George Ivanovitch Gurdjieff, entitled *All and Everything: An Objectively Impartial Criticism of the Life of Man*, or *Beelzebub's Tales to His Grandson* (hereafter, *Beelzebub's Tales*).[26] This book is an allegorical novel that claims to contain a body of sacred knowledge concerning the laws of the universe. The book is difficult to read because its structure and language were carefully designed to avoid loose interpretation. It has, in effect, to be translated.[27] But one of the important disclosures contained in the book is the existence of the Law of Three and the Law of Seven.

The differences in content between *Tunnel* and *Beelzebub's Tales* could not – literally! – be greater. Nevertheless, there are some significant parallels between the two books. Mr. Gann and Mr. Gurdjieff both claim that their books contain secrets that can only be accessed if they are read three times. Both authors indicate that the first reading is essentially an ordinary process; both indicate that the second reading should be approached as part of a learning process; and both maintain that the secret will start to become apparent on the third reading. Of course, the fact that both authors suggest that their book be read three times may just be a coincidence, based on the desire to transmit the idea that the number 3 itself is important.

What will also become apparent is that *Tunnel* and *Beelzebub's Tales* both use the same, very specific, technique to hide the particular pattern that is intrinsic to the law of vibration/*Law of Seven* within their books. Once the code has been broken, both books reveal the same pattern. Furthermore – and as a most amazing confirmation – the pattern is the same as that contained within "the sign of the prophet Jonas".[28]

A COMMON SOURCE

Although these parallels suggest that Mr. Gann may have obtained his knowledge from Mr. Gurdjieff, such contact seems unlikely. Mr. Gann claimed that he knew about a law of vibration in 1909. At that stage, Mr. Gurdjieff (who was only about five years older than Mr. Gann) was living in Eastern Europe and had not even made a known public appearance.[29] Moreover, although Mr.

---

[26] Gurdjieff, *Beelzebub's Tales*.

[27] The earliest and most complete summary of Mr. Gurdjieff's work, written in an understandable form, is contained in Pyotr D. Ouspensky, *In Search of the Miraculous: Fragments of an Unknown Teaching* (Harcourt, Brace & World, New York, 1949).

[28] There are other parallels that are worth noting. Both books contain references to astrology – *Tunnel* explicitly and *Beelzebub's Tales* implicitly. Both books use Roman numerals for chapter headings.

[29] Colin Wilson, *G. I. Gurdjieff: The War Against Sleep* (The Aquarian Press, Wellingborough, 1986).

Gurdjieff started to write *Beelzebub's Tales* in late 1924, it was not available to the general public until 1950. Mr. Gann published *Tunnel* in 1927, so he could not have read Mr. Gurdjieff's finished book.[30]

This is by no means conclusive, but it does raise the possibility of the existence of another – common – originating source, which would have pre-dated both men. Mr. Gann was a highly-placed Freemason, which may have given him access to information that was not otherwise generally available[31] and Mr. Gurdjieff was always quite clear that he had obtained his knowledge from elsewhere.[32]

The truth is that we'll probably never know precisely where the information came from, how Mr. Gann obtained it, or why he ended up hiding it. But there is no question that Mr. Gann and Mr. Gurdjieff were somehow on a parallel path, and that their respective insights about the functioning of a law of vibration emerged almost simultaneously.

More tellingly, both men chose to bury a particular aspect of their insights, either as a challenge to their students or for future use. *Tunnel* and *Beelzebub's Tales* both use the same specific method of transmitting vital information; both hid the same particular pattern relating to natural cycles; and both accepted the existence of cosmic laws that, in the 1920s, would have been regarded with suspicion. The coincidences are far too meaningful to be totally ignored.

So, what are these *cosmic laws*, and how are they hidden in the Bible?

---

[30] There are other points of potential contact. It is quite possible, for example, that Mr. Gann knew about Mr. Gurdjieff's teachings, and was attracted to them because of his interest in the law of vibration. There were lectures – given by Alfred Orage and other high calibre followers of Mr. Gurdjieff – both in New York and London in the early 1920s. Indeed, Mr Gurdjieff himself was in New York in 1924 and 1925-26. In addition, draft copies of what eventually became the final text of *Beelzebub's Tales* were also circulated amongst students for instruction and for comment. Further, Mr. Gann's 1909 version of the law may not have been the same as the one that he subsequently hid in *Tunnel*. The 1909 version of the law of vibration is described by him in very mechanistic terms. He argues that "the law of vibration is the fundamental law upon which wireless telegraphy, wireless telephone and photographs are based." *The Ticker and Investment Digest* (December 1909). This indicates a focus on *periodic* fluctuations rather than the variable *pattern* of fluctuations in living systems. At the time, periodic fluctuations were not thought to be applicable to stocks and commodities.

[31] Mr. Gann was a 32nd Degree Freemason of the Scottish Rite Order and it is highly likely that this gave him access to material that was considered to be secret. See David Keller (Ed.), *Breakthroughs in Technical Analysis* (Bloomberg Press, New York, 2007). Mr. Gann's contention that the Bible was the source of his knowledge could therefore have been a defence against any criticism that he had broken his vows of secrecy. It is also possible that Mr. Gann received the ideas relating to the law of vibration by accessing alternative states of consciousness. Mr. Gann's unusual book *The Magic Word* contains instructions for chanting the seven-letter word "Jehovah" in three separate syllables as part of a prayer routine. If used over a sustained period of time, concentration on the rhythmic word (or words) of a mantra can suppress the brain's tendency to generate random thoughts. This enables the meditator to access not just alternative states of consciousness, but also (sometimes) alternative states of reality. The former has significant – and known – benefits in terms of relaxation; the latter has benefits – albeit less well documented – in terms of *knowledge*. Mr. Gann himself mentions his "many blessings by applying the *Magic Word*" in terms of "health, happiness and prosperity".

[32] It is alleged that Mr. Gurdjieff's teachings can be traced back – albeit somewhat subjectively – to very early Christianity, in the first five centuries C.E. The knowledge is, for example, said to have been preserved by a group known as the "Saurmong Brotherhood". Unfortunately, the only evidence for the existence of this group appears to be the body of teachings attributed to it. See, for example, Wilson, *Gurdjieff*.

CHAPTER 2

THE GOLDEN RATIO AND THE CHRISTIAN SCRIPTURES

"I hold that the Bible contains the key to the process by which man may know all there is to know of the future."

W. D. Gann

THE NUMBER 666

In Chapter 13 of the *Book of Revelation* in the Christian Bible, there is an explicit arithmetical number that has been the cause of much anguish, confusion and academic debate. That number is **666**.[1]

Misunderstandings have been caused by the fact that, despite the groundbreaking work of Bligh Bond and Simcox Lea as long ago as 1917, very few people are aware of the science of *gematria* that was used in the writing of Holy Scriptures.[2] Gematria is the technique of assigning specific numbers to each letter of an alphabet, thereby allowing the calculation of the numerical value of certain words. These numerical values give additional meaning to each word, because they can be cross-referenced with other words.

A great deal of open-minded research still needs to be done on the subject, but the evidence already suggests that the main purpose of gematria was essentially twofold: first to give an harmonic structure to spiritual texts; and second, to

---

[1] *Revelation*, Chapter 13, verse 18.
[2] Bligh Bond and Simcox Lea, *Gematria* (Basil Blackwell, Oxford, 1917). See also John Michell, *City of Revelation: On the Proportions and Symbolic Numbers of the Cosmic Temple* (Garnstone Press Ltd., London, 1972). The word "gematria" is derived from the Greek word γεομετρια, or "geometria", meaning geometry.

ensure that an additional – and higher – form of knowledge was transmitted within those texts.

In the context of early versions of the Christian New Testament, the relevant alphabet was Greek[3] and the number assigned to each letter is shown in Appendix 1. Quite obviously, all of the numeric wisdom contained in the original Greek text was lost when it was translated into other languages. Hence the phrase "let him who has understanding count (or calculate) the number of the beast", in *Revelation*, Chapter 13, Verse 18, will take on a totally different meaning when it is realised that each of the letters in the Greek rendition of the subsequent phrase carries a number from gematria.[4]

The request to "count" is obviously a literal one. This means that the number appropriate to the infamous "beast" is not 666 at all, but something totally different.[5] However, in the absence of the necessary key – that is, a knowledge of gematria – the number 666 has come to be specifically, and incorrectly, associated with the power of *evil*.

In fact, the number 666 was originally used by ancient authorities to denote a particular type of energy – namely, the type of energy that is symbolised by the sun. For example, the number 666 can be found in the specific *matrix* of numbers that was traditionally associated with the sun. This matrix is one of a family of matrices known as *magic* squares that are associated with the planets.[6] Magic squares are so-called because each and every row, column and diagonal in the square adds up to an identical number. This helps to confirm an extraordinary, but definite, order underlying the structure of numbers. Hence, in the sun Square, which is shown below in Figure 2-1, there are 6 rows and 6 columns; and each row, column or diagonal adds up to 111.

The second important feature of each magic square is that the sum of all the numbers in the square creates a *characteristic* number for the square. Hence, in the Sun Square, the sum of all the numbers (i.e. 1 to 36) creates the characteristic

---

[3] Aland, *New Testament*.

[4] The subsequent phrase reads: "for it is the number of a man and his number is six hundred threescore and six". *The Holy Bible* (Authorised (King James), English Revised Version, 1881). Later versions of the Bible refer to the number 666 as being "man's number" or "a human number", rather than the number of a particular individual.

[5] Interested readers are referred to John Michell's *The Dimensions of Paradise* (Thames and Hudson, London, 1988) for a full discussion of this point. The veracity of the number 666 – at least in this context – has, in any case, been challenged. A possible alternative is 612. See Hugh Schonfield, *The Original New Testament: A Radical Reinterpretation and New Translation* (Waterstone & Co, London, 1985).

[6] See Jim Moran, *The Wonders of Magic Squares* (Vintage Books, New York, 1982). Hence:
- Saturn: 3 x 3 square; rows, columns, and diagonals sum to 15; characteristic number, 45; quotient, 3.
- Jupiter: 4 x 4; 34; 136; 4.
- Mars: 5 x 5; 65; 325; 5.
- Sun: 6 x 6; 111; 666; 6.
- Venus: 7 x 7; 175; 1225; 7.
- Mercury: 8 x 8; 260; 2080; 8.
- Moon: 9 x 9; 369; 3321; 9.

number for the sun itself – namely, 666. This is the number that cross references to the number 666 in Greek gematria.[7]

6	32	3	34	35	1	*111*
7	11	27	28	8	30	*111*
19	14	16	15	23	24	*111*
18	20	22	21	17	13	*111*
25	29	10	9	26	12	*111*
36	5	33	4	2	31	*111*
111	*111*	*111*	*111*	*111*	*111*	**666**

FIGURE 2-1: THE *MAGIC* SUN SQUARE

This relationship between magic squares and the science of gematria extends the underlying order of numbers into the very structure of language and therefore into the dimensions of communication and learning. Hence, the use of the number 666 could either be taken by association to imply *the sun*, or it could be taken to mean those aspects of the archetypal energy represented by the sun. In the latter case, the appropriate attributes were those of dynamism, expansion and fertilisation – basically, actively creative energy. This, indeed, is why the *Book of Revelation* calls the number 666 "the number of a man": it is an explicit reference to male energy.

The sun, therefore, was taken to represent the *positive* half of the polarity split that characterises activity throughout the universe. The moon, meanwhile, was taken to represent the other half – the *negative* half.[8]

It is important to recognise right here that these two polarities were understood to represent complementary energies. They did not incorporate any value

---

[7] It also cross references to the number 666 in Hebrew gematria. It is the value of "Sorath", the Spirit of the sun. See David Fideler, *Jesus Christ, Sun of God: Ancient Cosmology and Early Christian Symbolism* (Quest, Wheaton (Il.), 1993).
[8] There is no obvious direct relationship between the Sun Square and the Moon Square, except as part of the progression through the hierarchy of planets.

judgements whatsoever, but were concepts that dealt with the ebb and flow of change. Every movement in Nature was seen as consisting of a combination of both types of energy. Where the positive energy dominated, a system would be described as being active, expanding, growing, or moving. Where the negative energy dominated, the system was seen as being passive, contracting, dying, or standing still. The necessary coexistence of both types of energy meant – and still means – that it was totally inappropriate and misleading to denote solar energy and its corresponding attributes as being *evil*.

In fact, these concepts are now better understood by modern Western philosophers, mainly because of the influence of Eastern thought. Hence, solar-type activity corresponds to the *yang* of Chinese philosophy and to the *rajasic guna⁹* of Indian philosophy. The mathematical symbol of solar energy is therefore a plus sign; its sex is male; its sphere of activity is mental; the character of its activity is (broadly-speaking) logical and rational; its dynamic attributes are expansion and penetration; its associated mineral is gold; and its arena is the light. In Greek biblical texts the sum by gematria of the letters in words or phrases having these attributes was 666. For example, the sum of the letters in the Greek phrase meaning "the mind" or "reason" is 666.[10]

THE NUMBER 1080

In contradistinction to the positive solar-type of energy stands the negative lunar-type of energy. Activity here is understood to be receptive. It corresponds to the *yin* of Chinese philosophy and the *tamasic guna* of Indian philosophy. Its mathematical symbol is a minus sign; its sex is female; its sphere of activity is emotional; the character of its activity is intuitive and non-rational; its dynamic attributes are contraction and absorption; its associated mineral is silver; and its arena is the dark.

Unlike the solar number, however, the lunar number is not explicit in the Christian Scriptures. This, in fact, is one of the reasons why both numbers have been misunderstood. Nevertheless, writers such as the late John Michell,[11] who spent many years researching the subject, have concluded that biblical words and phrases that have lunar attributes[12] yield a very precise number. That number is **1080**.

---

[9] A guna is an energy attribute. Traditionally, there are three gunas: rajasic (active), tamasic (passive) and sattwic (equilibrating). See text.

[10] That is, $\eta \phi \rho \eta \nu$ = 8+500+100+8+50 = 666.

[11] Michell, *City of Revelation*. See also Michell, *Dimensions of Paradise*. Michell's findings have provided the basis for a new generation of research into the sacred doctrines hidden within the Scriptures. As a result, it is now possible to trace the relationship between early Christian gnostics and the teachings of the ancient mystery cults. See Fideler, *Jesus Christ*.

[12] Although not the word "moon" itself. The Greek equivalent is $\sigma \varepsilon \lambda \eta \nu \eta$, which has a gematrian value of 301.

The importance of this number is highlighted by the fact that it is – very specifically – the number by gematria of the Greek phrase το αγιον πνευμα, meaning "the Holy Spirit".[13] Furthermore, it is the calculated number for the Greek rendering of such well-known phrases as the "Fountain of Wisdom", and the "Abyss". It seems more than just a coincidence that the radius of the moon itself is just over 1080 miles[14] and that the atomic weight of silver is 108.0.

Although very important, most of this might seem basically irrelevant to the subject matter in hand. However, it is not. There is a very significant relationship between the solar number, 666, and the lunar number, 1080. If the former number is divided by the latter, then the resulting ratio between them is 0.62:1. That is:

666 / 1080 = 0.62

Alternatively, the ratio between the two numbers can be shown the other way around, so that:

1080 / 666 = 1.62

Philosophically, the ratios 0.62:1 and 1.62:1 are regarded as being interchangeable: either can be denoted by the 21st letter of the Greek alphabet φ (= phi), and both are called the *Golden Ratio*.

THE GOLDEN RATIO

The Golden Ratio – more accurately defined as 0.618:1 or its inverse 1.618:1 – is an extraordinary phenomenon. Its presence in Nature is now very well attested: it can be found both in natural structures[15] (such as the human body) and in natural processes[16] (such as growth spirals). The presence of the Ratio in the Bible suggests that it has long been understood as being sacred. Certainly it seems, in some mysterious way, to be a part of Nature's *blueprint* with respect to space and time.

The starting point for any analysis of the Golden Ratio is the fact that it is the only ratio that will divide a straight line in such a way that the ratio of the smaller part to the larger part is exactly equal to the ratio of the larger part to the whole.

---

[13] That is, το αγιον πνευμα = 300 + 70 + 1 + 3 + 10 + 70 + 50 + 80 + 50 + 5 + 400 + 40 + 1 = 1080.
[14] The equatorial radius of the moon is 1,086.3 miles. The English mile is thus a truly "natural" measure. The purposes and wisdom relating to such measures are, of course, becoming lost to us as we embrace the apparently *easier* method of measurement using metres and kilometres. This is a point well made by John Michell, *The New View Over Atlantis* (Thames and Hudson, London, 1983).
[15] See, for example, Livio, Golden Ratio.
[16] *Ibid.*

Hence, in the following diagram (Figure 2-2):

BC / AB = AB / AC = 0.618

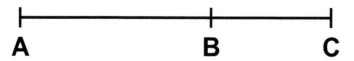

A   B   C

FIGURE 2-2: THE GOLDEN RATIO

The importance of the diagram is that it uses a Golden Measure that expresses three concepts simultaneously:

1. The Measure is a *number*, albeit an irrational one, (i.e. 0.618);

2. It is a *ratio* between two numbers (i.e. 0.618:1); and

3. It is a continuous *proportion* between three numbers (represented by the lengths AC, AB and BC in Figure 2).

The Golden Measure therefore simultaneously expresses the ideas of unity (number), duality (ratio) and trinity (proportion). Hence, it can be called the Golden Number, the Golden Ratio or the Golden Proportion.

The equivalency between the two ratios BC:AB and AB:AC means that the three values AB, BC and AC always bear the same relationship to one another. However, AC is equal to the sum of AB and BC. Hence the equation defining the Golden Proportion expresses the relationship between three terms by the relationship between two of those terms. In other words, if:

BC is to AB as AB is to AC

and if:

AC = AB + BC

then:

AB / (AB + BC) = BC / AB = 0.618

Ancient theological authorities considered these aspects of the Golden Measure to be very significant.[17] Indeed, they considered that the Measure directly reflected the essential nature of God, or The Source of All Things. For this

---

[17] See Robert Lawlor, Sacred Geometry: Philosophy and Practice (Thames and Hudson, London, 1982). In addition to the spatial relationship defining ϕ (as shown in Figure 2-2), there is another aspect to ϕ which is important. This is the uniqueness of the equation:

reason, and because it could be found at all levels of Nature, it was also known as The *Divine* Proportion. Hence, in analysing the Golden Measure, it is important that we understand the veneration with which it was treated. Otherwise, we run the danger of missing its essential function.

Implications of the Golden Ratio

First, since the larger of the elements in the above equations is equal to the sum of the other two elements, the Golden Ratio was considered to be an expression of the way that *The One* divided itself into *Two*. Second, because the proportion between the ratios was constant, the Golden Proportion was considered to be an expression of the way that change could occur without involving chaos. The Golden Measure was therefore taken to mirror the presumed relationship between God and the phenomenal world, because it embodied the reconciliation between Unity and Duality – that is, between The Whole and Its Parts.

The logic behind this conclusion is very revealing. In the first place, and as has already been observed, duality is an intrinsic feature of life. All movement is defined in terms of an oscillation between two opposite polarities. Implicit in the idea of oscillation, however, is the related concept of *differences*. Differences convey information to an observer and therefore provide the basis for a response.[18] Without differences between structures, and between states of being, there would be nothing to perceive, nothing to respond to, and therefore no movement or evolution.

From this it follows that any mathematical symbol that was to be taken by Christian philosophers as reflecting the primary division of God into two parts had to incorporate the idea of active difference – i.e. something other than a fifty/fifty split. On the one hand, just dividing something into two halves means the creation of two *identical* parts. This in turn means that there would be no differences to trigger a reaction from a system. On the other hand, therefore, bisecting something along the lines of the Golden Ratio incorporates the idea not only of duality but also of the presence of genuine information.

In the second place, harmony between structures, and between different states of being, is essential to the preservation of life through both time and space. Without harmony, there would be chaos and destruction, and (except for very briefly, perhaps) there would be no existence. Ancient authorities saw harmony

---

$1/\phi + (1/\phi \times 1/\phi) = 1/\phi \times (1/\phi \times 1/\phi)$
which is equivalent to:

$1/\phi + (1/\phi)^2 = 1/\phi \times (1/\phi)^2$

The resulting value is 4.236, which is $(1/\phi)^3$. This is the only equation where a summation involving two terms (i.e. $1/\phi$ and $(1/\phi)^2$) is identical to the value obtained from the multiplication of the same two terms.

[18] See Gregory Bateson, *Mind and Nature – An Essential Unity* (Wildwood House, London, 1979). In the phenomenal world, activity is generated by information. Bateson defines information as "differences which make a difference".

as being a result of proportion, so that movement in one area would be responded to by a movement in another area: the parts would adjust, and the whole would reflect this adjustment. The application of the Golden Proportion to the cosmology of Being implicitly allows for co-dependent adjustment throughout a system so that any potential conflict between the parts is effectively contained.

This is a profound conclusion and, among other things, involves two clear insights into the nature of life on Earth. First, it implies that apparently destructive forces among the *parts* of Nature actually only have a very limited potential to destroy the *whole* of Nature. Second, this in turn suggests the explicit operation of a harmonising, or equilibrating, force. In fact, and as we shall see in Chapter 3, the Golden Ratio provides direct information relating to this equilibrating force and also provides indirect information relating to the very structure of Creation itself.

CHAPTER 3

THE LAW OF THREE

"In every law of nature there is a major and a minor; a positive, a negative and a neutral."

W. D. Gann

"Every action, every phenomenon in all worlds without exception, is the result of the simultaneous action of three forces – the positive, the negative, and the neutralising."

P. D. Ouspensky

THREE CREATIVE FORCES

The use of the Golden Ratio by early Christian writers implies a deep understanding of the cosmological forces operating within the universe. Specifically, the use of the number 666 to denote *mental* energy with active attributes, and the use of the number 1080 to denote *spiritual* energy with passive (or receptive) attributes, suggests an understanding of the universe as an interplay of opposing, but nevertheless complementary, forces.

However, harmony requires some method of reconciling these opposing forces. It is not sufficient to look just at the influence of the positive and negative energy polarities. There has to be a third force that resolves their differences. In Eastern philosophy, the existence of this third force has always been accepted. In Chinese thought, for example, it is recognised as an aspect of *The Tao*, while in India it is more clearly identified as the *sattwic guna*.[1]

---

[1] The sattwic guna is regarded as being of the same hierarchical order as the tamasic and rajasic gunas.

In fact, the third force – and the *Law of Three* – can be inferred from the Golden Ratio. According to the formulation of the Golden Ratio, two terms can be used to define the relationship between three terms. Hence, it follows that the third term can be deduced from the first two. The implication is that a combination of the dual forces of spiritual and mental energies contributes to a greater whole. The number of this greater whole, by deduction is **1746** (i.e. 1080 + 666). John Michell called this the "number of fusion".[2] In this arrangement, it follows that:

$$1080 / 1746 = 666 / 1080 = 0.62$$

The Golden Ratio is thus consistent with the presence of the three creative forces recognised by general religious tradition – namely, spiritual energy, mental energy, and a combination of both that constitutes a Whole or Unity. According to this tradition, Spirit is the receptive matrix of all possibilities, Creative Mind is its generative counterpart that produces specific dynamic processes from within the matrix of spiritual potential,[3] and the combined force of Spirit and Mind is both the *result* of the Whole and the *cause* of the Whole. This, it can be argued, is the Mystery of Creation.

The mystery of the third force

The difficulty, of course, is that – being a mystery – the presence of the third energy is impossible to prove through discursive thought, since the result is always a paradox.[4] In the West, therefore, the attitude towards the existence of a third force, or energy, is somewhat ambivalent. Christianity clearly views the source of harmony as being God, but cannot be definitive about the operation of harmony because of a hostile attitude towards the forces of dissolution that are contained within Nature.

On the other hand, Western scientific authorities explicitly recognise the operation of the laws of creation and dissolution – unchanging laws of Nature – but do not, generally (or necessarily), accept the role of a higher power in these laws. They do not therefore explicitly accept the role of a third force.

Philosophically, of course, it is not possible (at a level) to distinguish between the concept of God and the idea of unchanging laws of Nature. If God is

---

[2] The number 1746 is, by gematria, the value of a *grain of mustard seed*, which is mentioned in St. Matthew's Gospel (Chapter 13, verse 31). It is also the value of the phrase the 'Same and the Other' used by Plato to denote opposite polarities; and of the Greek for 'Father, Son, Spirit'. See Michell, *Dimensions of Paradise*.
[3] The relationship between Spirit and Mind thus parallels the implications of Schrodinger's wave equation in the New Physics. An infinite profusion of possibilities is actualised into a specific outcome by mental *perception*. See, for example, Gary Zukav, *The Dancing Wu Li Masters: An Overview of the New Physics* (William Morrow, New York, 1979).
[4] The application of mental reasoning to the phenomenon of God results in the paradox of opposite truths – namely, God is *both* immanent and transcendent, is *both* part and whole, and is *both* devolution and evolution. The problem is that mental reasoning can only relate to, experience, and understand levels of consciousness that are at the same or lower levels than itself. It can therefore understand mind and matter, but it cannot experience spirit.

expressed in terms of the operation of unchanging and universal laws, there will inevitably be a point where scientific endeavour actually becomes impotent: it becomes impossible to reduce the laws any further and we can only point to the fact that certain laws exist in the first place.

Whatever one's attitude to the concept of God, it seems logical to conclude that, without some form of a third force that generates, maintains, and participates in the coherence of the universe, nothing that exists could exist.[5] So, if the existence of this force is accepted as a working hypothesis, then we can look at the phenomenon of the three forces – active, passive and reconciling – from two perspectives. First, we can see it *horizontally*, in terms of the diagram shown in Figure 2-2, and reproduced as Figure 3-1.

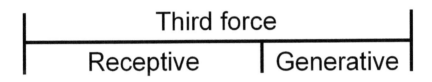

FIGURE 3-1: THE GOLDEN RATIO EXPRESSED IN TERMS OF THE THREE FORCES

In this format, the third force contains the other two energies. Its wholistic authority embraces both the active force of generative change and the passive force of fertile and receptive potential. It would therefore embrace, reflect, and stimulate the other two forces: actively, it would ensure that vibration and change exist in the first place; passively, it would ensure that the resulting perturbations are subject to compensatory adjustments. In short, it would ensure harmony.[6] On this hypothesis, it is difficult to miss the idea that the third force would be a specific attribute of the conscious energy field that humankind has traditionally called *The Creator*.[7]

---

[5] Science – particularly in the area of quantum physics – is getting closer and closer to incorporating the concept of an overarching self-organising force. On this, and many related aspects of the search for an integral 'theory of everything', see Ervin Laszlo, *Science and the Re-enchantment of the Cosmos: The Rise of the Integral Vision of Reality* (Inner Traditions, Rochester (Vt.), USA, 2006).

[6] Since the *third force* cannot allow total chaos, all living organisms respond to its imperative to merge with greater wholes. The third force thus provides both the basic impulse to coexist and the impulse to evolve. See Ken Wilber, *Up from Eden: A Transpersonal View of Human Evolution* (Routledge & Kegan Paul, London, 1983).

[7] The active and passive forces would also be fundamental aspects of The Creator. There are, therefore, three distinct conclusions that could be drawn. First, the universe is actualised *from* fertile Spirit *by* generative Mind. Second, the universe necessarily contains opposing energy forces. Third, if the two energies remain in a constant relationship to the Source from which they arise, then the Source itself would likely retain an influence during the process of creation.

Hierarchical order

The second way in which the triad of energies contained in the Golden Ratio can be viewed is *vertically*. This approach accepts that, although the whole is bounded by the third force, the structure of that whole is in some way hierarchical. This idea of a hierarchy of power was reflected in the ancient hermetic formula: "as above, so below". Whatever takes place at one level of being will also occur in some form at another (lower) level of being.

However, this phenomenon is only possible if each level of being is in some way a stepped-down version of the level above it. There would be an *analogue* law that would transmit changes down through the hierarchy of being.[8] Importantly, this principle would necessarily guarantee the existence of harmony within the whole; and the Golden Measure is, in fact, a perfect representation of this harmony.

This certainly appears to have been the attitude of the early Christian philosophers.[9] First, the way that the number series 1746, 1080, 666 reduces in size is suggestive of a *hierarchical* structure to the triad of energies implicit in their concept of God.[10] Second, the critical mediating role of the force represented by the number 1080 is implicit in the fact that the number 1080 is the geometric mean of the numbers 1746 and 666.[11] According to Plato and Pythagoras, a geometric mean was not only the product of two extremes but it also *reconciled* the two extremes. It thereby produced harmony. Third, harmony is produced from proportion – i.e. from equivalency between ratios. In this case, the ratio is not just any old ratio, it is specifically the Golden Ratio and, if each level is a stepped-down version of the level above it, then each level would maintain a constant relationship to the level above and below it.[12]

The question that arises from this presentation is: what would be the nature of each of the forces represented by the three numbers 1746, 1080 and 666 when they are placed in a *vertical* framework? In principle, they should correspond to

---

[8] See Ken Wilber, 'Reflections on the New-Age Paradigm' in Ken Wilber (Ed.), *The Holographic Paradigm* (Shambhala, Boston (Ma.), 1985). It is important to recognise that the flow of authority is essentially *downwards*. Creativity at the highest levels is reflected in some degree of flexibility (or randomness) at the lower levels. But apparent randomness at the lower levels does not mean that the highest levels are therefore themselves random. This downward flow of authority also means that the lower levels are unlikely to recognise the *purposes* of the higher and are likely therefore to regard change only in their own context.

[9] See Lawlor, *Sacred Geometry*. Indeed, traditional *esoteric* teachings in most of the world's main religions (e.g. Christian mysticism, Sufism, Hinduism, Buddhism) argue that the universe was created by a progressive reduction in spiritual vibrations.

[10] This presentation would not mean that there are three Gods, only that there are three 'dimensions', or aspects, to God. Christianity sees the three dimensions as being 'consubstantial' – i.e. of the same essence.

[11] That is, 1080 = (1746 x 666). The number 1080 thus mediates between the two extremes.

[12] As if to confirm this analysis, the process of summing the digits in each of the numbers 1746, 1080 and 666 reduces them all to the number 9. This latter number was always associated with initiation and completion. Hence, $1 + 7 + 4 + 6 = 1 + 8 = 9$; $1 + 0 + 8 + 0 = 9$; and $6 + 6 + 6 = 1 + 8 = 9$.

the three primary divisions (or gradations) of Being that are recognised by most religious traditions – namely, The Source, the First Emanation from The Source (i.e. Spirit) and the Realm of Time (i.e. Creative Mind).

It is quite clear from John Michell's work on gematria that this was, indeed, the intended implication.[13] The number 1080 is the intermediate term between 1746 and 666, and the Holy Spirit can thus be seen as the dynamic linkage between what is Above and what is Below.[14] In other words, ancient authorities were able to visualise the Holy Spirit as being the vehicle that transmitted the powers of the Creator throughout the universe. Spirit became Creative Mind, animated by Itself.

NATURE'S LAWS

This use of the three numbers 1746, 1080 and 666 thus helps to explain why the Golden Ratio was known as the Divine Proportion. Nevertheless, attempting to unravel the insights of the early Christian writers about the Golden Ratio is not necessarily the same thing as saying that their conclusions were correct. Indeed, for many in this scientific age, the operation of the equilibrating powers of God through the agency of Spirit is an intellectually unsatisfying explanation for the intrinsic harmony of Life.

The fact remains, however, that life on Earth does appear to be bounded by certain inviolable laws that synchronistically incorporate fluctuation and harmony. We may not yet fully understand why this should be so but, at the very least, we can usefully acknowledge that these laws are built upon three forces that can be defined respectively as active, passive, and reconciling. Taken together, these forces constitute what George Gurdjieff called "the *Law of Three*".[15]

As will become increasingly apparent, the *Law of Three* expresses itself in various ways in life on this Earth, and it is central to the evolution of natural cycles.

---

[13] The Greek texts of the New Testaments were written before the First Council of Nicea (which sat in 325 C.E.). It is possible that this Council – which established subsequent Christian orthodox teaching concerning the Trinity – knew that the scriptures themselves could not be altered and so suppressed the idea that gematria in the texts carried deeper meanings.

[14] The three numbers therefore provide a very clear exposition of early understandings about the Trinity. The number 1746 would have corresponded to *The Father*, 1080 would have referred to *The Holy Spirit* and 666 would have implied *The Son*. On the face of it, this is an awkward conclusion because the history of 666 means that, for many Christians, the number is almost irrevocably equated with the power of evil. The critical point, however, is that the numbers 1746, 1080 and 666 relate to the *cosmogony* of Being. Under this schema, there is no implied relationship between any particular individual and the Source. Difficulties of interpretation arise because Christian theology equates The Son to Jesus Christ and thus blurs the distinction between the different concepts of "the Son of man" (see Chapter 4, and note 13), "the Son of God" (i.e. Christ) and "The Son" (i.e. Creation). Furthermore, the number 666 references the stepped-down version of what the ancients thought of as being The Holy Spirit, and thus means the created world of time and space.

[15] Ouspensky, *In Search*.

This was why Mr. Gann found it so important. However, before looking at the law in more depth, we need to delve a little further into the Christian scriptures in order to shed light on Mr. Gann's extraordinary claim that a certain passage in the Bible embodies hidden information that is directly applicable to a law of vibration – and, by inference, to collective human behaviour.[16]

It turns out that the passage in question contains a number of layers of meaning and that the significance of the final revelation is enhanced by the genius of the structure on which it is built.

---

[16] Gann, *Tunnel.*

CHAPTER 4

THE SIGN OF THE PROPHET JONAS

"I believe that that is the key to the interpretation of the future."

W. D. Gann

ST MATTHEW'S GOSPEL

It has been shown that the Bible contains hidden information in the form of symbolic numbers and that these numbers contain references to the energy of a third force encapsulated within the Golden Ratio. The task now is to follow the lead provided by William Gann and analyse certain specific references that he made to the Bible. In so doing it will be possible to reveal not only the extraordinary nature of the Bible itself, but also the remarkable perceptions of those who were involved in producing it. Some of the resulting information is beyond current scientific understanding.

As was mentioned in Chapter 1, in *Tunnel* Mr. Gann – in the guise of Robert Gordon[1] – was quite specific in declaring that he had the key to the interpretation of the future. He argues that the key can be found in Chapter 12 of St. Matthew's Gospel, verses 38-40, under "the sign of the prophet Jonas".[2] The original Greek text is shown in Appendix 2. The text, as translated by Mr. Gann, reads:

---

[1] Gann, *Tunnel.*
[2] The same "sign" is referred to a second time in St. Matthew, Chapter 16, verses 1-4. The reason for this is not clear. The repetition may be designed to highlight its importance.

Then some scribes and Pharisees said to him, "Teacher, we wish to see a sign from you." But he answered them:

"An evil and adulterous generation seeks for a sign; but no sign shall be given to it except the sign of the prophet Jonas. For as Jonas was three days and three nights in the belly of the whale, so shall the Son of man be three days and three nights in the heart of the earth."

It was shown in Chapter 2 that examining a biblical text in terms of gematria can yield some astonishing insights into the hidden meanings and purposes of the text. The obscure nature of "the sign of the prophet Jonas" certainly suggests that it might contain hidden dimensions based on gematria. This possibility can now be explored in some detail. By demonstrating the integrity and credibility of St. Matthew's text, it is also possible to establish the authority of the eventual revelations.

"JONAH" OR "JONAS"

The first point to make is that, in gematria, not only is every letter important, but also the words and sentences need to be seen in terms of logical clusters. Extra information is carried by the mathematical relationships between specific phrases.

The second point to make is that there is something very significant about the original Greek text[1] from which the above translation is derived. This is that the name of the individual being referenced actually *changes* between verse 39 and verse 40. In the original Greek, verse 39 concludes:

το	σημειον	**ιωνα**	του	προφητου
the	sign	Jonah	of the	prophet

While the beginning of verse 40 includes the phrase:

ιωνας	εν	τη	κοιλια	του	κητους
Jonas	in	the	belly	of the	whale

In other words, the name changes from Jon*ah* to Jon*as*.

In practice, most translators use either Jonah or Jonas in both places in the text without explicitly acknowledging that there is a difference: the Nestle-Aland *Greek-English New Testament*, for example, uses "Jonah" in its translation; while Mr. Gann himself uses "Jonas". In terms of gematria, however, such differences are usually of critical importance. So, the question is: why does the difference exist in the first place? There are at least three answers.

---

[1] Aland, *New Testament.*

First, there is always the possibility that a mistake was made during the process of hand-copying the original Greek texts and then translating them. Second, the name could have been changed on purpose to divert attention from the esoteric nature of "the sign of the prophet". Finally, if the original text is held as being strictly accurate, then the distinction between *Ιωνα* and *Ιωνας* could be a clue to breaking an underlying code.[4]

The value of "ς"

It is therefore unlikely to be an accident that, in *Tunnel*, Mr Gann explicitly contrasts the names "Jonah" and "Jonas". Mr Gann has Robert Gordon state that he has "read the book of Jon*ah* thru very carefully, and [has understood] what the Saviour meant when he said: 'No sign shall be given, but the sign of the prophet Jon*as*.'" Mr Gann thus differentiates between "Jonah" (from the book of Jonah) and the prophet "Jonas" (in verse 39 of St. Matthew's text). The direct inference is that Mr. Gann believed that it was necessary to include the Greek letter "ς" in the phrase "the sign of the prophet Jonas".

Whatever the original reason for the letter "ς" being excluded from verse 39, the results both of allowing the difference, and of then including (or re-including) it in the "sign of the prophet", are extraordinary: on the one hand, allowing the difference has the same effect as inserting – and turning – a key in a lock and opening a door onto a hidden world; on the other hand, using "*Ιωνας*" instead of "*Ιωνα*" in "the sign of the prophet Jonas" offers a potential revelation about the nature of Time.

The reason that the letter "ς" is so important is that it has a gematrian value of 200; and this has – to put it mildly – a dramatic effect on the analysis. First, the symbolic value of *Ιωνας* is **1061** (i.e. 10 + 800 + 50 + 1 + 200). Second, the symbolic value of the "sign of the prophet" increases from 3912 in the case of "Jonah" to **4112** in the case of "Jonas". That is:

the	sign	Jonas	of the	prophet	
το	σημειον	Ιωνας	του	προφητου	
370	383	1061	770	1528	= 4112

As will be shown in Chapter 5, the number 1061 is at the very centre of a remarkable and important section of sacred geometry in the ancient world, while the number 4112 progresses the analysis into the modern world.

---

[4] An important consideration here is that the two names need not refer to the same individual. In the absence of a knowledge of gematria, it would be logical to presume that the Jonas in the whale's belly is also the same as the prophet Jonah. However, in gematria, such a logical presumption might actually distort the intended message.

SIGNIFICANT PHRASEOLOGY

Looking at the full text of verses 39 and 40 in Chapter 12 of St. Matthew's Gospel, it is quite obvious that the phrases "Jonas in the belly of the whale" and "the Son of man in the heart of the earth" have a resonance with one another. In both phrases, important individuals are placed symbolically within identifiable constructs. Once account is taken of the joint use of the phrase "three days and three nights", it is apparent that sentient beings (who?) are being placed in a particular place (where?) in the context of time (for how long?). The relationships between the two phrases are obviously going to be important.

By gematria, the numerical value of the phrase "Jonas in the belly of the whale" is **3333**. That is:

Jonas	in	the	belly	of the	whale	
Ιωνας	εν	τη	κοιλια	του	κητους	
1061	55	308	141	770	998	= 3333

Meanwhile the numerical value of the phrase "the Son of man in the heart of the earth" is **4248**. That is:

the	Son	of (the)	man	in	the	heart	of the	earth	
ο	υιος	του	ανθρωπου	εν	τη	καρδια	της	γης	
70	680	770	1510	55	308	136	508	211	= 4248

Finally, it can be seen that these two phrases (and hence the numbers 3333 and 4248) are directly linked to each other, not only by the harmonic construction of the text, but also by the phrase "three days and three nights". That is, the text explicitly incorporates the passage of time (i.e. "for how long"). By gematria, this third phrase has a numerical value of **2586**. That is:

three	days	and	three	nights	
τρεις	ημερας	και	τρεις	νυκτας	
615	354	31	615	971	= 2586

CONNECTIONS TO GEOMETRY

We now need to analyse the connections that are implicit in these three pieces of text. Initially, however, let us concentrate on the "who" and "where" aspects. The first important relationship concerns the name "Jonas" and the associated phrase "Jonas in the belly of the whale". It turns out that the number for "Jonas" (i.e. 1061) is related to the number of the total phrase (i.e. 3333) by the irrational number **3.1416**.

That is, rounded to the nearest whole number:

1061 **x 3.1416** = 3333

The number 3.1416 is, of course, well known. It is usually referred to as π (= *pi)* and is crucial to the calculation of various aspects of a circle. Hence, the situation is quite clear: we are dealing with **the formula for the circumference of a circle** whose diameter is 1061 units.[5] See Figure 4-1.

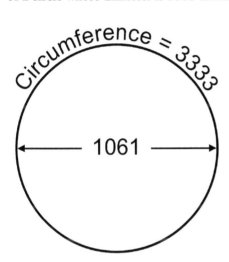

FIGURE 4-1: JONAS IN THE BELLY OF THE WHALE

This relationship between the numeric value of words and important geometric constructs is no coincidence. The word "gematria" derives from the Greek word γεωμετρια meaning "geometry", or "measuring the earth", and the Greek philosophers readily accepted that natural numbers and natural structures were intimately related. It should, therefore, come as no surprise to find this close relationship expressed in the Greek texts of the Christian Gospels.

The second important relationship concerns the connection between the phrase "the Son of man in the heart of the earth" and the name "Jonas". It turns out that the number 4248 is also related to the number 1061. The relevant equation is:

4248 = 1062 x 4

Following the same idea as that for the circle, we can deduce that we are dealing with **the formula for the perimeter of a square** whose sides are 1062 units in length. See Figure 4-2.

---

[5] There is some debate about how accurately π could be calculated 2000 years ago. The evidence is that it could be calculated *very* accurately.

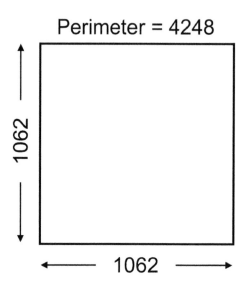

FIGURE 4-2: THE SON OF MAN IN THE HEART OF THE EARTH

The question now is whether or not the one unit difference between 1061 and 1062 is important. In fact, the answer is no. As already mentioned, the prime function of gematria was to indicate *relationships* between words and expressions, in order to draw out hidden associations and symbolic meanings. If, for example, the numbers for two different words are identical, then it indicates an important relationship between those words that would warrant further analysis. Obviously, however, the nature of language and number requires some degree of flexibility in establishing these relationships. Flexibility was achieved by allowing one unit to be added or subtracted from the numeric value of a word without altering its symbolic meaning. This extra unit was known as a *colel*.

Allowing for the flexibility provided by the colel, therefore, we can deduce that the phrase "the Son of man in the heart of the earth" can be seen a symbolic reference to a square whose sides are 1061 units in length.

THE CIRCLE AND THE SQUARE

The fact that the circle of Jonas and the square of the Son of man are both based on the number 1061 suggests that they should be constructed together. There are two ways in which this can be done. The first way is to make the square *embrace* the circle. See Figure 4-3. This is, in fact, one version of the concept of "squaring the circle".[6]

---

[6] The other two versions, which are usually regarded as being more important, are: drawing the square with the same *area* as the circle; and drawing the square with the same *perimeter* as the circle. The process symbolically matches the evolution of consciousness: the physical world (the square) becomes equivalent to the spiritual world (the circle).

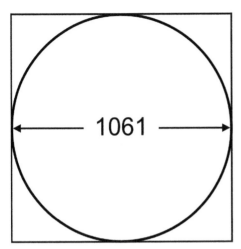

FIGURE 4-3: THE SQUARE EMBRACING THE CIRCLE

The alternative method of integrating the two diagrams is to use the diameter of the circle as the *top edge* of the square. See Figure 4–4. The diagram in Figure 4-4 is one of the ancient representations of the relationship between the spiritual world and the physical world.

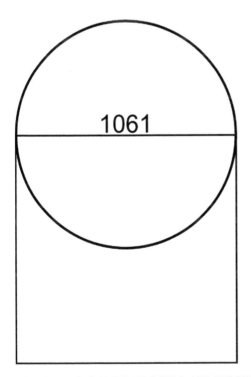

FIGURE 4-4: THE SPIRITUAL WORLD AND THE PHYSICAL WORLD

In ancient cosmology, heaven was represented as a circle and the earth was always represented as a square.[7] Indeed, in St. Matthew's text, Jesus refers directly to "the earth".

Hence, in the diagram, the spiritual realm penetrates the physical realm. Note, however, that the penetration is only halfway. In other words, the physical realm is not completely synchronised with the spiritual realm. This is consistent with Jesus' reference to "an evil and unfaithful generation" – if consciousness was sufficiently evolved, the sign would have been a squared circle similar to that in Figure 4-3.

THE HEART OF THE EARTH

At this point, there is a specific question that needs to be answered: what exactly is meant by "the Son of man" being "in the heart of the earth"? It may be remembered that the name "Jonas" implicated the *diameter* of the circle. It would therefore be logical to conclude that "the Son of man" should somehow refer to the *width* of the square. And this is, indeed, the case – although the reference is more subtle than in the case of "Jonas" because the reference is to the *diagonal* width. The formula for the diagonal width of a square is given as:

√2 x horizontal width

So, in this case, the diagonal of a square whose horizontal width is 1061 is:

1.414 x 1061 = 1500

This is shown in Figure 4-5.

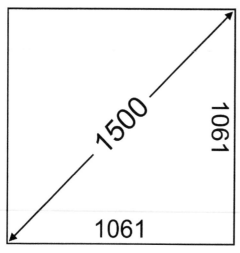

FIGURE 4-5: THE DIAGONAL OF A SQUARE

---

[7] This is one of the meanings behind the phrase: "the four corners of the earth".

On the face of it, this bears no relationship to the phrase "the Son of man", whose value by gematria is **3030**:

the	Son	of (the)	man
o	υιος	του	ανθρωπου

However, if the width of the square is *divided*, rather than multiplied, by √2, the result is **750**. That is:

1061 / 1.414 = 750

This is equivalent to *half* of the length of the diagonal of the square. It thereby references the point at the very *centre* of the square – the "heart of the earth" – where the diagonals intersect. It is also relevant that, in St. Matthew's Gospel, Jesus appears to refer to himself simply as o υιος (i.e. "the Son")[8] and the numeric value of this title is **750**. These concepts can be placed together in Figure 4-6 so that "the Son (of man)" is "in the heart of the earth".

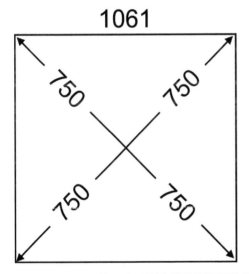

FIGURE 4-6: THE SON (OF MAN) IN THE HEART OF THE EARTH

Hence, Figures 4-3 and 4-4 can be amended to include this idea. This is done in Figures 4-7 and 4-8. In the former, "Jonas" (i.e. 1061 as the diameter of the circle) intersects "the Son" (750, as half the diagonal of the square) in the "heart of the earth" (the centre of the square). So, the diameter of the circle bisects the square. In Figure 4-8, on the other hand, "the Son" in "the heart of the earth" is intersected by the locus of Jonas's circle.

---

[8] For example, St. Matthew, Chapter 11, verse 27.

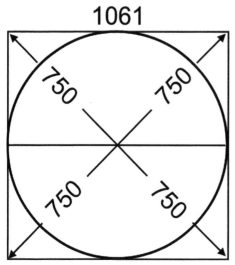

FIGURE 4-7: DIAMETER OF THE CIRCLE BISECTING THE SQUARE

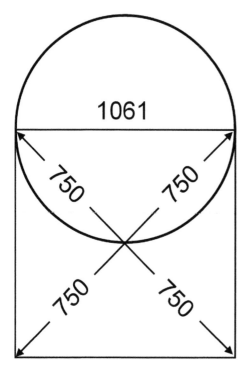

FIGURE 4-8: THE CIRCLE OF JONAS INTERSECTING THE SON IN THE HEART OF THE EARTH

As the analysis stands, there is no way of knowing for certain which of the two diagrams in Figures 4-7 and 4-8 was actually the one that was intended by St Matthew's text. In addition, it can be noted that, although there is a reference in the diagrams to "the heart of the earth" as being the location for the "Son of man", there is no comparable reference to "the belly of the whale" for "Jonas" to occupy.

The reason, it turns out, is that neither of the diagrams takes account of *time*. It will be remembered that the two phrases "Jonas in the belly of the whale" and "the Son of man in the heart of the earth" were linked by a third phrase, namely "three days and three nights". The symbolic value of the latter is 2586. If we now add this number to each of the numbers 3333 and 4248, the results are as follows:

"Jonas in the belly of the whale three days and three nights" = 5919

"the Son of man in the heart of the earth three days and three nights" = 6834

The conclusions to be drawn from these two numbers are simply extraordinary. The relationship between them hinges on the fact that:

$$5919 / \sqrt{3} = 6834 / 2$$

such that:

$$5919 / 6834 = \sqrt{3} / 2 = \textbf{0.866 / 1}$$

The ratio 0.866:1 is central to an ancient diagram known as the *vesica piscis*, or the "vessel of the fish".

THE VESSEL OF THE FISH

The *vesica* is the geometric area that is shared by two circles of equal diameter, where the centre of each circle is located on the circumference of the other. This common area looks very much like the outline of a fish. Hence, in Figure 4-9, a diagram is constructed from a pair of interlocking circles, each with a diameter of 6834 (i.e. the symbolic equivalent of "the Son of man in the heart of the earth three days and three nights"). Because the horizontal length of the resulting common area is 0.866 of 6834, the length of the *vesica* can be no other number than 5919.

In other words, the phrase "Jonas in the belly of the whale three days and three nights" in St. Matthew's text *literally* refers to the horizontal width of a geometric symbol known as the "vessel of the fish". We have a direct visual representation of Jonas's location.

The *vesica piscis* is well known to Christianity, being identified with the man called Jesus. The reason usually put forward for this relationship is that the first two letters of the Greek word for "fish" (i.e. ιχθυς) correspond to the initials of the Greek for Jesus Christ (i.e. Ιησους Χριστος).[9] However, in 1969 Giorgio de Santallina and Hertha von Dechend brought attention to the historical

---

[9] More completely, the initials can be taken as an acronym representing the Greek for "Jesus Christ, Son of God, Saviour".

relationship between astrological *ages* and mythological symbolism.[10] Other researchers subsequently added more evidence.[11]

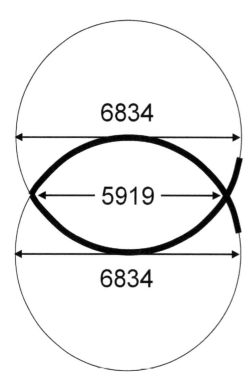

FIGURE 4-9: THE VESSEL OF THE FISH

It seems that, in the ancient world, it was customary to relate the zodiacal sign for a particular astrological age to a specific symbolic representation of God. Hence, for example, during the Age of Taurus (i.e. 4000 to 2000 B.C.) the Egyptians of the Old Kingdom employed the symbol of the Sacred Bull of the Heavens (named Apis), and during the Age of Aries (i.e. 2000 to 1 B.C.) the Egyptians of the New Kingdom used the symbol of the ram.[12] We are currently in the astrological Age of Pisces (by convention, 0 C.E. to date), represented by

---

[10] Giorgio de Santillana and Hertha von Dechend, *Hamlet's Mill: An Essay on Myth and the Frame of Time* (Gambit, Boston, 1969). Astrological ages occur because of the phenomenon of *the precession of the equinoxes*, caused by the Earth's wobble. The spring rising point of the sun moves backwards through the Zodiac, changing sign approximately every 2160 years. There is, however, a great deal of disagreement about the start and end dates of the various Ages, partly due to the fact that stars in some of the constellations overlap. The Age of Pisces may have started anytime between 1 A.D. and 500 A.D., and could end anytime between 2062 A.D. and 2720 A.D.

[11] See, for example, David Ulansey, *The Origins of the Mithraic Mysteries* (Oxford University Press, London, 1989).

[12] This raises the question of when ancient societies knew about the precession of the equinoxes and how they discovered it. There is evidence that knowledge of the phenomenon is at least 4000 years old. In the transition from the Age of Taurus to the Age of Aries, for example, the artwork oriented, first, to killing the bull (at the end of the Age of Taurus) and, then, progressed to such activities as searching for the ram's fleece (at the start of the Age of Aries).

a pair of fish set head to tail with one another. This means that the *vesica piscis* is a perfect vehicle for transmitting the symbolism of the Piscean Age: it is literally the vessel of the fish; and the fish image can be either left facing or right facing (see Figure 4-10).[13]

It can now also be shown that Figure 4-4 and Figure 4-5, showing the potential relationships between the circle and the square, are both applicable. The use of two circles in constructing the *vesica piscis* suggests the accompanying presence of two squares. These are shown in Figure 4-11 as ABCD and abcd. The top circle can be associated either with the square abcd (as in Figure 4-4) or with the square ABCD (as in Figure 4-5).

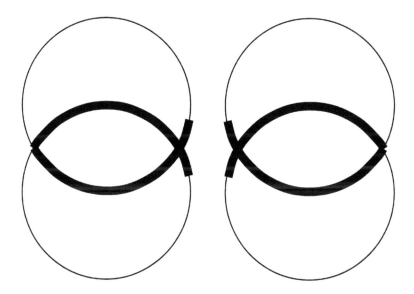

FIGURE 4-10: THE PISCEAN IMAGE OF TWO FISHES

---

[13] The *vesica piscis* was not specifically a Christian innovation (see Chapter 5). Nevertheless, the adoption of the *vesica* in Christian symbolism undoubtedly marked a new order of understanding, both about the nature of life in general and about the nature of humankind in particular. With the bull and the ram, God was seen as being an *external* force assigned to the vault of the heavens. With the fish, however, God was seen as being in some way *internal* to the experience of life. The *vesica* represented the point where the external God (The Father – i.e. the top circle) met the internal Life Force (The Holy Spirit – i.e. the lower circle) to become a perfect, God-realised, human being (The Son). The latter is an accurate description of "the Son of man", which was essentially a Jewish conception. Alternative epithets were *Adam Kadmon* and "Sky Man". It was taken to mean the archetypal – or "perfect" – man, whose consciousness spanned Heaven and Earth. See Hugh Schonfield, *The Essene Odyssey* (Element, Shaftesbury (Dorset), 1984).

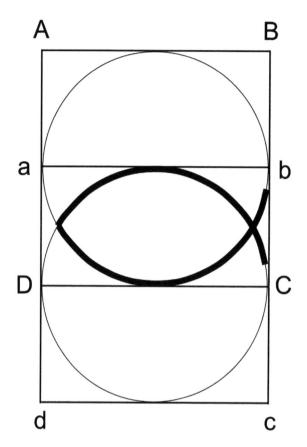

FIGURE 4-11: DOUBLE CIRCLE AND DOUBLE SQUARE

THE NUMBER 666 AND TIME

This particular representation of the *vesica* is important because it contains a reference to the active energy of creation that was discussed in Chapter 3, via the number 666. This is shown in Figure 4-12, which reflects the dimensions used in Figure 4-7. Half the width of a circle in the diagram is:

6834 / 2 = 3417

Hence, the *height* of the rectangle enclosing the two circles is three times this number. That is:

3417 x 3 = 10,250

At the same time, the *width* of the rectangle is 6834. Hence the ratio of the width to the height is:

6834 / 10,250 = **0.666**[14]

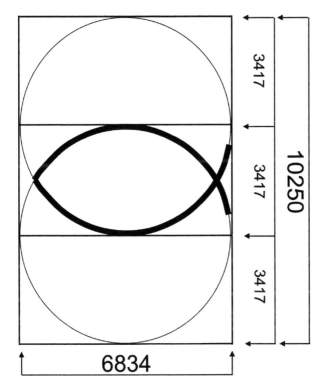

FIGURE 4-12: THE 666 RECTANGLE AND THE VESICA PISCIS

It is also important to remember that this particular version of the *vesica piscis* emerges when the numerology of "Jonas in the belly of the whale" and "the Son of man in the heart of the earth" are linked together through the use of the phrase "three days and three nights". In other words, the *vesica* emerges only once account is taken of the *passage of time*. Appendix 3 demonstrates how the dimensions of the *vesica* in St. Matthew's text can be correlated with gematrian values for "three days and three nights".

So, let us recapitulate. We now know that the reference to "Jonas" and to "the Son of man" in St. Matthew's Gospel is a reference – veiled through the science of gematria – to an ancient geometric symbol known as the *vesica piscis*. The presence of this "vessel of the fish" is confirmed by the explicit reference in the text to the "belly of the whale".

---

[14] In gematria, the *symbolism* of the number always overrides the nature of its presentation – that is, decimal points are ignored.

Furthermore, the symbol is implicitly associated with two aspects of the phenomenon of Life. First, the *vesica* is encapsulated by a rectangle whose dimensions reflect the number 666. It is, therefore, associated with the active energy of creation. Second, the *vesica* was generated with the help of the phrase "three days and three nights". It is, therefore, associated in some way with the dimension of time.

We can now look at this revelation in a little more detail.

CHAPTER 5

THE SON OF MAN IN THE HEART OF THE EARTH

"I believe there was a secret meaning in what [Christ] said; that the Son of man be three days and three nights in the heart of the earth."

W. D. Gann

THE NUMBER 1061

In the previous three Chapters, I demonstrated the importance of symbolic numbers in ancient Greek texts. I also concluded that, in Chapter 12 of St. Matthew's Gospel, there was a clear textual distinction between the name *Ιωνα* (i.e. "Jonah" in "the sign of the prophet Jonah") and the name *Ιωνας* (i.e. "Jonas" in "Jonas in the belly of the whale"). This distinction is of immense importance. The addition of the "*ς*" in the original Greek has the effect of adding 200 to the gematrian – or symbolic – value of the name.

The symbolic number for "Jonas" is thus **1061**; and this number yields either a circle when it is combined with the spatial number of "the belly of the whale", or it yields a square when it is associated with the subject-spatial numbers of the "Son of man" in "the heart of the earth".

In addition, I concluded that, once an account was taken of the symbolic numbers for the passage of time (i.e. **2586**), the relationships between the numbers reveals the presence of a *vesica piscis* – the vessel of the fish.

It can now be shown that the reference to the passage of time represented a new philosophical development, and a potential *revelation* about the structure of the cosmos.

To understand this, it is first necessary to analyse the role of the number 1061 in gematria. The important piece of information is that this number is also the symbolic number for the Greek god Apollo (i.e. $A\pi o\lambda\lambda\omega\nu$). That is:

$A\pi o\lambda\lambda\omega\nu$ = 1 + 80 + 70 + 30 + 30 + 800 + 50 = 1061

In the Greek pantheon, Apollo was the god of light and reason. But the point here is that he was always associated specifically with two other gods: Zeus (i.e. $Z\epsilon\nu\varsigma$), the father god who reigned on Mount Olympus; and Hermes (i.e. $E\pi\mu\eta\varsigma$), the messenger of the gods. The symbolic number of Zeus is **612** and the symbolic number of Hermes is **353**. That is:

$Z\epsilon\nu\varsigma$ = 7 + 5 + 400 + 200 = 612

$E\pi\mu\eta\varsigma$ = 5 + 100 + 40 + 8 + 200 = 353

The startling fact here is that the numbers 1061, 612 and 353 are related to one another in two distinct ways. First, they are related by a common ratio. That is:

1061 / 612 = 1.733/1

612 / 353 = 1.733/1

Second, and as a result of this relationship, the gematrian number for "Zeus" (i.e. 612) represents the *geometric* mean between the numbers for "Apollo" (i.e. 1061) and "Hermes" (i.e. 353). Specifically:

612 = √(1061 x 353)

These relationships throw up a striking parallel between the three Greek gods (placed in the hierarchical order of: Zeus, Hermes, and Apollo) and the Christian Trinity as analysed in Chapter 2 (i.e. Father, Holy Spirit, and Son). These parallels are emphasised by the fact that the three Greek gods are linked together by the ratio 1.733:1, and the three aspects of the Trinity are linked through the Golden Ratio 1.618:1. In both cases, therefore, a triad of forces are linked symbolically and mathematically.

THE LAW OF THREE IN GREEK PHILOSOPHY

As will be shown, Chapter 12 of St. Matthew's Gospel focuses on the difference between the two presentations and, in doing so, offers a revelation concerning the nature of time itself. In the meantime, however, the fact that "Jonas" and "Apollo" have the same symbolic numbers is unlikely to be just a coincidence. The number 1061 links "Jonas" to the god "Apollo", and therefore assigns to the former the attributes of latter. But, in linking "Jonas" to the three Greek gods, it also symbolically linked St. Matthew's text to the *Law of Three*.

The additional clue here is the ratio 1.733:1, which was of tremendous importance in Greek philosophy. The number 1.733 itself is virtually identical to the irrational number √3 = 1.7320508…,[1] which in turn was an explicit reference to the importance of the interrelationship of three forces. This interrelationship was the Greek version of the *Law of Three*.

There were three main images of these three forces – and therefore of the *Law of Three* – in Greek geometry. Each of these images involved the irrational number √3. The first was the perfect *equilateral triangle*. In such a triangle, the lengths of the sides are equal, and the height is √3 multiplied by half the width of the base. See the left-hand diagram of Figure 5-1. The equality of the sides emphasised the equivalence of the positive, negative and equilibrating energies in Creation. Usually, the equilateral triangle was shown in the context of a circle. Such a triangle would therefore divide the circumference of the circle into three equal parts. See the right-hand diagram of Figure 5-1. This triangle/circle combination will be revisited in Chapter 8.

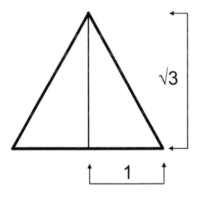 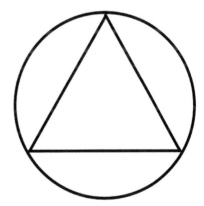

FIGURE 5-1: THE PERFECT EQUILATERAL TRIANGLE

The second image of the Greek *Law of Three* was the simple formative image of volume in three-dimensional space – namely, the cube. The square and the cube were associated with the solidity of matter and of earthly existence. The diagonal width of a cube, split from one corner to the opposite corner, is measured by the ratio √3:1. See Figure 5-2.

---

[1] The inference always was that the number 1.733 was a representation of the value of √3. See Fideler, *Jesus Christ*.

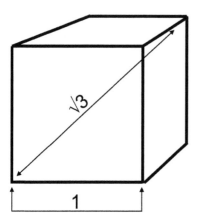

FIGURE 5-2: THE CUBE

But the third image is the most important in the immediate context – it is the *vesica piscis*. The *vesica*, like the perfect equilateral triangle, is defined by the ratio √3:1. This is shown in Figure 5-3 below. Here, the width of the *vesica* is √3 multiplied by the height of the *vesica*. Despite the use made of the *vesica piscis* in Christian symbolism, it had a much earlier origin. It signified the interaction of opposites, with the area formed by the interlocking circles representing the region where pre-existent form fused with manifest creation.

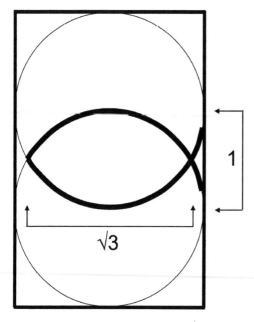

FIGURE 5-3: THE VESICA PISCIS AND √3

A break with tradition

The seminal work of David Fideler has made it very clear that the number 1061 would automatically evoke the numbers 612 and 353 (with their symbolic references to the forces of the gods), the ratio √3:1 (with its geometric implications), and the *vesica piscis* (with its pre-Christian ideas of the fusion of opposites).[2] As a cross-check, if the width of the *vesica* is Apollo (1061), then the height is going to be Zeus (612); and if the width is Zeus, then the height is going to be Hermes (353). This is precisely why the number 1061 was so important.

So, whilst it could now take modern researchers many hours to disinter the *vesica* from any given piece of text, an ancient Greek theologian with a knowledge of gematria would almost certainly have intuited its presence just from the number 1061.[3] And, in this case, St. Matthew's text actually emphasises the presence of the *vesica* (in the context of the number 1061) by using the phrase "in the belly of the whale". Ordinarily, this would have been enough.

In this particular case, however, there was also something else. The initial construction of the *vesica* in Chapter 4 used the numbers 5919 and 6834. In other words, the specific *vesica* that was hidden within St. Matthew's text depended, not just on Jonas, but *also* on the Son of man. This suggests that an important message was intended. The phrase "Jonas in the belly of the whale" was undoubtedly a direct reference to the *known* geometry of the *vesica piscis*. However, the use of the numbers 5919 and 6834 suggests a reference to an *unknown* aspect of the *vesica* deriving from a higher order. If correct, this represents a major development from tradition.

THE GOLDEN RATIO AT WORK

St. Matthew's text draws all these concepts into focus, but its brilliance lies in using the associated Greek philosophy and geometry as a stepping stone to a revelation. As has already been discussed, "the sign of the prophet Jonah" depends for its interpretation on the relationship between two phrases – namely, "Jonas in the belly of the whale for three days and three nights" and "the Son of man in the heart of the earth for three days and three nights". Each of these phrases consists of a person, in a place, and for a given length of time. Each phrase, therefore, is an *event* that lasts for a fixed period of time. If we calculate the symbolic numbers for each of the sub-phrases relevant to each event, Table 5-1 emerges.

---

[2] *Ibid.*
[3] The number 1061 was undoubtedly a particularly sacred number.

	Jonas event	Proportion of total (%)	Son of man event	Proportion of total (%)
Who	1061	18	3030	44
Where	2272	38	1218	18
How long	2586	44	2586	38
Totals	5919	100	6834	100

TABLE 5-1: SYMBOLIC NUMBERS RELATING "JONAS" TO THE "SON OF MAN"

What is interesting here is the existence of specific internal resonances between the two events. In *both* events, each sub-phrase represents 18%, 38% or 44% of the total. Furthermore, note that 18% + 44% = 62%. In the case of the Jonas event, "who" and "how long" together form 62% of the phrase; while "where" forms 38%. In the case of the Son of man event, "who" and "where" form 62% of the total phrase, while "how long" forms 38%. So St. Matthew's text incorporates the Golden Ratio, **38:62**.

In Chapter 2, it was shown that, when looking at energies of Creation within the context of the Christian scriptures, the active generative force can be represented by the number 666 and that the passive receptive force can be represented by 1080. It was also shown that, in relation to their originating Source, these numbers were reflected, respectively, in the ratios 0.382:1 (i.e. 666:1746) and 0.618:1 (i.e. 1080:1746). The functions of these ratios are not restricted just to their immediate context, which means that the ratio 0.382:1 can be used to isolate those elements in St. Matthew's text that are "active" in relation to the hidden message.

Hence, in the case of the Jonas event, the active energy is represented by the *location* – i.e. in "the belly of the whale" (see Table 5-1). It has already been shown that this is true because "the belly of the whale" is a direct reference to the *vesica piscis*. If the same logic is then applied to the case of the Son of man event, the obvious conclusion to be drawn is that the active energy is provided by the *time* dimension (see Table 5-1 again). The focus has therefore shifted from "where" to "how long".

"JONAH" VERSUS "JONAS" AGAIN

This insight can be validated by another very important symbolic relationship within the text. But the detail of the text itself first needs some attention. In Chapter 4, I raised the possibility that it might be necessary to reconcile the difference between "Jonah" in verse 39 and "Jonas" in verse 40, by making them identical. The whole of the foregoing analysis would, of course, be irrelevant if the name "Jonas" was reduced to "Jonah". The mathematical relationships would disappear.

If, on the other hand, the correct appellation for the prophet was "Jonas" rather than "Jonah", then the hugely symbolic number **1061** would be applicable. As shown in Chapter 4, the gematrian value of "the sign of the prophet Jonas" would be increased from 3912 to **4112**. Although there is no obvious peripheral evidence that such a reconciliation was intended, the direct evidence from making the adjustment is compelling.

In Chapter 4, the sign given by Jesus was quite specifically categorised: it belonged not just to "Jonah", but to the "*prophet* Jonah/Jonas". Hence, the word προφητου (i.e. "prophet") is obviously relevant to the analysis. By gematria, the value of προφητου is **1528**. This means that the gematrian value for the epithet "prophet Jonas" becomes (1528 + 1061 =) **2589**. This is virtually equivalent to the number **2586,** which is the gematrian value of τρεις ημερας και τρεις νυκτας, meaning "three days and three nights".

Indeed, the flexibility permitted by the colel allows the two numbers to be matched. Therefore, the phrase "prophet Jonas" has, in effect, the same symbolic meaning as "three days and three nights". It also implies that, since the "prophet Jonas" is interchangeable with "three days and three nights", "the sign of the prophet" can be read as being "the sign of the *three days and three nights*". In other words, the text is placing the purpose of "the sign of the prophet Jonas" within the dimension of time.[4]

Three important points have thus been established. First, the sign to which Jesus was referring in St. Matthew's text involves the *vesica piscis*. Second, however, the precise form of this *vesica* was not the traditional one because it is created using the phrase "the Son of man in the heart of the earth for three days and three nights"; it therefore implies a new dimension to the symbol. Third, this additional dimension in some way involved the phenomenon of time. It is now necessary to establish how the latter expresses itself in the context of geometry.

THE GOLDEN RATIO AND TIME

It was shown in Table 5-1 that once St. Matthew's text is broken down into its constituent parts the Golden Ratio emerges. For example, the value of the phrase "the Son of man in the heart of the earth" (i.e. 4248) is related to the value of the *total* phrase "the Son of man in the heart of the earth, three days and three nights" (i.e. 6834) by the Golden Ratio. That is:

4248 / 6834 = **0.62**

---

[4] There are other relationships here. For example, the number for "three days" (i.e. 969) is equal, by gematria, to the number for "nights". So the phrase could read "three days and three {three days}", thereby suggesting a period of (3 + (3 x 3)), or *twelve*, days. The number 12 is one of the important numbers in the context both of time and of circular measurement.

It is the addition of the crucial phrase "three days and three nights" to the denominator that reveals the presence of the Golden Ratio. Time and the Golden Ratio are therefore related in some way. Now suppose that the phrase "three days and three nights" is a literal reference to a specific transit of clock-time – that is, to a period defined as "three days" followed by "three nights". The symbolic number for "three days" (i.e. τρεις ημερας) is **969** and the number for "three nights" (i.e. τρεις νυκτας) is **1586**. Hence, the arithmetic sum of "three days" (i.e. 969) plus "three nights" (i.e. 1586) is **2555**, such that:

969 / 2555 = **0.38**

1586 / 2555 = **0.62**

And this is exactly what is to be expected from the general symbolism of the words "day" and "night": the former is associated with light and action, and therefore with the ratio 0.382:1; the latter is associated with darkness and passivity, and therefore with the ratio 0.618:1.[5]

The evolution of thought

However, the critical evidence confirming the influence of the Golden Ratio lies (again) within the symbolic number for "the sign of the prophet Jonas". The fact is that 4112 is bound to the Golden Ratio by the formula:

4112 = (**666 x 0.6174**) x 10

Hence, "the sign of the prophet Jonas" is defined by the combination of the active energy of Creation (i.e. 666) and the Golden Ratio (i.e. 0.62).[6]

This last formula isolates something new and important in St. Matthew's text. Although the symbol of the *vesica piscis* was well known at the time the text was written in the first century A.D., its relationship to the numbers 666 and 0.618 was essentially a secret. The revelation therefore has two implications. The first – which is philosophical, but which needs to be highlighted – is that it closes a loop that the original Greek version of the *vesica piscis* left open. The symbolic numbers of Apollo, Zeus and Hermes reflect a continuous proportion in *three* terms (i.e. a:b::b:c). Traditionally, such a proportion represents the use of understanding by *analogy* and requires the application of a type of intelligence that is classically human.

---

[5] See Chapter 2.
[6] Furthermore, "the sign of the prophet Jonas" is on the same *ray* as the symbolic numbers 1746, 1080 and 666. This is because the ratio 411.2:666 is equivalent to 666:1080 and 1080:1746, or 0.618:1.

This type of proportional relationship is to be distinguished from a simple proportion in *two* terms (i.e. a:b), which represents understanding by *comparison*. The resulting recognition of "differences"[7] is necessary to Life, but is not sufficient for human intelligence. The Golden Ratio, however, is a continuous proportion in *two* terms (i.e. a:b::b:(a+b)). If this is taken to involve a jump to a higher order of mental functioning – that is, to the level beyond comparison and analogy – then the Golden Ratio implies *intuitive* understandings, arrived at within the context of a prior Unity. The "sign of the prophet", therefore, can be interpreted as an affirmation of the drive within evolution to create the conditions for higher intelligence.

The second implication, however, may be a genuine revelation: it concerns the *geometry* of time itself. Remember that the number 666 is a symbolic number in Greek gematria. In the double circle diagram of the *vesica piscis* it arises in the form of a ratio. However, in gematria, the symbolism of the number always overrides the nature of its presentation – that is, decimal points are ignored. This means that, symbolically, "the sign of the prophet Jonas" is equal to 666 x 0.62 and there is only one way to interpret this statement. This is that, for some reason, **the active energy of Creation is to be multiplied by the Golden Number**. The question then is: what exactly does this mean?

Squaring output with input

The active energy within any process can be measured either in terms of what goes into the process (i.e. inputs) or in terms of what comes out of it (i.e. outputs). As a generalisation, it is consistent with the analysis of Chapters 2 and 3 that the number 666 (and hence the ratio 0.382:1) is representative of *output* energy, while the number 1080 (and hence the ratio 0.618:1) is representative of *input* energy. The logical conclusion, therefore, is that "the sign of the prophet Jonas" requires that the measured output from any process is multiplied by the Golden Number.

At the same time, the use of the words "day" and "night" in the phrase "three days and three nights" is suggestive, respectively, of the processes of activity and rest. And symbolic numbers often represent energies of some sort. If these two ideas are put together, it also seems logical that the symbolic number for "three days" (i.e. 969) can be taken to represent the active process of creation, while the number for "three nights" (i.e. 1586) might represent the passive, rest, phase of creation. Then multiplying 969 and 1586 by 0.62 yields the following equation:

$$(969 \times 0.62) + (1586 \times 0.62) = 1584$$

---

[7] In Gregory Bateson's sense of a "difference which makes a difference". See Bateson, *Mind and Nature*.

In other words, the *result* of the calculation (i.e. 1584) is virtually identical to the *largest number* (1586) used in the calculation.

This is a stunning result because it means that, if this equation is transferred onto a geometric diagram, the result is a *square*. Each calculation on the left-hand side of the equation represents a Golden Rectangle – namely, a rectangle of 969 x 0.62 and a rectangle of 1586 x 0.62. If these rectangles are then placed on a chart, so that their widths are registered horizontally and their heights are measured vertically, then the sum of their widths – when they are placed contiguously – is equal to the height of the largest rectangle. This is shown in Figure 5-4.

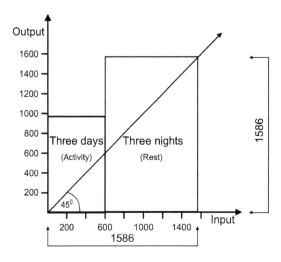

FIGURE 5-4: THE INPUT-OUTPUT SQUARE OF 666 AND 0.62

Squaring activity with Time

To repeat: this is stunning. The Jonas event and the Son of man event each have a particular beginning and a particular end – i.e. each has a *specific* life span. Each event transits *two* rectangles – i.e. one lasting three days and one lasting three nights. Each event therefore terminates when a *square* has been formed. Indeed, if it is assumed that the vertical axis represents some form of *output*, and that the horizontal axis represents an as yet undefined form of *input*, the event terminates when output meets input on the 45° diagonal line. The work of Creation is therefore literally "squared off" and completed when the extent of creativity is equal to the sum of the creativity in each time frame multiplied by the Golden Ratio.

As presented, Figure 5-4 assumes that activity is followed by rest. There is, however, another way of looking at "three days and three nights". Any active process in the mundane world is necessarily preceded by a stimulus of some sort. This means that the organism has to go through a passive adjustment phase *before* its own internal energy is activated. This phenomenon will be revisited again in Chapter 8, but it means that the Golden Rectangles within Figure 5-4 could be reversed. The outcome is shown in Figure 5-5.

In both diagrams, the phenomenon of time – better written as "Time", with a capital "T" – is shown to have an *objective* dimension. Movement in the manifest world is related – through the influence of the Golden Ratio – to an unseen creative energy. This energy is not yet properly known to science; but, by tradition, it has been known as "spirit". The phenomenon of Time is a reflection of the influence of a hidden creative energy.[8]

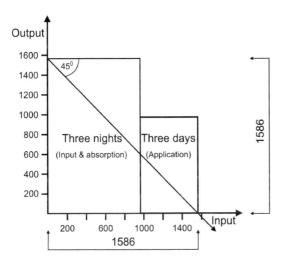

FIGURE 5-5: THE PASSIVE-ACTIVE SQUARE OF 666 AND 0.62

UNKNOWN SOURCE OF ORDER?

In the original Greek, St. Matthew's "sign of the prophet Jonah/Jonas" consists of only 48 words.[9] Even now, it seems extraordinary that such a small number of words could be used to hold a complex set of geometric diagrams. In ancient times, these diagrams could only have been exhumed by the select few who had access to geometry and mathematics. In the early stages of the Christian era, attention would undoubtedly have focused on the connections between the man Jesus, the concept of the Son of man, and the image of the *vesica piscis*. These

---

[8] It is my belief that this is the true basis of William D. Gann's formula for "squaring price with time".

[9] The number 48 itself is very significant because – via the number 12 (i.e. 4 x 12 = 48) – it alludes to the heavens and the zodiac. See Michell, *Dimensions of Paradise*.

connections would have been regarded as a *natural* proof that Jesus was to be the true representation of the Divine during the Age of Pisces.

But there seems to be something else: hidden in the text are two diagrams that – even if identified – could not easily have been understood by ancient geometers. There would have been no context within which to put them. The first diagram suggests that there is an objective dimension to Time. The second diagram, which will be addressed shortly, suggests that time-bound natural processes exhibit a very specific pattern of vibration.

Taken together, these two diagrams indicate that St. Matthew's text reveals not just a hidden form of order behind the phenomenon of Life, but a form of order that modern scientific research does not yet recognise. This conclusion could, of course, be misplaced; but, if it isn't, either St. Matthew's text is an unbelievably clever fabrication or science has a paradigm shift to negotiate.

CHAPTER 6

THE STRUCTURE OF THE MUSICAL OCTAVE

"A study of the seven-tone musical scale gives a very good foundation for understanding the cosmic law of octaves."

P. D. Ouspensky

THE OCTAVE

In Chapter 3, it was argued that the *Law of Three* is an essential aspect of Life. It will be shown that this law – which embraces active, passive, and neutralising forces – is not the only one that is involved with the concept of vibration. Nevertheless, if it is a fundamental law, it must be present in all aspects of vibration. One direct way of exploring this idea is to see how it exists within the vibrations of music – in particular, within the musical *octave*. This chapter will therefore analyse the simple mathematics of the octave in search of the *Law of Three* and, in so doing, provide a crucial link to Chapter 7.

The first point is that Western music is based on a particular set of notes, centred on a vibration of 256 cycles per second. This vibration, which is traditionally referred to as "Middle C" because of its location on a piano keyboard, evokes a sympathetic response in human beings: the human body literally resonates with it and harmonises with it.[1]

The second point is that the minimum number of notes that can be used to create a practical set is eight. This is the octave. The set starts with one note and

---

[1] Theo Gimbel, *Form, Sound, Colour and Healing* (C.W. Daniel Company Ltd, Saffron Walden (Essex), 1987).

ends where the vibration of a note has either doubled or halved. If we use an octave based on Middle C (hereafter 'C^{MID}'), the ascending octave stops with a vibration of 512 cycles per second (at 'C^{HI}'), and the descending octave finishes with a vibration of 128 cycles per second (at 'C^{LO}').

The third point is that each note in the octave bears a constant relationship to C^{MID}. There are therefore *six* ratios in any particular octave that do not involve either a doubling or a halving of vibrations. Table 6-1 shows a full set of notes in an ascending and in a descending octave based on C^{MID}, together with the relevant ratios. The vibrations of the descending octave are calculated by using half the diatonic ratios.

Ascending octave			Descending octave		
Note	Vibration	Ratio to C	Note	Vibration	Ratio to C
C^{HI}	512	2	C^{MID}	256	1
B	480	1.875	B	240	0.9375
A	426.666	1.666	A	213.248	0.8333
G	384	1.5	G	192	0.75
F	341.333	1.333	F	170.496	0.666
E	320	1.25	E	160	0.625
D	288	1.125	D	144	0.5625
C^{MID}	256	1	C^{LO}	128	0.5

TABLE 6-1: THE ASCENDING AND DESCENDING OCTAVE

By tradition, an octave is referred to as being *diatonic* (from the Greek διατονικος, meaning "through the tones"). Moreover, the musical notes are referenced by a form of notation, known as the *tonic sol-fa* – namely, Do, Re Me, Fa, So, La, Ti, Do.[2] Table 6-2 shows the ascending and descending octaves, using the tonic sol-fa.

Ascending octave			Descending octave		
Note	Tonic Sol-fa	Ratio to C	Note	Tonic Sol-fa	Ratio to C
C^{HI}	Do^{HI}	2	C^{MID}	Do	1
B	Ti	1.875	B	Ti	0.9375
A	La	1.666	A	La	0.8333
G	So	1.5	G	So	0.75
F	Fa	1.333	F	Fa	0.666
E	Mi	1.25	E	Me	0.625
D	Re	1.125	D	Re	0.5625
C^{MID}	Do	1	C^{LO}	Do^{LO}	0.5

TABLE 6-2: THE TONIC SOL-FA

---

[2] The tonic sol-fa was originally introduced to help sight reading.

THREE INNER OCTAVES

So far, this is standard information. What is not so well known is that a basic ascending octave contains *three* inner octaves. In the ascending octave in Tables 6-1 and 6-2, the move from Do to Do^{HI} involves a doubling of vibrations from 256 cycles per second to 512 cycles per second. In other words, there is an increase in vibrations of 256 cycles per second. As Russell Smith has shown[3] we can therefore look at the tonic sol-fa in a slightly different way, using the fact of an increase of 256 in vibrations, but starting from zero. Although the ratios in Tables 6-1 and 6-2 hold true when compared with C^{MID} as Do, the ratios are different when they are calculated in relation to the whole range of vibrations, from 0 to 256. This is shown in Figure 6-3. The vibrations follow the sequence 0, 1/8, 1/4, 1/3, 1/2, 2/3, 7/8, 1.

Ascending octave		
Tonic Sol-fa	**Vibrations**	**Ratio within whole**
Do^{HI}	256	1
Ti	224	0.875
La	170.666	0.666
So	128	0.5
Fa	85.333	0.333
Me	64	0.25
Re	32	0.125
Do	0	0

TABLE 6-3: THE TOTALITY OF 256 VIBRATIONS

Table 6-3 contains three important pieces of information concerning the *Law of Three*. First, the diatonic octave that covers the whole phenomenon of 0 to 256 vibrations contains *three* doublings in vibration, starting at Re (32) – that is, at Me (64), So (128) and Do^{HI} (256). Since the basic idea of an octave is the doubling and halving of vibrations, the whole phenomenon of 0-256 vibrations can therefore be seen as spanning three octaves starting, respectively, at Re, Me and So. This is shown in Table 6-4.

The fact that each octave contains three *inner* octaves reflects the operation of the *Law of Three*. Each inner octave represents one of the three creative forces – active/neutral/passive – that define the *Law of Three*. Each of the three forces has to undergo the exigencies of climbing through its own octave. This is not as easy as it sounds because, as will be shown in Chapter 7, each octave has points of retardation – or energy gaps – which have to be surmounted. Only the completion of three successive octaves produces the whole phenomenon.

---

[3] Russell A. Smith, *Gurdjieff: Cosmic Secrets* (The Dog, Sanger (Tx.), 1993).

PI AND THE LAW OF SEVEN

Second, these three *inner* octaves span 22 notes. This is because:

1. Each octave consists of 7 tones;

2. The end of each inner octave is also the beginning of the next octave; and

3. The whole higher level octave can only be complete when the final Do is struck.

We thus have 21 (3 x 7) notes in the three inner octaves plus the final Do. See Table 6-4. Importantly, the numbers 22 and 7 reference the *classical* ratio that defines the relationship between the circumference of a circle and its diameter. This ratio, denoted by the Greek letter π (or *pi*), is 22/7.[4] As Michael Hayes has demonstrated,[5] this ratio links the *Law of Three* to another law – the *Law of Seven* – that is intimately linked to the evolution of cycles and rhythms. The *Law of Seven* will be dealt with in the next chapter.

Mr. Hayes' insight was that the numerator in the ratio refers to the number of notes in three octaves, and the denominator references the number of intervals, or tones, in an octave. And, as was shown in Chapter 4, the formula for a circle can be found in St. Matthew's text in the context of the passage of time.[6]

Third, the range of vibrations can be divided into *thirds*, also starting at Re – namely, at Fa (0.333), La (0.666) and Do^{HI} (1.000). These are highlighted in Figure 6-3. The vibration of Fa is 85.333 cycles per second, that of La is 170.666 cycles per second, and the vibration of Do^{HI} is 256 cycles per second. The vibrations are thus 85.333 cycles per second apart. See Table 6-4. As will be shown in Chapter 8, these points are important to an understanding of inflexions within any genuine cycle.

SUPPORT AND RESISTANCE IN FINANCIAL MARKETS

In Chapter 14, I shall deal with the triple octave within the context of Mr. Gann's approach to cycles. Here, it can be noted that Mr. Gann appears to have used the ratios within an octave to calculate points at which a financial market trend might hesitate or reverse. The first step was to divide trading ranges into

---

[4] The quotient of the ratio 22/7 is 3.142857... etc. However, the more precise representation of π is 3.14159265358979... etc. It is also relevant that, first, the gematrian value for π is 80, so that 8 + 0 = 8 (the notes in a complete octave) and that, second, π is the 16th letter of the Greek alphabet, so that 1 + 6 = 7 (the tones in an octave).
[5] Michael Hayes, *The Infinite Harmony: Musical Structures in Science and Theology* (Weidenfeld and Nicolson, London, 1994).
[6] It seems appropriate that the Greek word for "circle" – κυκλος – also means "cycle".

eighths and thirds[7] in order to isolate potential support and resistance levels. The second step was to focus on halvings and doublings – in terms both of retracements and of absolute moves – on the grounds that they were potential reversal points.

Whole phenomenon		Triple octave	
Tonic Sol-fa	Vibration	Tonic Sol-fa	Vibration
Do^{HI}	256	Do^4	256
		Ti^3	240
Ti	224		
		La^3	213.333
		So^3	192
La	170.666	Fa^3	170.666
		Me^3	160
		Re^3	144
So	128	Do^3	128
		Ti^2	120
		La^2	106.666
		So^2	96
Fa	85.333	Fa^2	85.333
		Me^2	80
		Re^2	72
Me	64	Do^2	64
		Ti^1	60
		La^1	53.333
		So^1	48
		Fa^1	42.666
		Me^1	40
		Re^1	36
Re	32	Do^1	32
Do	0		

TABLE 6-4: THE WHOLE PHENOMENON AND THE TRIPLE OCTAVE

Since the purpose of this book is to focus on the dynamics of human behaviour rather than to isolate profitable trading techniques, these ideas will not be

---

[7] My own research suggests that the 38.2% and 61.8% levels are more important. Mr. Gann's use of thirds may have been related to his caution about advertising the power of the Golden Ratio.

analysed here. Nevertheless, it is worth emphasising the importance of 50% and 100% moves. The former would be the full extent of a descending octave and the latter would be the full extent of an ascending octave. Of the two, Mr. Gann considered that a halving was far and away the most powerful in terms of its potential for a reversal.[8] Falls of 50% were, for example, experienced in equity markets during the financial collapse of 2007-09.

The point is that a completed octave would be a natural stopping point in a trend, and an extension of the trend would therefore require some form of additional energy to move it onwards. This is why – uniquely – changes in government policy can be so important after a doubling or halving: an expansionary policy can help to extend an advance or halt a fall. Conversely, however, a failure to act appropriately, or at all, can stop an advance or extend a fall.[9]

THE OCTAVE AND THE LAW OF THREE

There is much more that could be said about the diatonic octave, not least because the notes Mi and So of each inner octave will form the starting point for octaves of even finer vibration.[10] The immediate conclusion, however, is that the eight notes of an octave contain *three* inner octaves, or sections; and this, in turn, specifically implies that any complete phenomenon can be seen in terms of *three* phases.

Hence, we have two distinct concepts relating to the *Law of Three*: one where the third element is not obvious; and one where it is. First, all oscillations between the active and passive polarities in a natural system are organised by a hidden reconciling force (Chapter 3). Second, a natural process will evolve in three clear stages (this Chapter). As will be shown, each of these three stages can be classified in terms of their active, passive and reconciling functions.

The interplay of these two perspectives on the *Law of Three* has great relevance to an understanding of cyclical behaviour. In particular, the *Law of Three* co-arises and co-exists with another fundamental law of the universe that can be found in the octave. Mr. Gurdjieff called it the *Law of Seven*. This is the law that is the essence of William Gann's law of vibration.

---

[8] See, for example, William D. Gann, *45 Years in Wall Street* (Library of Gann Publishing Co., Pomeroy (Wa.), 1949).
[9] My own research suggests that a 50% fall or retracement in broad equity indices is probably the only point where direct government intervention can reverse a trend.
[10] Interested readers are referred to Smith, *Gurdjieff*.

CHAPTER 7

THE LAW OF SEVEN

"He had learnt that the '7th' was a sacred day, and had often talked to Marie about the number 7, and the number of times it was spoken of in the Bible."

W. D. Gann

"Even our division of time, that is, the days of the week into work days and Sundays, is connected with the same properties and inner conditions of our activity which depend upon the general law [of octaves]."

P. D. Ouspensky

UNCOMMON KNOWLEDGE

Current scientific methodology does not allow much deviation from the constraint of *accepted wisdom*. Our understanding of reality can therefore only proceed through a kind of common consensus, where people accept something as being true because others do as well. This understanding is passed on through parents, peer groups and professional educators. All reality testing is done within the framework of this common consensus, so that *paradigm shifts* – fundamental changes in beliefs – only occur when there is a crisis of some sort. Such a crisis may take the form of an overwhelming number of observations failing to accord with reality, or it may take the form of a contradiction in the theoretical framework of a belief system.[1] Either way, progress can be painfully slow.[2]

---

[1] Thomas Kuhn, *The Theory of Scientific Revolutions* (University of Chicago Press, Chicago (Ill.), 1962). A paradigm is not just a set of ideas. It is an actual research practice that generates data. New paradigms are therefore a response to contradictory data brought up by old paradigms. They also disclose new data in their own right.

[2] Even where research has clearly established a new paradigm, large numbers may still be convinced that the old

Hence, new ideas – or old ideas, newly presented – are likely to encounter strong emotional resistance, particularly if the ideas are derived from a totally different culture or context. Sometimes, however – and despite the potential hostility – the ideas are sufficiently extraordinary to warrant their disclosure. So it is with *The Law of Seven*.

This fundamental law, and the teaching diagram used to communicate it,[3] has probably been known to humanity for thousands of years. However, it is also likely that – because knowledge represents power – the details of the law (and its associated cosmogony) have periodically been suppressed by those who presume to authority over others. In any case, the *Law of Seven* has been generally unknown in the West until well into the last century, but it is now making a reappearance.

It appears initially to have been brought to the attention of Western thinkers during the inter-war years by George Gurdjieff. Subsequently, a number of associates – notably Pyotr Ouspensky,[4] John G. Bennett,[5] Kenneth Walker[6] and Charles S. Nott[7] – devoted a great deal of time to analysing the implications and applications of the law. Their findings were released into the public domain during the 1950s, 1960s and 1970s. Even more recently, others – such as Oschar Ichazo[8] and Robert Campbell[9] – appear separately to have found the same phenomenon and have also chosen to disclose it. So the workings of this alleged cosmic law are no longer a secret.

UNIVERSAL VIBRATIONS

The *Law of Seven* is the law that regulates vibrations and cycles. Its first assertion is that everything in the universe vibrates. In the modern era, when theoretical physicists are wrestling with the concepts of String Theory,[10] this statement does not seem especially strange. However, in the older, more mechanical, *billiard ball* world of Newtonian physics, the idea would have been regarded as absurd.

The second assertion of the *Law of Seven* is that vibrations stimulate movement elsewhere. This means that, first, every cause is itself a vibration and that, second,

defunct theories are actually *the truth*. In fact, while the emotions of a large majority are actively engaged in following a particular belief system, that majority is likely to persecute individuals with alternative information. John Stuart Mill once observed that even the most self-evident axiom would cause a war if it threatened someone's beliefs.

[3] See Chapter 8.

[4] Ouspensky, *In Search*.

[5] John G. Bennett, *Enneagram Studies* (Coombe Springs Press, Masham, 1974).

[6] Kenneth Walker, *A Study of Gurdjieff's Teaching* (Jonathan Cape, London, 1957).

[7] Charles S. Nott, *Journey Through This World* (Routledge & Kegan Paul, London, 1969).

[8] Reported in Claudio Naranjo, *Ennea-Type Structures* (Gateways/IDHHB inc, Nevada City (Ca.), 1990).

[9] Robert Campbell, *Fisherman's Guide: A Systems Approach to Creativity and Organization* (Shambhala, Boston (Ma.), 1985).

[10] See, for example, Shing-Tung Yau and Steve Nadis, *The Shape of Inner Space: String Theory and the Geometry of the Universe's Hidden Dimensions* (Basic Books, New York, 2010).

every cause will have a history and will have an effect that depends on that history. The third assertion of the *Law of Seven* is that, once a movement (i.e. an effect) has been initiated, it will be subject to retardations, or *energy gaps*, at two very precisely-defined points in its evolution.[11] After the second energy gap, the movement will be travelling in precisely the opposite direction from that in which it started and, after the process has repeated, the movement will return to travelling in its original direction. See Figure 7-1. In other words, movement tends to occur in *cycles*.[12]

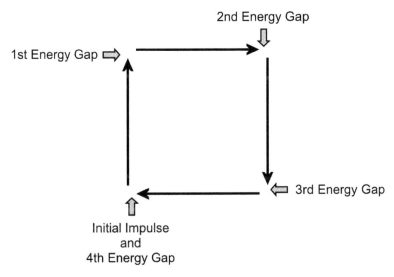

FIGURE 7-1: THE FOUR ENERGY GAPS IN A CYCLE

Figure 7-1 is somewhat misleading in the sense that it implies that both energy gaps in a successive pair of energy gaps are similar in nature. As we shall see in the next chapter, this is not correct. Crossing the first energy gap involves an evolution through the re-structuring of information that is already within a system, but crossing the second energy gap involves evolution through the input of new information from outside the system.[13] The very nature of cycles involves a successful crossing of the first gap and a failure to cross the second one. Figure 7-1 only states therefore that four important points have to be confronted for a cycle to complete itself.

---

[11] This is a slight oversimplification. The *Law of Seven* states that the vibrations develop discontinuously, with accelerations, as well as decelerations at specific points. However, it is the decelerations that are important in the current context. For fuller details see, for example, Walker, *Gurdjieff's Teaching*.

[12] The idea that four points of deviation have to be passed through to complete of cycle is one of the hidden meanings behind the concept of *squaring a circle*.

[13] That is, it involves a paradigm shift.

VIBRATION AND TIME

The importance of cycles is that they literally *retard* the effects of the passage of time. Time is usually measured in relation to the movement of the moon around the Earth, and of the Earth around the sun. But the *phenomenon* of Time is the irreversible process of change; some have called it the "arrow of time", implicitly aligning it with self-organising systems;[14] others have called it "energetic causation", thereby explicitly equating it with an energetic process.[15] Since change basically involves the dissolution of prior states, Time is intimately linked with the movement towards entropy, or chaos. The operation of the *Law of Seven* (or law of vibration) retards the collapse into chaos. In other words, cycles slow the process of change.

This retardation can be viewed in either of two ways: cycles either insert a *rest* period into the process of creation, or they insert a period of creativity into the natural drawdown into chaos. In both cases, the process between beginning and end becomes elongated. Indeed, although difficult to conceptualise, it can be argued that Time is *curved* in a long cycle,[16] which lasts from initial impulse to final accomplishment.[17] This Cycle of Time, which is a function of creative energy, contains and controls all subordinate cycles.[18]

The *Law of Seven* is so called for two distinct, but related, reasons. The first of these derives from the fact that the law is indeed a direct expression of the relationships between musical notes in an octave. Specifically, the existence of two critical energy gaps can be found within the *seven* gaps between the eight notes of a musical octave.[19] The second reason why the law is called the *Law of Seven* is that its working can be explained with the help of a geometric diagram whose interrelationships are defined by the *number* seven. We shall look at each of these in turn. The rest of this chapter will outline the *Law of Seven* within the context of the musical octave and the next chapter will explore the relevant geometric diagram.

---

[14] See, for example, Peter Coveney and Roger Highfield, *The Arrow of Time* (W.H. Allen, London, 1990). The authors propose that Time is the factor that draws together unpredictable parts into a predictable whole, which implicitly equates Time with self-organising systems and with some form of equilibrating energy. However, Time is better regarded as a *restriction* on existence. In this context, the *Law of Seven* regards Time as being the movement from one state of being to another. It therefore explicitly equates Time with change.

[15] Alfred North Whitehead, *Process and Reality* (Free Press, New York, 1969).

[16] This has been called "The Cycle of Eternity". Boris Mouravieff, *Gnosis* (Praxis Institute Press, Newbury (Ma.), 1992).

[17] This cycle is reiterated at all levels of being for humanity. It operates through *history* in the evolution of consciousness; it operates *physically* in the form of an individual's life cycle; and it operates *psychologically* in personal development. For a detailed analysis of this process, see Ken Wilber, *The Atman Project* (Quest Books, Wheaton (Ill.), 1989).

[18] There is obviously a big question here about the nature of this creative energy. See Chapter 3.

[19] Seven tones and eight notes because 'Do' appears twice in an octave.

THE LAW OF SEVEN AND THE MUSICAL OCTAVE

The *Law of Seven* controls the formation both of vibrations and of sound. This follows logically – in the sense that, if it controls one, then it must control the other – because all vibration creates sound waves.[20] Since everything vibrates, it follows that the whole universe is saturated with sound waves. Most of these waves are either so high or so low in pitch that they are outside the normal hearing range of the human ear; but being unable to hear the vibration does not mean that the vibration does not exist in the first place.[21]

One of the essential qualities of vibration is that – if it interacts with its environment[22] in a periodic or rhythmic manner[23] – it will strike a musical note. As mentioned in Chapter 6, one of the most important is 'Middle C' of the so-called diatonic scale.[24] Middle C (hereafter, 'C^{MID}') is the note that sounds when a vibration of 256 cycles per second is started, and it has been found that the human body responds to it.[25]

Other notes harmonise with C^{MID} via a series of ratios. The note that has double the vibration of C^{MID} will be eight notes higher, and the note that has half of the vibration will be eight notes lower. A set of eight notes is thus the basis of the diatonic octave. This is shown in Table 7-1, which reproduces some of the information from Chapter 6.

In theory, this octave is based on the musical proportion 6:8::9:12, which is known as the *perfect fourth*. In terms of the vibration rates given in Table 7-1, this is equivalent to 256:341.33, or 384:512. This proportion also encompasses the other perfect harmonic ratios of Western music – namely, the octave itself (i.e. 6:12) and the perfect fifth (i.e. 6:9 or 8:12). It has been found that these ratios, being *perfect*, are universal. They provide the framework for music of all cultures, even though these cultures may use different syntaxes and different intervals, and prefer different tuning systems.[26] The direct implication is that music reflects universal laws of harmony.

Points of deceleration

The diatonic octave is important because it contains within it the essence of the

---

[20] Or, more precisely, longitudinal waves (as opposed to transverse light waves) that have the potential for being heard.

[21] The ancient teaching behind the *Law of Seven* is that all vibration and all sound – whether hidden or not – is sourced in God. Hence, sound is one of the main characteristics of the initial creative emanation of God – known to Christianity as the Holy Spirit. This is why religions refer to the phenomenon as "The Word" or "The Sound Current". It is thought to resound through the universe, bearing with it the essence and characteristics of its Source.

[22] A solid, liquid or gaseous medium.

[23] See Itzhak Bentov, *Stalking the Wild Pendulum* (Wildwood House, London, 1978).

[24] Middle C is so called because it is physically closest C to the middle of a piano keyboard. Guy Murchie, *Music of the Spheres* (Dover Publications, New York, 1961). The discovery of the diatonic scale is attributed to Pythagoras.

[25] Gimbel, *Form, Sound, Colour and Healing*.

[26] Sigmund Levarie and Ernst Levy, *Tone: A Study in Musical Acoustics* (Kent State University Press (Kent), 1980).

Law of Seven. The law indicates that progress upwards through the octave decelerates at two precise points. This can be expressed in either of two ways. First, the octave consists of seven different tones (i.e. gaps between notes), but only five semi-tones. Hence, two semi-tones are missing – namely, those between E and F and between B and C^{HI} (see Table 7-1). In the terminology of the tonic sol-fa, progress upwards through the octave is retarded between Me and Fa, and between Ti and Do^{HI}.

Second, and in another way of making the same point, there are seven points of potential change in vibration between the eight notes in the octave – namely C-D, D-E, E-F, F-G, G-A, A-B, and B-C^{HI}. In Table 7-1, the vibrations are given in column 6 as ratios, with the rate of vibration of the note C as the numeraire. The difference between ratios, upwards through the octave, is retarded at E-F and at B-C^{HI}.

Note	Semi-tone	Tonic Solfa	Tonal Vibrations		Relation to C	
			Cycles/second	Difference	Ratio	Difference
C^{HI}		Do^{HI}	512		2	
B		Ti	480	32	1.875	0.125
A	A#	La	426.666	53.333	1.666	0.209
G	G#	So	384	42.666	1.5	0.166
F	F#	Fa	341.333	42.66	1.333	0.166
E		Me	320	21.333	1.25	0.083
D	D#	Re	288	32	1.125	0.125
C	C#	Do	256	32	1	0.125

TABLE 7-1: THE DIATONIC SCALE AND THE TONIC SOL-FA

This retardation, or deceleration, is also very clear if we plot either the cumulative amount of the difference between vibrations, or the difference between the ratios, in the octave. See Figure 7-2. There is a marked moderation in the upward slope of the graph between E and F (i.e. Me and Fa) and then between B and C^{HI} (i.e. Ti and Do^{HI}).

The octave and the solar system

These decelerations obviously interrupt the smooth advance of vibrations up through the octave. It's as if the process falls into a gap of some sort. At one level, this may seem to be no more than an interesting function of the way that musical notes are structured. However, the phenomenon announces its ubiquity by presenting itself in the most unlikely of places. The solar system, for example, appears to contain parallel dislocations within the orbits of the planets.

This is shown below in Table 7-2, which measures the average distances from the sun of each of the planets *excluding* the Earth. On this presentation, the solar system consists of eight planets plus the asteroid belt that lies between Mars and Jupiter.[27] If the sun is assumed in some way to act as the note Do, such that it *initiates* an octave, then that octave appears to be complete at Uranus.

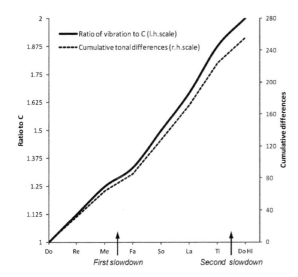

FIGURE 7-2: THE SLOWDOWN POINTS

The important point is that the ratio of the distances between successive planets and the sun is essentially a constant of 1.85, except for Venus-Mars and Uranus-Saturn where the ratio is in excess of 2.00. Hence an increase in the ratio of distances occurs precisely where the diatonic octave predicts that they should occur – namely, between Me and Fa, and between Ti and Do[HI].[28]

	Note in octave	Planet	Average distance from sun (m miles)	Ratio of distances
1	Do	Sun		
2	Re	Mercury	36.25	
				1.85
3	Me	Venus	67.20	
				2.10
4	Fa	Mars	141.68	
				1.84
5	So	Asteroid belt	261.00	
				1.85
6	La	Jupiter	484.00	
				1.83
7	Ti	Saturn	887.10	
				2.01
8	Do[HI]	Uranus	1783.90	
9		Neptune	2796.30	

TABLE 7-2: THE ENERGY GAPS IN THE SOLAR SYSTEM

[27] The average distance of the asteroid belt from the sun is calculated from Bode's Law. In 1772, Johann E. Bode

The implications of the planetary octave within our solar system obviously lie far beyond the scope of this book. Nevertheless, the existence of such a clear parallel with the diatonic octave attests to the latter's extraordinary ubiquity. In particular, it confirms the natural existence of very precisely defined points of retardation within non-linear systems. According to the *Law of Seven*, these points of deceleration are critical both to our understanding of the interaction of living organisms with their environment and to the unfolding of the associated cyclical behaviour. It is to this phenomenon that we now turn.

---

formulated this law and predicted that there should be a planet between Mars and Jupiter. This space is now known to be filled by the asteroid belt. This suggests that the asteroid belt is either a planet that has been destroyed or debris that was unable to accrete into a planet. Bode's Law works only for planets up to Uranus. Neptune and Pluto do not adhere to Bode's calculations.

[28] These observations raise some interesting questions. The Earth orbits between Venus and Mars, and therefore in some way fills the gap between those two planets. What, therefore, is the Earth's function within the *octave* of the Solar System? Meanwhile, the Earth has an average distance of 93 million miles from the sun, which means that the ratio of that distance to Venus's distance from the sun is just over 1.38 and the ratio of Mars's distance from the sun to that of the Earth is just under 1.62. Does this mean that the influence of the Golden Ratio extends into the relationship between the Earth and its neighbouring planets? Finally, Neptune lies beyond the sun-Uranus octave (and outside of the mathematics of Bode's law). Does this mean that it somehow starts a *new* octave?

CHAPTER 8

THE OCTAVE AND
THE ENNEAGRAM

"I believe that a man who understands the meaning of that has all the power under heaven and earth."

W. D. Gann

"The understanding of this symbol and the ability to make use of it give man very great power."

P. D. Ouspensky

A TEACHING DIAGRAM

In Chapter 3, it was proposed that oscillations in the universe were subject to the interplay of three creative forces. In Chapter 4, it was shown that the circle seemed to have a central role to play in part of the hidden knowledge of the ancients. In Chapter 6, it was argued that the laws governing the pattern of vibration were implicit in the musical octave and in the circle-related ratio, 22/7. In Chapter 7, a theoretical base was laid for the defining vibrations in terms of the interplay of energy gaps, as revealed in the musical octave.

These three ideas – of three forces, energy gaps and a circle – now need to be pulled together into a model that can generate cyclical oscillations. This model is known as the *enneagram*.

The enneagram has been known about in the West for less than 100 years, although it has a significantly longer history of influence. It was specifically used by George Gurdjieff in the 1920s to instruct his pupils,[1] but it reached a wider audience after one of those pupils – Pyotr Ouspensky – produced a written record.[2]

The enneagram derives its name from the Greek word ΕΝΝΕΑ or *ennea*, meaning *nine*.[3] It consists of an outer circle and an inner triangle, and a six-lined pattern that is both contained by the circle and controlled by the triangle. See Figure 8-1 below. The teaching behind the diagram is that it is an accurate representation of *every* vibration within the universe, at all hierarchical levels, and over all time periods. It is *powered* (if that is the right word) by an energy that is currently unknown to science and is thus the representation of a sacred truth.[4] More prosaically, it is the representation of perpetual motion through eternity.

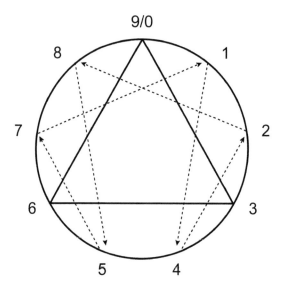

FIGURE 8-1: THE ENNEAGRAM

MOVEMENT AROUND THE ENNEAGRAM

The outer periphery of the enneagram is a circle whose circumference is divided into *nine* equal segments. The division between each segment of the

---

[1] See, for example, Walker, *Gurdjieff's Teaching*.
[2] Ouspensky, *In Search*.
[3] The numeric value, by gematria, of *ennea* (ΕΝΝΕΑ) is 111. The three equal unities reference the *Law of Three*. And, of course, 1 + 1 + 1 = 3.
[4] Ouspensky, *In Search*.

circumference is given a number from 1 to 9. See Figure 8-2. The northern point – which coincides with the apex of the triangle – is usually given the number 9. The numbers 1 to 8 are then placed at equal distances around the circumference of the circle. As was observed in Chapter 3, the number 9 represents initiation *and* completion – that is, the start *and* the finish. Hence, a movement around the circle in a clockwise direction, starting with 9 and ending with 9, represents a complete cycle.

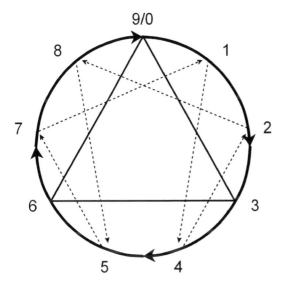

FIGURE 8-2: MOVEMENT AROUND THE CIRCUMFERENCE OF THE ENNEAGRAM

However, the circle also represents a *spiral*. Viewed from above, the movement appears as a circle; but viewed from the side, the movement may be seen as a spiral. See Figure 8-3.

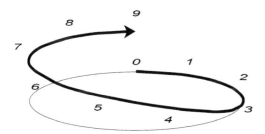

FIGURE 8-3: THE CIRCULAR SPIRAL AROUND THE OUTSIDE OF THE ENNEAGRAM

This is an oversimplification, but the point 9 that represents completion certainly has a *higher* level of vibration than the point 9 that represents initiation. Hence, a complete movement around the circle represents an *evolution* in quality as well as a movement in quantity. This idea of evolution means that point 9 is sometimes also denominated point 0. In this way it is made clear that the movement from 0 to 9 represents some form of progress.

The importance of the enneagram, however, lies not *on* the circle but *inside* it. Specifically, the *movement* of energy – which forces the cycle around the periphery of the circle – does not actually progress sequentially from point 9 (or point 0) back to point 9. The energy instead flows from point to point around the diagram in the repeating sequence, 1-4-2-8-5-7. This is represented by the six arrowed lines within the circle in Figure 8-4.

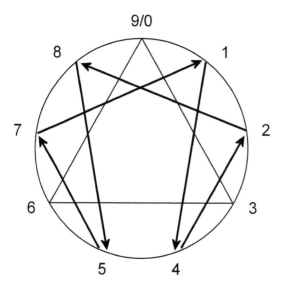

FIGURE 8-4: THE MOVEMENT OF ENERGY WITHIN THE ENNEAGRAM

This movement of energy is the most important aspect of the *Law of Seven*, but it is also the most difficult to understand. Therefore, before looking at the process in more detail, it might be useful to demonstrate how it looks if it is shown in a two-dimensional diagram that explicitly includes *time*. Let us assume that a point on the enneagram with a higher number represents (in some sense) a more evolved state than a point with a lower number.

Then, if we translate the number sequence 1-4-2-8-5-7 into a two-dimensional diagram that relates each number to its occurrence at a specific moment in time, the result is as shown in Figure 8-5 below. At time 1, the process is at point 1 on the circle; at time 2, the process is at point 4; at time 3, it is at point 2; at time 4, it is at point 8; and so forth. The movement takes no account of the time units used, or of distances travelled. Nevertheless, the fundamental *pattern* traced out by the enneagram is that of a three-up/three-down movement. And this pattern is precisely the one that, in the 1980s,[5] I had suggested existed in financial markets. I called it *the price pulse.*

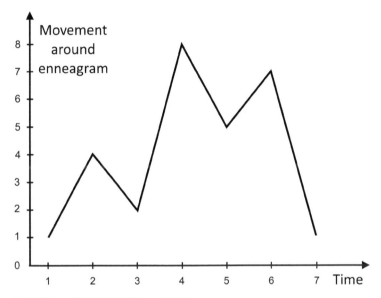

FIGURE 8-5: THE ENNEAGRAM PULSE

THE ENNEAGRAM AND THE LAW OF SEVEN

We can now look at the interaction of the enneagram and the *Law of Seven* in more detail. It was stated earlier that there are essentially *two* reasons why the law of vibration was named the *Law of Seven*. The first derives from the law's relevance to (and its analogy with) the musical octave. The octave is not only a truly natural phenomenon; it is also a metaphor for the process of transformation and change. Specifically, evolution can be described by a sequence of *seven* steps between eight points. Hence, an initial impulse (metaphorically described as Do) is then followed by *seven* separate steps – namely, Do-Re, Re-Me, Me-Fa, Fa-So, So-La, La-Ti and Ti-Do[HI]. The whole process involves an increase in vibrations and the process is complete when (or if) the vibrations *double.*[6]

---

[5] Plummer, *Forecasting Financial Markets.*
[6] At this point, however, the process also *begins* again – but on a higher level – because, in order for the vibrations to double, a new impulse (Do[1]) has to occur. This new impulse arises from *outside* the closed system of the original cycle. In other words, evolution is controlled by, and harmonises with, the environment.

However, as was shown in Chapter 7, the *Law of Seven* clearly states that the vibrations do *not* increase at a constant rate; rather, the increase accelerates and decelerates at very specific points. In the context of cycles, it is the points of *deceleration* that are the most important. The *Law of Seven* states that the vibrations will decelerate at *two* of the seven steps after the initial impulse – namely, between the equivalents of the steps Me-Fa and Ti-Do[HI] – thereby introducing energy gaps into the process of growth. This is a fundamental law of the universe.

The second reason why the *Law of Seven* has been given its name relates not to the *steps* between the notes in the octave, but to the *relationship* between the initial stimulus and the subsequent six energy points in the enneagram. As has already been mentioned, energy flows around the enneagram in the sequence 1-4-2-8-5-7. This recurring sequence of numbers can be found within the result of dividing unity by the number seven. That is:

$$1 / 7 = 0.142857142857^r$$

The sequence also emerges when the triple octave of 22 is divided by the seven tones in an octave.[7] That is:

$$22 / 7 = 3.142857142857^r$$

So, if unity, or the three octaves that create unity, are divided by seven, the result is the sequence of numbers that describe the flow of energy around the enneagram.

The number 7 has a variety of unique features that were taken by early religious authorities to be very meaningful. Of these, two in particular were important. First, the number 7 cannot be derived as the product of two other whole numbers (other than unity and the number 7 itself). Second, the number 7 cannot be divided by any other number (other than itself) to yield a whole number. For these two reasons, the number 7 was known as the *virgin* number and was seen as representing the Eternal.[8]

THE ENNEAGRAM AND THE LAW OF THREE

We can now return to the details of the enneagram itself. Following the arrows around the diagram, it can be seen that the flow does not include points 9 (or 0), 3, or 6. See Figure 8-6. These points have a specific function, which needs some explanation.

---

[7] Dividing any number by seven will reveal the presence of this same sequence, although it would not necessarily start with 1.

[8] See, for example, Michell, *Dimensions of Paradise*.

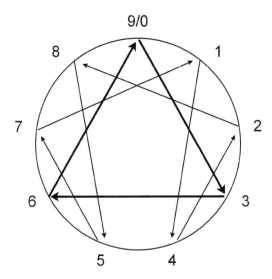

FIGURE 8-6: THE TRIANGLE WITHIN THE ENNEAGRAM

As normally presented, points 9 (or 0), 3 and 6 are joined together to form a *triangle*.[9] This confirms that they are related. In fact, the three points represent the active-passive-reconciling forces of the *Law of Three*, which were discussed in Chapter 3. At the start of the process around the enneagram, point 9/0 represents the *initial stimulus* from outside the energy circuit. Point 3 then automatically represents the *active* force of the initial stimulus, but within the energy circuit, and point 6 represents the *passive* force of that stimulus, again within the energy circuit.

To complete the balance, point 9/0 also assumes the responsibility of the *reconciling* force within the energy circuit.[10] The enneagram thus incorporates *both* the law of reconciled opposites (the *Law of Three*) *and* the law of vibration (the *Law of Seven*): it reconciles the spiral of evolution with the cycle of recurrence. As we shall now see, the reconciliation comes about as a result of the response to information shocks.

If we continue to use the analogy of the tonic sol-fa, the note Do occurs at point 9/0 and *starts* the cyclical process moving. This can be viewed as the initial *shock*, or the initial creative act. Successive points around the circumference of the circle – Re, Me, Fa, etc. – represent the attempt of the system to transform its energies into higher notes, or higher vibrations. That is, they represent the process of evolution as a *response* to the initial creative act. However, the *internal* dynamics of the evolutionary process are not smooth. The flow of internal

---

[9] Ouspensky, *In Search*.
[10] This is consistent with the argument presented in Chapter 2 – namely, that the creative force also reconciles the associated active/passive polarities.

energy stands at point 1 (or Re) after the initial shock, but then it jumps to point 4 (or Fa). This jump is too much for the system, which then begins to fade. In other words, there is an *energy gap* (see Figure 8-7) that restricts the smooth transition from one level of vibration to the next.

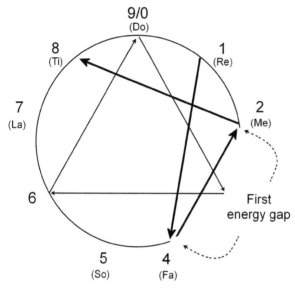

FIGURE 8-7: THE FIRST ENERGY GAP

The movement between points 1, 4, 2 and 8 therefore exhibits a three-wave pattern. Accordingly the energy flow drops back to point 2 (or Me). It is during this drop – which traverses point 3 (the gap between Me and Fa) on the enneagram – that extra energy, or information, has to be received. Otherwise the process stops. The extra information shock is, in fact, provided at this point by the *active force* of the initial stimulus at point 3. When it has been received, the energy flow can jump to point 8.

THE PATTERN OF LEARNING

This pattern is the basic profile of adjustment that all self-organising systems have to undergo in response to perceived changes in their environment. It reflects the threefold process of:

1. The initial learning response to new information;

2. The consolidation and restructuring of internal response mechanisms; and

3. The application of new learnt abilities to the receipt of further information.

In terms of the system's relationship to its environment, these three phases may be denoted as being active, passive and reconciled. In the first phase, the system responds dynamically to the receipt of new information. The system moves as far as it can under its old structure but does not yet change that structure. In the middle phase, the system becomes *passive* and allows external energy to reorganise it and thereby create change. This passivity is usually marked by a drop in the index being used to measure the internal energy of the system. But, critically, the re-structuring *cannot* take place unless a higher degree of energy is input.[11] Finally, the system can adopt a neutral relationship to the environment, adjusting quickly and easily to additional information as it becomes available.

This adjustment process mirrors the archetypal learning pattern proposed by Henry Mills.[12] See Figure 8-8. Learning is a form of mutation as energy is diverted away from the receipt of new information towards re-structuring the internal automatic response systems. This automation of the ability to respond represents the *acceptance*, or internalisation, of a paradigm shift. As a corollary, the movement after this internalisation process does not represent true learning in the sense of further structural adjustments – it merely represents the ability of the organism to respond quickly and effectively to further information.

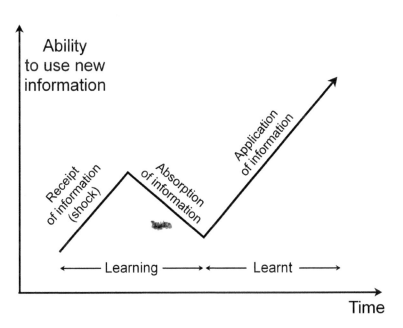

FIGURE 8-8: THE THREE-PHASE LEARNING PROCESS

---

[11] How a system accepts the need to change its structure, and is then able to do so with the help of 'external' energy, is not yet understood.

[12] Henry Mills, *Teaching and Training* (Macmillan, London, 1967).

The processes involved in this mutation are still not fully understood. Donald Hebb proposed that the adjustment involves the transfer of information from short-term memory to long-term memory. The former depends on electrical impulses within the brain, the latter depends on the structure of the neurons in the brain. Hebb's specific thesis was that persistent electrical activity associated with the receipt of new information eventually alters the connections between brain cells and thereby consolidates the information into long-term memory.[13]

It is important to note that additional information received *after* the learning has occurred, and *during* the subsequent growth phase, is no longer treated as a *shock* by the system. It is, instead, seen as confirming the validity of the context within which it is placed.[14] This phenomenon will be dealt with in more detail in the next chapter, in the context of the behaviour of financial markets. In the meantime, we can note that the main thrust of a bull or bear movement in a financial market will take place when the market is *neutral* in relation to its environment.

THE SECOND ENERGY GAP

However, the logic of the enneagram reveals that there is a *natural* limit to the process of environment-neutral growth. In terms of the three-phase learning process, satiation and tiredness eventually set in, and a period of rest and recuperation is required. See Figure 8-5 again. However, there is an alternative. The environment may deliver an unexpected shock to a system.[15] This requires more than just a minor adjustment in the latter. There is, therefore, an important distinction to be drawn between change as a learnt response to fluctuations in the environment and evolution as a revolutionary jump into a *different* state of being.

This distinction is reflected in the fact that there is a *second* energy gap, which coincides precisely with the missing semi-tone between Ti and Do[HI]. See Figure 8-9 below. This means that, in the absence of a new revolutionary impulse between Ti and Do[HI], the power within the organism is insufficient to start a new circuit at a higher level on the spiral: it is insufficient to push it from point 8, past point 9, and on to point 1. The energy flow therefore *reverses* after point 8. It drops to point 5.

---

[13] Donald Hebb, *The Organisation of Behaviour* (John Wiley, New York, 1949). Interestingly, the process of adjustment involves a temporary 'forgetting' of the initiating information.

[14] In the initial stages of a bull market, for example, the new information is placed in the context of bear sentiment; but in the later stages, bullish information is placed in the context of bullish sentiment.

[15] This raises the very relevant question about higher purposes. A shock, transmitted from outside the system, will simultaneously destroy the old structures and raise the system to a higher level of being. Hence that which appears *bad* from the lower point of view, is actually *good* from a higher point of view.

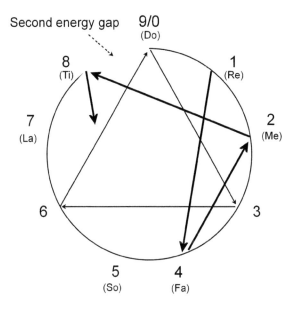

FIGURE 8-9: THE SECOND ENERGY GAP

This *failure* to bridge the gap between point 8 and point 9 of the enneagram (i.e. between Ti and Do^HI), highlights an important feature of the *Law of Seven* that is often missed. This is that there is a critical difference between the second energy gap and its predecessor, making it more difficult to offset. Whereas the first gap was easily bridged by the influence of the *active* force of the initial stimulus, the second gap is *protected* from being bridged by the influence of the passive force of the initial stimulus. The second gap is thus a great barrier. In terms of our analogy with the musical scale, the system cannot jump from Ti to Do^HI unless a quality of energy that is *higher* than that of the initial stimulus is received. Otherwise, the movement still remains under the control of the initial creative shock and starts to travel in the opposite direction.

This point can be better explained by looking again at the tonic sol-fa in the context of the enneagram. The initial shock or creative impulse, Do, occurs at the apex of the enneagram's triangle. The system traverses Re, Me and Fa by moving through points 1, 4 and 2. As already mentioned, the *active force* (which is a function of the initial impulse) delivers the necessary energy to the system at point 3, encouraging the system to rise to point 8. However, note what happens to the follow-through from this point 3 energy shock. *It* now assumes the status of being an *initiating* stimulus (Do*) (see Chapter 6). Point 6 accordingly becomes the *active* force in the context of this stimulus (bridging the gap at Me*-Fa*). This is shown in Figure 8-10.

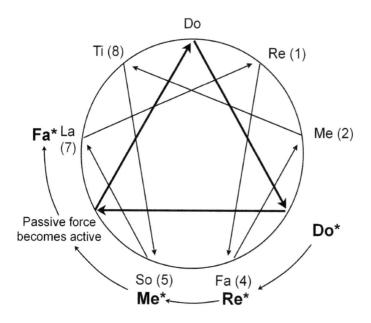

FIGURE 8-10: THE PASSIVE FORCE REVERSAL

The next step in the logic of this process is shown in Figure 8-11. The now activated passive force generates a new octave starting at Do**. The result is that the retardation, or energy gap, between Me** and Fa** in this octave coincides with the original second energy gap between Ti and Do^{HI}. Unless a new energy source is received at this point from outside the system, the energy flow will have met a barrier and will drop from point 8 to point 5. The movement up along the growth spiral is thereby terminated.

ENERGY FLOWS, BARRIERS AND SHOCKS

The enneagram reflects the processes within a self-contained energy system. No new energy is received by it, but the energy itself assumes different roles as it transits through each complete oscillation. Consequently, an original creative impulse, or shock, sets up a repetitive oscillation. The system will continue around the circle of the enneagram unless, or until, a *new* shock from outside the system can bridge the second energy gap between Ti and the higher Do^{HI}. This would represent evolution through *revolution* and would take the system to a higher point on the open ended spiral. Otherwise, the system remains in a cycle of recurrence.

There is one last point that needs to be made about the enneagram before we move on. This is that, as presented so far in this chapter, the six-wave energy pulse is shown separately from the triangle of forces. That is, the 1-4-2-8-5-7(-1) pulse is separate from the 0-3-6(-9) triangle. This helps to explain some of the theoretical processes that are involved, but it is an oversimplification.

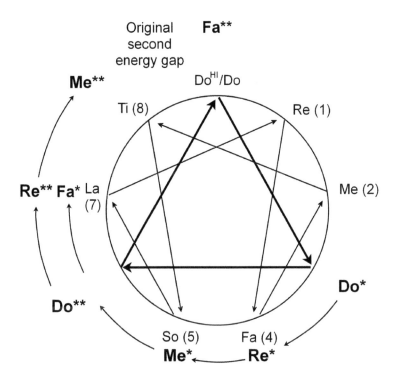

FIGURE 8-11: THIRD OCTAVE ENERGY GAP

If, instead, the notes of the tonic sol-fa are placed *diatonically* around the circle of the enneagram, the notes Fa, La and Do^{HI} coincide with the corners of the equilateral triangle. This is shown in Figure 8-12, where the notes are placed on the circumference of the enneagram according to the ratios shown in Table 6-3 of Chapter 6. The result is that Fa coincides with the corner of the triangle that defines the active force and La coincides with the corner that defines the passive force. This means that, in the absence of an (internally-generated) shock at Me, or an (externally imposed) shock at So, the energy forces at Fa and La will act as barriers. This keeps the energy trapped in the circuit and the system cannot ascend to the peak of the triangle.

The conclusions from Figure 8-12 are that: first, a clear distinction needs to be drawn between the active, passive and neutral forces that drive a system, and the energetic shocks that are necessary to take a system over an energy gap; and, second, a system is receptive to transformational shocks only at very specific moments in its evolution.

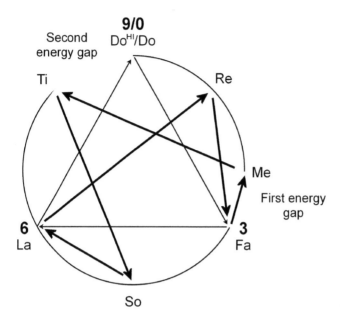

FIGURE 8-12: THE DIATONIC ENNEAGRAM

CONCLUSION

Mr. Gurdjieff thus used a very clear teaching tool, based on the *Law of Seven* and the *Law of Three*, to demonstrate the forces involved in creating recurring cyclical behaviour. This is something so much more than either just a recognition of non-linearity or only a belief that external shocks create vibrations. The message is that the vibrations are ordered, non-random, processes, and that they are an essential part, not just of biological systems, but of life generally. This implies that – no matter how difficult it is to understand – the *Law of Three* and the *Law of Seven* apply to collective human behaviour.

CHAPTER 9

THE ENNEAGRAM AND FINANCIAL MARKETS

"Remember, everything in this universe is elliptical or circular in motion; that applies both to the abstract and the concrete."

W. D. Gann

"This law explains why there are no straight lines in nature."

P. D. Ouspensky

SELF-ORGANISING SYSTEMS

Before proceeding further, it may be useful to take a detour away from esoteric literature into the arena of scientific research and practical application. The ultimate purpose of this book is to establish whether the possible existence of hitherto unrecognised natural laws can actually be applied to human behaviour – particularly collective human behaviour. We therefore need to establish a bridge between abstruse ideas that, as yet, have no grounding in fact and areas of human behaviour that can be measured in some way. For example, can the oscillations that are intrinsic to the enneagram be found in financial market speculation or in economic activity?

At this stage, therefore, it may be useful to introduce some ideas from modern systems and behavioural theory and then consider the characteristics of oscillations in financial markets. This should ultimately provide the basis for direct comparison of theoretical vibrations – as derived from St. Matthew's Gospel, *Beelzebub's Tales*, and *Tunnel* – with the reality of price movements in markets.

Modern researchers are very familiar with the idea that the universe is a *hierarchy* of competence and power, which utilises a dynamic two-way relationship between the higher and lower levels. Within this view, every level of the universe exerts a controlling influence over its subordinate parts, including the damping down of anarchic fluctuations; yet every part contributes to the nature of the level above it, including the evolution of the higher level through un-damped (or increasing) oscillations generated from below.

The direct inference is that each level of the hierarchy is something very much greater than the sum of its parts: quality is, in some way, derived from quantity. This quality is reflected in the *self-organising* ability of each element in the hierarchical structure, and in the *responsiveness and adaptability* of these elements to changes in their environment. The central characteristic[1] of a self-organising system is its ability to use *negative feedback loops* to transmit information[2] throughout the hierarchy – both horizontally (on the same level) and vertically (between levels).

GREATER WHOLES

The problem is that the *cause* of this self-organising ability is, as yet, not generally recognised. Its existence is evidenced by the presence of order; and the evidence is more convincing the less likely it is that order exists in the first place. But quantitative science cannot yet bring itself to suggest that some form of unknown (super-natural, or sub-quantifiable) power is involved. Consequently, scientific debate recognises the *result* of the energies involved, without necessarily dealing with the *source* of those energies. The cause of self-organisation remains, for most, a mysterious *fact* of life.

Nevertheless, it is at least a useful working hypothesis to postulate that the source of self-organisation may be some form of pervasive energy with which we are not yet familiar. Ancient traditions – which were very well aware of the equilibrating forces in the universe – allocated to this energy the attribute of consciousness, albeit not in the way that it arises in the human brain. If correct,

---

[1] Bateson, *Mind and Nature*. In this seminal book, Bateson observed five characteristics of self-organising systems, or of mental processes. These are:
1. Self-organising systems are aggregates of interacting parts;
2. The interaction is triggered by difference;
3. Self-organising systems require an input of energy;
4. They use negative feedback loops; and
5. Each stage in any feedback loop transforms information.

[2] *Ibid.* Information is defined as "change which makes a change".

it follows that the more closely that human perception is aligned to greater wholes, the more closely can it approach this mysterious energy, or force.[3] This alignment – or widening – of perception may be viewed in either, or both, of two ways: first, it may be obtained by expanding consciousness to embrace ever-greater units of self-organisation; second, it may simply be recognised by accepting the implications of the dynamic stability of revealed life processes.

Whether or not the source of self-organisation can be experienced directly is not strictly relevant here. However, the effects of its power – in terms, particularly, of control of its lower levels – are continuously available for observation and repeated verification. The fact is that, from the perspective of higher levels of the hierarchy, the lower levels are highly organised and are responsive to apparently simple laws. For example, in a sample of blood, a white blood cell may appear to be a separate entity and its movements may appear to be random; but in its natural environment, the same cell would be completely responsive to the body's survival needs. The simple law is: if the body is invaded by a threatening organism, the white blood cell – as the body's agent – will attempt to destroy it.

The really important point in the current context – and the idea that represents the greatest challenge to economic theorists – is that human beings themselves are also subject to controlling forces from higher-level groupings. That is, we each have a *self-assertive tendency* (a drive towards individuality) but we also all have an *integrative tendency* (a drive to take part in greater wholes).[4]

On the one hand, therefore, we each perceive ourselves as being independent, unique and therefore important. But, on the other hand, we are continually being influenced by social pressures that treat us as being dependent, undifferentiated and therefore dispensable. As a result, we are continually being presented with a choice (whether actual or metaphorical) between creative isolation and unconscious immolation. We are, each of us, caught between opposite polarities that can either stimulate us to the greatest achievements in art and science or sweep us to revolution and war.

COLLECTIVE BEHAVIOUR

The central fact that emerges from modern neuro-scientific research is that there is an observable form of order in collective behaviour that co-exists with – or overrides – the otherwise non-predictable behaviour of individuals.[5] We are social

---

[3] Wilber, Atman Project.

[4] Arthur Koestler, *Janus: A Summing Up* (Hutchinson, London, 1978).

[5] The evidence can be regarded as more convincing the less likely it is that order exists in the first place.

beings; this is a function not just of rational choice, but also of evolutionary necessity. Most of us need contact with others both to validate the mental construct of the ego and to enhance our chances of personal survival. In the business and investment world, the latter is essential.

We are literally programmed to rely on others to provide us with information that we cannot get directly for ourselves.[6] We are, therefore, programmed to be open and vulnerable to the reactions of others so that any new information can quickly be absorbed through the emotional brain. Necessarily and constantly – and unconsciously as well as consciously – we scan the behavioural patterns of others to see what, if anything, is changing.

This implies that the personal ego – the sense of self – has a weakness in its structure: it has to remain permeable to collective needs in order to deal with an actual or perceived threat. Under normal circumstances, there is always some degree of group influence, but under conditions of immediate threat or of prolonged stress, the ego boundaries can collapse completely, and allow the psyche to be overrun by simple group objectives and beliefs. This latter is the primary process associated with major social, economic and/or political change.[7] It creates single-minded tribal groups whose fanatical members have the power to destroy actual and imagined *enemies*. The psychological and physical havoc wreaked by such groups – which on a smaller scale are *crowds* – helps to break down the old social orders and provides the raw material for the new ones to emerge.[8] It is a process that oscillates between the polarities of *fission* and *fusion*.

Measuring collective behaviour

This is all well and good, but the next question is, how can group behaviour actually be quantified? Noise levels and numbers involved might be one way forward. However, the problem becomes even more insoluble when the group is not actually physical, but is instead widely dispersed. How, for example, can the integrative force of patriotism be measured?

The starting point is to recognise that coherent collective groups (hereafter, for simplicity, *crowds*) are *psychological* phenomena, not physical ones. Membership of a crowd is determined, not by a physical presence, but by a willingness to accept the crowd's belief system uncritically and by a willingness to identify with other crowd members. In this way alternative points of view are filtered out and

---

[6] See, for example, Albert Bandura, *Social Learning Theory* (General Learning Press, New York, 1977).

[7] Neumann, *Depth Psychology*. The only defence against this problem is active self-awareness, which broadens and strengthens the ego boundaries. It is my belief that Mr. Gann's success was partly related to his pursuit of self-awareness. See Gann, *The Magic Word*.

[8] Social groupings are an *essential* part of the human condition, because they facilitate co-operation. However, it is also arguable that *crowd* behaviour (in all its forms) is basically a reflection of humankind's inherent *inability* to evolve to higher levels of consciousness.

the rational thought processes of participants are effectively suppressed. There is a diminution of awareness and responsibility,[9] and personal freedom is sacrificed to the purposes of the crowd.[10] In such a condition, crowd members are very responsive to instructions from the crowd leadership, which acts as the catalyst for crowd activity.

In this context, one of the very best areas to research is financial markets. Not only do such markets develop a distinct crowd mentality, but the behaviour of the crowd can be researched – and then tracked in real time – by movements in explicit and readily available *activity* indicators such as asset prices, and by movements in certain *energy* indicators such as trading volumes.

A financial crowd's belief system relates to views about the *future* direction of price movements: the bullish crowd thinks that prices will rise; the bearish crowd thinks that prices will fall. Having adopted a particular belief system, all that each crowd member will then tend to concentrate on (at first sub-consciously and then increasingly consciously) is the *actual* movement in prices. This is, quite simply, because it is the *movement* in prices that determines the success or otherwise of a trading position – *not* the quality of the so-called *rational* analysis that preceded it. Accordingly, rising prices encourage bulls and falling prices encourage bears.[11] In this way, moving prices fulfil the *leadership* function in a financial market crowd: the crowd *chases* the prevailing trend because that is what they are effectively being told to do by a linear projection of the most recent move in prices.[12]

Constraints on rational decision-making

Hence, crowd psychology ensures that the ability of investors to arrive at *independent* decisions waxes and wanes over the course of a bull/bear life cycle. At major turning points in markets, the crowd-mind is at its most effective. The majority of investors will still be prepared to buy as a market approaches its peak; while the majority of investors will still want to sell as a market nears its trough. At these turning points, the *integrative* force operating within the crowd will be strong and will ensure that individuals are experiencing minimal fear towards the prevailing trend. In effect, the crowd has become complacent.

Conversely of course, as a new price trend emerges, the *new* crowd is in its infancy. Hence its grip on individuals is very weak and profitable positions will

---

[9] Gustave le Bon, *Psychologie des Foules*. Reprinted as *The Crowd* (Macmillan, New York, 1922).

[10] As a result, it is possible for people to commit all sorts of crimes that, as individuals, they would not even contemplate.

[11] This, of course, directly contradicts traditional economic theory, which only allows for changes in net demand to influence prices, not for prices to influence net demand. However, the two-way feedback mechanism, which actually occurs in the price-demand relationship, is a natural characteristic of life.

[12] Plummer, *Forecasting Financial Markets*.

tend to be closed off very quickly. Not surprisingly, therefore, there is often a prolonged period of price volatility before a new trend is clearly seen to emerge. The integrative tendency of the new crowd will be weak and the fear about the re-emergence of the old trend will be high.

FINANCIAL MARKET DYNAMICS

In *Forecasting Financial Markets*,[13] I argued that, because moving prices generate a crowd-type environment, every financial market has natural metabolic price oscillations with three observable characteristics:

1. They have regular periodicities;

2. They each have a basic pattern; and

3. They each contain segmented price movements that are mathematically related to each other. I called this matrix of phenomena *the price pulse*.

The basic concepts involved may be demonstrated by the use of a very simple model that combines the influence of rhythmic oscillations with the operation of a spiral.[14] In Figure 9-1, the change in financial asset prices is related to a notional index of investor sentiment (such as, for example, the ratio of bulls to bears).

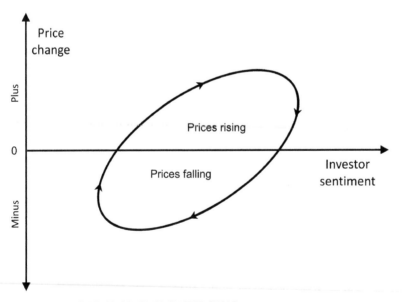

FIGURE 9-1: THE PRICE-SENTIMENT LIMIT CYCLE

---

[13] *Ibid.*
[14] *Ibid.*

Above the horizontal line, prices are rising in absolute terms; below the line, they are falling. The two-way relationship between prices and sentiment is expressed by a construct known as a *limit cycle*.[15] Such a cycle describes the co-evolution through time of two inter-dependent variables. As shown, this cycle is biased to the right. Hence, during the main part of a trend, price changes and sentiment will move together, with no clear-cut direction of causation; moving prices stimulate investor activity and investor activity stimulates price movements. At turning points, however, the relationship breaks down. Changing prices cannot stimulate further investor involvement because the market has become overbought or oversold. Technical analysts will note the divergence and call it a *non-confirmation*.

Information shocks and re-tests

However – and this is crucial – behaviour does not stay on the limit cycle. As profit-taking develops (whether by closing longs or shorts), prices change direction and a *shock* – specifically, an information shock – is delivered to the limit cycle system. See Figure 9-2. This is the sort of behaviour that is easily recognisable during a financial market *crash*, but is less noticeable under normal circumstances. Nevertheless, it is ubiquitous: it occurs at all levels of the market's hierarchy of cycles.

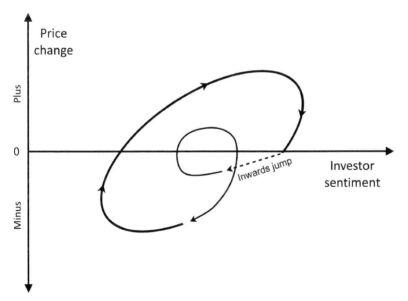

FIGURE 9-2: THE SHOCK-INDUCED SPIRAL

---

[15] A limit cycle is defined as the periodic oscillation between two variables and is represented by a closed non-linear path. See, for example, D.W. Jordan and P. Smith, *Nonlinear Ordinary Differential Equations* (Oxford University Press, Oxford, UK, 1977).

Next, the shock sets up a series of potentially destabilising oscillations, caused by negative feedback. These oscillations translate into a spiral that continues until the self-organising limit cycle processes re-assert themselves. See Figure 9-2 again. This spiral movement actually involves a re-test of the price levels from which the shock occurred. It may therefore occur either in a falling market (as shown in Figure 9-2) or it may occur in a rising market (not shown).

Such re-tests may, in fact, involve a new high in a bull market, or a new low in a bear market, depending on the strength of the limit cycles operating at the next higher level in the hierarchy. Whether it does or not, however, it is not normally accompanied by a strong improvement in the indicators of investor sentiment. This is also a *non-confirmation*, but it is much the more powerful of the two types of divergence because the subsequent move will be a dynamic thrust in the direction indicated by the limit cycle.

Three-phase movements

What emerges from this brief consideration of market dynamics is that price movements – in terms of both momentum and level – are likely to evolve in three-wave patterns. A bull move will start with bears closing positions in an oversold market. This is the information shock that the market will have to absorb. Prices advance further as rising momentum encourages additional bear closing. Nevertheless, a point will come where the short-term traders will judge that the market has travelled far enough. Prices start to pull back, and there will be a surge in short-term selling as traders attempt to take their profits. Consequently, a 'retest' of the low occurs.

It is during this retest that market participants will start to consider the possibility that a reversal might actually be occurring. In other words, the retest of the low corresponds to the absorption stage of the learning process. There need not be an active restructuring of trading and investment positions, and prices may even move out to new highs. The important development is that the certainty of the bear trend has been undermined and that some degree of doubt will have crept in. Consequently, market participants will be just that much more willing to reverse their bear positions and open bull positions when prices start to recover again. The learning has been done; all that is required is for the market to lead the way.

This process will, of course, be reversed in a bear trend, or in a correction within a bull trend. That is to say falling markets, too, will exhibit a basic three-wave profile. Hence, financial markets can be seen as an oscillating process that moves between extremes of overbought and oversold. Each swing is an outward expression of an inner process that moves through the sequence of: information shock, information absorption and information application. The result is the cycle pattern shown in Figure 9-3. This is the price pulse.

FIGURE 9-3: THE PRICE PULSE

The extraordinary fact is that the price pulse – which represents the shape of a cycle in a particular aspect of collective human behaviour – exactly matches the pattern of oscillation that evolves from Mr. Gurdjieff's enneagram. See Chapter 8.

This conclusion has consequences that are potentially profound. Mr. Gurdjieff maintained the enneagram was "the fundamental hieroglyph of a universal language" and "a schematic diagram of perpetual motion". He argued that it contained "the eternal laws of the universe" and that if a person truly understands something, then he or she should be able to put it into the enneagram. Hence, if the pattern of the price pulse – or enneagram – holds true within the context of financial markets, it is likely that it also holds true for economic activity, cultural evolution, and even the rise and fall of civilisations. The basic points are:

1. The pattern is universal, so it can apply to all sorts of processes ranging from psychological dynamics to biological systems; and

2. The cycle pattern is fractal,[16] such that it reproduces itself at all levels of the hierarchy and over multiple time frames.[17]

We shall be looking at the presence of this pattern in collective human behaviour in later chapters. At this point, however, it will be useful to register that the

---

[16] See Benoit Mandelbrot, *The Fractal Geometry of Nature* (Freeman, New York, 1977).

[17] This fact is not intuitively obvious. However, observers such as Ralph Nelson Elliott have been able to catalogue a *strictly limited* number of price patterns in financial markets. Ralph Nelson Elliott, *The Wave Principle* (Elliott, New York, 1938). Reprinted in Robert R. Prechter (Ed.), *The Major Works of R.N. Elliott* (New Classics Library, New York, 1980).

pattern does indeed exist in financial markets. Figure 9-4 shows the profile of the 3.5-year cycle in the Dow Jones Industrial Average.[18] The cycle is tracked in terms of six-month percentage rates of change in closing prices. Each beat of the cycle inevitably varies in terms of time elapse from the average, so the shorter cycles have been mathematically stretched to match the time elapse of the longest cycle in the matrix. Then, 18 beats of the cycle – starting in November 1946 and ending in February 2009 – have been averaged together and compared with an *ideal* cycle.

The ideal cycle deduced from the enneagram/price pulse is as shown by the dashed line in Figure 9-4. The upswing (denoted 1-2-3) peaks about 50% of the way along the length of the cycle, the downswing (A-B-C) ends with a deep low, and the intra-cycle lows at the end of waves 2 and A impact at around 33% and 66% of the way into the cycle. In reality, each beat of the cycle will have its own unique characteristics, but it is quite clear that the average of all 18 beats produces a pattern that is consistent with the ideal.

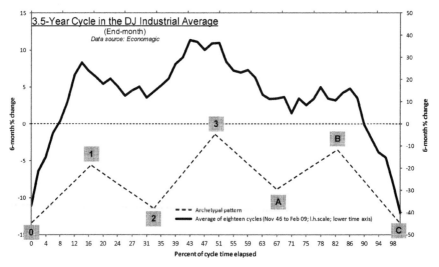

FIGURE 9-4: THE PRICE PULSE IN THE DJIA

However, the real power of what is being presented can be seen when the evolving 19th beat of the cycle is overlaid on the chart (see Figure 9-5). This beat started in February 2009. At the time of writing, the cycle is some way from finishing. However, there can be no question that the broad swings of the cycle are a sufficiently close match to the average and the ideal to know that the enneagram/price pulse can be used for anticipating the future.

---

[18] The cycle is often identified as a 40-month cycle. See, for example, Louise L. Wilson, *Catalogue of Cycles* (Foundation for the Study of Cycles, Pittsburgh (Pa.), 1964).

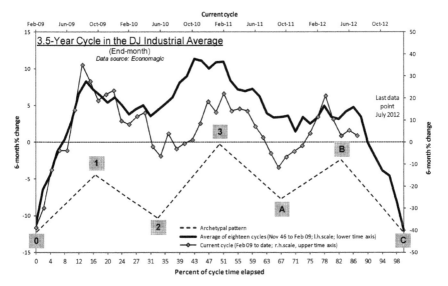

FIGURE 9-5: THE 2009 TO 2012 CYCLE

CONCLUSION

The purpose of this chapter has been to establish a link (via modern systems theory and the concept of collective psychology) between supposed natural laws and mass human behaviour. If the evidence contained in Figures 9-4 and 9-5 is correct, then such a link does indeed exist.

The *Law of Three* suggests that natural systems will always be either expanding or contracting, and the *Law of Seven* – i.e. the law of vibration – suggests that each swing will be characterised by a three-wave behaviour pattern. However, for these two laws to operate together – in a coherent way that can be recognised and anticipated – something profound needs to be acknowledged. This is that there has to be some form of *holding force* that generates the processes of expansion and contraction, and controls the patterns of the resulting oscillations. So far, this force is not recognised by science, but it is becoming increasingly difficult to argue that, because it exists beyond the boundaries of scientific observation, and cannot therefore be quantified, it does not exist.

There is much more research that needs to be to be done but, if the conclusions of this chapter are correct, we have the basis for an additional dimension to understanding about collective human behaviour.

CHAPTER 10

WILLIAM D. GANN AND
THE LAW OF VIBRATION

"The great law of vibration is based on like producing like."

W. D. Gann

"The enneagram is perpetual motion… [which] is part of another perpetual motion and cannot be created apart from it."

P. D. Ouspensky

HIDDEN PATTERNS

The claim that George Gurdjieff's enneagram describes an archetypal pattern of vibration is startling and intriguing. On the one hand, the enneagram is said to be based on fundamental principles that are without antecedent. This implies that we may have to accept that there are influences beyond the level of the individual human being that we cannot yet access through the power of discursive thought. Certainly, the *Law of Three* and the *Law of Seven* are not yet overtly recognised by science. On the other hand, if enneagram-type patterns can be found in nature, then Mr. Gurdjieff's claims need seriously to be considered. In the previous chapter, it was shown that these patterns can, in fact, be found in financial market price movements.

I have argued elsewhere[1] that financial market and economic activities demonstrate the existence of a rhythmic recurring pattern. The argument was

---

[1] Plummer, *Forecasting Financial Markets.*

that the basic three-up/three-down pattern that could be derived from financial market indices and from economic data was created by collective learning in response to changes in the environment. Furthermore, there seemed to be little doubt that the phenomenon was more consistent with non-rational group behaviour than with the aggregated decisions of rational individuals acting independently of one another.

The name that I originally gave to the archetypal pattern within the context of financial markets was *the price pulse*. This gave recognition to the idea that financial market prices did not move just in patterns but also oscillated rhythmically. As shown in the previous chapter, the price pulse is to all intents and purposes identical to Mr. Gurdjieff's enneagram vibration.

It also turns out, however, that the most important version of the three-up/three-down pattern may be one that has a pronounced bias in it. There are two reasons for believing this to be the case. Firstly, Mr. Gurdjieff hid such a pattern within the architecture of his book, *Beelzebub's Tales*, having told his pupils that his extant teaching enneagram was "incomplete".[2] Secondly, exactly the same biased pattern is contained in the mathematics of "sign of the prophet Jonas" in St Matthew's Gospel, and in the structure of William Gann's book, *The Tunnel Thru The Air*.

The fact that all three books contain a concealed reference to exactly the same – very specific – pattern is probably of monumental importance. What is not clear is the reason why the pattern has remained hidden for so long. One explanation is that a researcher would need to have some sense of the object of the search. But it is also true that it is first necessary to find the key that opens the lock.

THE PATTERN HIDDEN IN *TUNNEL THRU THE AIR*

Given the importance of Mr. Gann's work in directly referencing St. Matthew and indirectly referencing Mr. Gurdjieff, it seems appropriate to start with his presentation of the pattern in *The Tunnel Thru The Air*.[3] The clue about how to find it came from an unexpected source – namely, a research thesis by Sophia Wellbeloved[4] that dealt with (among other things) the way that Mr. Gurdjieff had been able to include the influences of the various planets in *Beelzebub's Tales*, but without making explicit reference to astrology.[5] Ms. Wellbeloved's argument – which was certainly consistent with her detailed analysis – was that those influences

---

[2] George Gurdjieff, quoted in Ouspensky, *In Search*.
[3] Gann, *Tunnel*.
[4] Wellbeloved, *Gurdjieff, Astrology & Beelzebub's Tales*.
[5] Gurdjieff, *Beelzebub's Tales*.

were implicit in the *structure* of that book. The question that immediately arose was: could Ms. Wellbeloved's idea be applied to Mr. Gann's book?

The first edition of *Tunnel* consists of 418 pages and spans 36 chapters.[6] As a piece of literature, it is tediously long and seemingly meaningless. It is full of irrelevant poems and apparently inappropriate quotations – especially from the Bible. This, however, turns out to be a clue, because the additional text is used as an artifice to control the number of pages in any given chapter. The details of the pages per chapter in *Tunnel* are shown in Appendix 4. It is apparent that the number of pages per chapter varies significantly, from a low of four to a high of 30.

Figure 10-1 plots the number of pages in each chapter against the chapter number itself. For ease of exposition, the chart includes some additional information. First, the top horizontal axis is used to measure the percentage of the whole book covered by each chapter. Second, a 45-degree line is drawn from the lower left-hand corner to the point on the upper horizontal axis that is equivalent to 100% of chapters. Third, a simple notation is added so that the rising part of the diagram is marked 1-2-3, the subsequent (falling) section is marked A-B-C, and the fluctuations within the interim (rising) wave B are marked a-b-c.

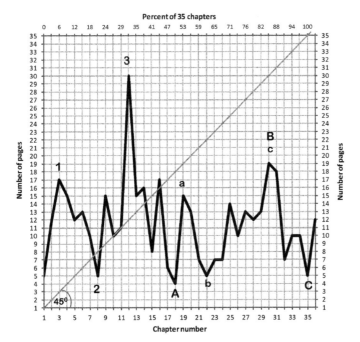

FIGURE 10-1: GANN'S HIDDEN PATTERN OF VIBRATION

---

[6] The information held in the physical structure of the book is inevitably lost in reproductions that take no account of the original typesetting. In recent years, insensitive alterations have effectively halted the transmission of some of Mr. Gann's more profound ideas.

The result is truly stunning: it is a *left-biased* enneagram-type pulse, placed within a square. There are three waves (1-2-3) into a very marked peak. This is followed by a sharp contraction (A), which would be an energy gap in terms of an enneagram pattern. There is then a long advance (B) that divides into three sub-waves (a-b-c). And, finally, there is a sharp fall (C) as the whole process comes to completion. Within the overall pattern, it is noticeable that the majority of waves themselves consist of three sub-waves.

The peak number of pages occurs in Chapter 12, which is exactly one-third of the way through *Tunnel*. So wave 3 peaks 33% of the way through the evolution of the whole pattern. Meanwhile, the end of the wave A downswing is emphasised. It is the lowest low on the chart, and it coincides with the halfway point (i.e. the 18th chapter) of the book.

As presented, the 45-degree line in Figure 10-1 bisects a 35 x 35 square. The line runs from the lower left-hand corner to the upper right-hand corner of the square, and intersects the point where the number of chapters in the book equals the natural extension of the scale that measures the number of pages in a chapter. Hence, 35 chapters equal 35 pages per chapter where the 1-2-3/A-B-C vibration reaches completion. The process is complete when the end of the cyclical pattern coincides with a geometric boundary.

The emphasis on the square, plus the fact that the lowest low occurs exactly halfway through the cycle, appears to split the cycle into two distinct parts. Indeed, the second half essentially recapitulates the oscillations of the first half, although the amplitudes of the fluctuations are significantly reduced. Hence, the 1-2 base of the first half is repeated in the a-b base of the second half; the dynamic wave 3 is mirrored in the slower wave c; and the A wave fall is echoed in the end-of-cycle wave C.

At first sight, the use of a dyadic structure seems to discount the *Law of Three*. However, a closer analysis reveals the presence of a threefold arrangement. It also reveals the presence of the Golden Ratio, which – as we saw in Chapter 3 – implicitly references the *Law of Three*. The details are shown in Figures 10-2 and 10-3. Firstly, the pattern contains *three* important swings (i.e. advances plus contractions) within the main cycle. Waves 1 and 2 are identified as the *first beat*; waves 3 and A are labelled the *second beat*; and waves B and C are denoted the *third beat*.

An initiating shock and the Golden Ratio

As presented, there is some evidence that the first beat of the pattern (i.e. waves 1 and 2) has a specific role to play in the evolution of the whole pattern. Firstly, it covers *eight* chapters (i.e. chapters 1 through 8 inclusive). The number 8 is almost certainly significant in this context because it references the metaphor of a completed octave. This, in turn, transmits the message that the interval between the seventh and eighth notes (i.e. Ti-Do) has been transcended and that another, higher, octave has been initiated. Hence, the first beat of the cycle can be seen as an information shock that then generates the other two cycle beats in the pattern. This reflects the idea – introduced in Chapter 9 – that living systems adjust to new information.

The second important piece of evidence that the first beat of the pattern is an information shock of some sort is that the subsequent two beats of the pattern are related to one another by the Golden Ratio, 0.382:0.618. Figure 10-2 uses the number 1 as the origin of both the lower horizontal axis and the vertical axis. If, however, the horizontal axis starts at zero, the presence of the Golden Ratio becomes clear (see upper axis). The second beat of the pattern (i.e. rising wave 3 and falling wave A) covers 10 chapters and the third beat (i.e. rising wave B and falling wave C) covers 17 chapters.

This means that the second beat is 37% of the length of the second and third beats taken together – i.e. (10/27) x 100. It also means that the third beat is 63% of that part of the pattern – i.e. (17/27) x 100. This division is as near to the Golden Ratio as can be achieved using whole numbers. On the basis of the arguments explored in Chapter 3, this suggests that the second beat of the pattern has an active energy, and the third beat has a passive energy. This is certainly consistent with the differences in the amplitudes of the vibrations.

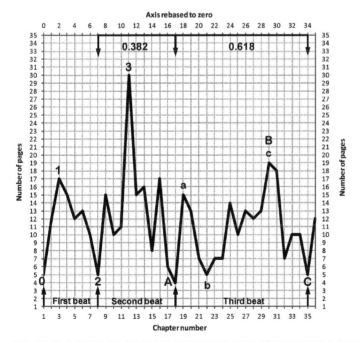

FIGURE 10-2: THE LAW OF THREE WITHIN AN APPARENTLY DYADIC STRUCTURE

This does not complete the evidence that the overall pattern references the Golden Ratio. Figure 10-3 shows that the length of pattern from the start of the first beat to the end of wave b within the third beat is 21 units (see upper horizontal axis), while waves c and C taken together cover 13 units.[7] This means that the horizontal distance from the start of the pattern to the low of wave b is 61.8% of the whole pattern – i.e. (21/34) x 100 – and that the horizontal distance from the low of wave b to the end of the pattern is 38.2% of the whole pattern – i.e. (13/34) x 100. Furthermore, the horizontal distance travelled by wave c is 61.8% of the length from the low of wave b to the end of the pattern – i.e. (8/13) x 100 – and the distance travelled by wave C is 38.2% of the length from the low of wave b to the end of the pattern – i.e. (5/13) x 100.

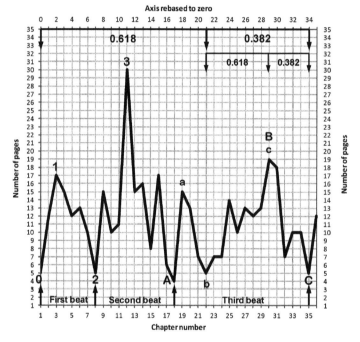

FIGURE 10-3: THE GOLDEN RATIO

It is clear that behind the dyadic structure of Mr. Gann's pattern lays a wealth of detail that emphasises the influence of the *Law of Three*: the pattern contains three inner cycles; the second and third cycles are related to one another by the Golden Ratio; and the whole pattern can be separated into two unequal parts that reflect the harmony of the Golden Ratio. This latter is particularly important because it separates the volatile part of the pattern (i.e. 0-b) from the

---

[7] These numbers come from the Fibonacci Series, 0,1,1,2,3,5,8,13,21,34,... etc. In this particular series each number is the sum of the two preceding numbers, and the ratio of each number to the subsequent number tends to the ratio 0.618:1. The Fibonacci Series therefore reflects the Golden Ratio.

subsequent advance (i.e. b-c). This advance is the longest individual section of the pattern. In some sense, therefore, the initial volatility establishes the base from which a sustainable advance emerges.

The emergence of additional information once attention is paid to the detail of Mr. Gann's pattern is very important. The pattern is complex and – as will become apparent – far-reaching. It is in direct contrast to the flaccid text and weak story line within *Tunnel*. What becomes apparent is that Mr. Gann's pattern is a type of *carrier wave*: it contains within it a profusion of important information, not just about the nature of vibration, but also about the evolutionary patterns that are involved. These features of Mr. Gann's pattern will be explored in more detail in Chapters 13, 14, and 15.

THE GANN PATTERN IN FINANCIAL MARKETS

The question at this stage, however, is: can the basic pattern that was concealed in *Tunnel* actually be found in financial markets (which were, after all, supposedly Mr. Gann's area of expertise)? The answer is in the affirmative, although it is not always obvious. One of the most dramatic examples of Mr. Gann's pattern occurred in the US Treasury bond market between 1981 and 1994, when inflationary expectations were being brought under control after the appalling experience of the 1970s.

FIGURE 10-4: US TREASURY BONDS, 1981-1996

Treasury bond price behaviour over this period is represented by Figure 10-4, which shows the movement in an index calculated by deducting the official constant maturity yield on US 10-year Treasury bonds from 100. The period started with a price explosion in the second half of 1982 and ended with a bond *crash* in 1994; in between, prices were very volatile. The whole 12-year cycle incorporated the shocks that were necessary to bring inflationary expectations back under control, and those traders and investors who lived through the cycle will readily attest to its brutality.

The price oscillations associated with the transformation of inflation expectations should provide an ideal set of data for testing the veracity of Mr. Gann's pattern. In particular, we should be able to see where the pattern matches actual experience and where there are differences. The raw price data in Figure 10-4 shows a distinct upward bias to US Treasury bond prices between 1981 and 1993. We can partially remove this bias by creating a 12-year (i.e. a 624-week) moving average of the data and then tracking the divergence of each of the data points from a centred version of that average. The results are shown in Figure 10-5.

FIGURE 10-5: DEVIATION OF TREASURY BOND INDEX FROM MOVING AVERAGE

Mr. Gann's pattern is then overlaid on the adjusted bond index, with the objective of matching the primary trends. There is an extraordinarily close match between the expected pattern and the actual movement in the Treasury bond market. Three waves (1-2-3) into a left-biased peak are followed by a sharp fall (A), a long three-wave recovery (a-b-c) and a final fall (C). The pattern of vibration hidden in *Tunnel* by Mr. Gann is obviously very meaningful in the context of change.

There are, however, some differences between Mr. Gann's pattern and actual behaviour. In practice, waves 1 and 2 evolved much more quickly than might have been expected; the final downswing within wave A was not as weak as might have been anticipated; and the end of wave C was much stronger than might have been expected. This strongly suggests that the overall picture provided by the pattern is more important than its precision at lower levels. Indeed, if Mr. Gann's objective was to deliver a great deal of information in a relatively small container, some degree of variability would be inevitable. As already mentioned, we shall address some of these issues in Chapters 13, 14 and 15.

CONCLUSION

The important conclusion is that the divergences do not seem significant enough to invalidate the overall correspondences. So, although every market cycle will undoubtedly have its own unique variations, caused by contemporaneous fluctuations in the wider environment, the overall cycle should exhibit a very specific pattern. Hence, there seems to be a non-random process at work that exerts some degree of control over how oscillations are going to progress. This is directly at odds with one of the persistent claims of economic theory.[8]

The structure of Mr. Gann's book, *The Tunnel Thru The Air*, seems to have been very carefully designed to ensure the transmission of esoteric information about a law of vibration. He was not explicit about how to interpret the pattern, or even about what it was for, but his implied hypothesis was that collective human activities – of which financial markets are a good example – are organised according to this pattern.

We shall unravel some of the details in later chapters. For the moment, it is sufficient to know that his version of the pattern is significantly more detailed than those presented by Mr. Gurdjieff and St. Matthew, and that the detail meant something. In order to make this apparent, we first need to look at the work of Mr. Gurdjieff and St. Matthew.

---

[8] See, for example, Burton G. Malkiel, *A Random Walk Down Wall Street* (W. W.Norton & Co., New York, 1973). Also, Eugene Fama, 'Random Walks in Stock Prices', *Financial Analysts Journal* (September/October, 1965).

CHAPTER 11

GEORGE I. GURDJIEFF AND THE LAW OF VIBRATION

"The knowledge of the enneagram has for a very long time been preserved in secret and if it is now, so to speak, made available to all, it is only in an incomplete and theoretical form."

P. D. Ouspensky, quoting G. I. Gurdjieff

BEELZEBUB'S TALES

Having established the pattern of vibrations as visualised by Mr. Gann, we can now have a look at the same pattern as it was defined by Mr. Gurdjieff. It is more deeply hidden in *Beelzebub's Tales* than it is in *Tunnel*, which is consistent with the fact that Mr. Gurdjieff was known to have made some of his important teachings as obscure as possible – a process that he called "burying the dog"[1] – so that students had to work hard for their knowledge.[2] However, this also means acknowledging that Mr. Gurdjieff intended to hide the pattern within the structure of the book itself, and then had sufficient control over the structure of the book in its published form to ensure that the information was included.

Both these assumptions are probably correct. Mr. Gurdjieff started to write *Beelzebub's Tales* in December 1924 and the final page proofs were made available in October 1949, a week before he died. The book was not written quickly! In

---

[1] That is, the whole dog and not just the bone. See Smith, *Gurdjieff*.
[2] Sections of the book were read aloud to pupils. If they were seen to understand the ideas too easily, then the text was changed. Wellbeloved, *Gurdjieff, Astrology & Beelzebub's Tales*.

fact, it is known that Mr. Gurdjieff persistently wrote and re-wrote *Beelzebub's Tales*, although he appears to have stopped doing so in 1935. This left him with another 14 years to find a publisher and finalise the proofs.[3] It is therefore entirely feasible that having formulated a structure for the book that could be used to transmit extra information, he worked towards creating that structure.

The second assumption – that Mr. Gurdjieff then had final control over the structure of the book – is difficult to verify.[4] There are bound to be some doubts, given that the publishers – Routledge & Kegan Paul in London, and Harcourt Brace in New York – had reputations to maintain. Nevertheless, the fact that these two companies were willing to publish *Beelzebub's Tales* in the first place, and in a very specific physical shape, implies that the publishers had some recognition of its importance.

The physical format of the original edition is unusual. If anything, it has the same dimensions as a personal bible: it is 4½" wide, 6¾" long and 2" thick. The front and back covers therefore each constitute a 2 x 3 rectangle, which in turn references the active solar – or male – energy of 666.[5] Finally, of course, it is also highly unlikely that Ms. Wellbeloved's research, which was mentioned in the previous chapter, would have been able to produce the conclusions that it did had there not been some form of pre-determined order in the chapter structure and page numbering.

Beelzebub's Tales consists of 48 chapters and 1238 pages. The details are shown in Appendix 5. The whole book is divided into three sub-books. This, according to Sophia Wellbeloved, mirrors the *Law of Three*.[6] The first book is 408 pages long, the second is 402 pages long and the third is 426 pages long. So, although not precisely equal, they are of broadly similar lengths.[7] However, the number of the chapters in each book differs significantly. The first book has 28 chapters, the second has 11 chapters and the third has 14 chapters. Furthermore, there are significant variations in the number of pages in each chapter. This gives ample opportunity for embedding patterns in a number series that tracks the quantities involved.

---

[3] A typescript was apparently available in 1929-30. Alfred Orage 'roneoed' one hundred copies for sale to people working in groups. See Nott, *Journey Through This World*.

[4] Mr. Gurdjieff would probably not have been able to make any major adjustments to the final page proofs, so we cannot be absolutely certain that the structure of the book is a completely accurate representation of his wishes.

[5] See Chapter 2. *Beelzebub's Tales* is considered to be the active psychological force in a triad of books. The other two books are *Meetings With Remarkable Men* (the reconciling force) and *Life is Real, Only Then, When 'I Am'* (the passive force). See Hayes, *Infinite Harmony*.

[6] It also represents the Biblical ideas of The Fall, Creation, and Redemption. Wellbeloved, *Gurdjieff, Astrology & Beelzebub's Tales*.

[7] It is also worth noting that Mr. Gann's *Tunnel* has 418 pages in total, of which 406 relate directly to the complete 1-2-3/A-B-C vibration.

THE HIDDEN PATTERN

Ms. Wellbeloved's research indicates that Mr. Gurdjieff used the structure of *Beelzebub's Tales* to convey valuable information about the influence of planetary cycles. This is beyond the subject matter covered here, but the important insight is that he did so by grouping the 48 chapters into sets of four. The reason for this – which will be re-emphasised in Chapter 12 – is based on the importance of the number 12 in ancient thought. This number, as John Michell pointed out in his book *Dimensions of Paradise*,[8] was associated with the gods, the zodiac and the majestic order of the heavens. Researchers would divide any large number that was associated with gematria and numerology by 12 in order to see what else might emerge. So it is with the number 48, where 48 divided by 12 equals 4. Some of the relevant data are shown in Table 11-1.

Chapter number	Number of pages	Proportion of total (%)	Change in pages (%)
1-4	67	8	0
5-8	11	17	-84
9-12	22	25	100
13-16	31	33	41
17-20	93	42	200
21-24	120	50	29
25-28	66	58	-45
29-32	166	67	152
33-36	84	75	-49
37-40	208	83	148
41-44	274	92	32
45-48	94	100	-66

TABLE 11-1: PAGE STRUCTURE OF *BEELZEBUB'S TALES*; FIRST, SECOND, AND THIRD BOOKS

The relationship between the number of pages in each set of four chapters and the location of that set within the book is shown in Figure 11-1. There is an overall rising trend, interrupted by contractions. The trend can be seen as an impulsive five-wave movement (1-2-3-4-5), with the second wave being a simple correction and the fourth wave formed from an irregular three-phase pattern (a-b-c). Financial market analysts will quickly recognise the overall pattern as being similar to the one identified as being a bull move by Ralph Nelson Elliott.[9]

Next, the changes in the number of pages between successive groups of four chapters (see fourth column of Table 11-1) are plotted in Figure 11-2. The result is really quite remarkable. The pattern is consistent with the configuration that was found in *Tunnel* (see Figure 9-1). The configuration is obviously different

---

[8] Michell, *Dimensions of Paradise*.
[9] Elliott, *Wave Principle*. Reprinted in Prechter, *R. N. Elliott*.

in terms of the extent of the swings, but it is nevertheless a left-biased enneagram-type pulse. There are three waves (1-2-3) into a very marked peak. This is followed by a sharp contraction (A), which ends halfway through the pattern. This would be an energy gap. Then there is a volatile advance (B) that divides into three sub-waves (a-b-c). And, finally, there is a sharp fall (C), which brings the whole process to completion.

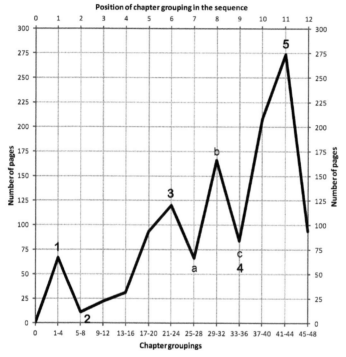

FIGURE 11-1: PAGES AND CHAPTER GROUPINGS

Pattern details

One point is that the enneagram pulse emerges clearly only when *momentum* is used. However, there are also other aspects of the pattern that need to be mentioned. First, if the horizontal and vertical axes are given the same-sized divisions, the pattern ends when the width of the whole pattern is equal to the contemporaneous height. This means that, except for the peak of wave 3, the whole pattern fits into a square. It also means that the pattern ends along the 45 degree line drawn from the start of the pattern. It is noteworthy that Mr. Gann's pattern also exhibits a squaring (Figure 10-1 in Chapter 10).

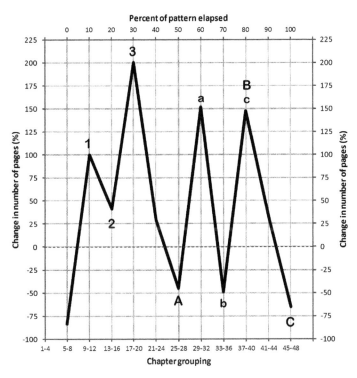

FIGURE 11-2: MR. GURDJIEFF'S HIDDEN VIBRATION

Second, the peak of wave 1 occurs at 100 units on the vertical axis and the peak of wave 3 occurs at 200 units. Meanwhile, the trough of wave A and the trough of sub-wave b occur around -50, and the peak of sub-wave a and the peak of wave B occur at around 150. The data thus resonate with a vital aspect of the *Law of Seven*: an octave has an inherent tendency to double and to halve. In the diagram, the move to 200 (which references a second doubling) takes the pattern out of the square. But the breakout is only temporary; it is followed by a sharp fall to -50 (which references a halving). Mr. Gann is well known for championing the use of doubling and halving to anticipate turning points in financial markets.[10]

Third, the peak of wave 3 occurs 30% of the way through the pattern and the trough of wave A (i.e. at the end of the energy gap) impacts at 50% of the way through it. This – unsurprisingly – resonates with Mr. Gann's pattern, where the wave 3 peak occurs 33% along the width of the pattern and the trough of wave A occurs 50% of the way along it. The peaks of wave A and wave B then occur 60% and 80% respectively of the way through pattern.

---

[10] See, for example, Gann, *45 Years*.

The fact that the architecture of a large and complex book like *Beelzebub's Tales* can be made to resonate with the detailed body of knowledge that is embedded within it almost defies imagination. It is certainly a testament to the genius of the man who conceptualised and implemented the project. But this is not the end of the matter.

The first point is that there is no evidence from the available literature that Mr. Gurdjieff included the concept of a left-biased enneagram pulse in his teachings. The extant teaching diagram is invariably a centred three-wave up/three-wave down pattern. It may be relevant, therefore, that Pyotr Ouspensky quotes Mr. Gurdjieff as saying: "The knowledge of the enneagram has for a very long time been preserved in secret and if it now is, so to speak, made available to all, it is only in an incomplete and theoretical form..."[11]

This strongly suggests that the left-biased pattern buried in the structure of Beelzebub was not just nearer to the truth, but sufficiently close to that truth to warrant preserving for subsequent researchers. The second point follows from this. Mr. Gurdjieff would only have ensured that this pattern was preserved if he considered that it carried genuine information about the very nature of our existence. And so it does.

The pattern in practice

Figure 11.3 shows the pattern of one beat of the (approximately) 10-year cycle in output that has been operating more or less continuously in the US since the American Declaration of Independence in 1776. The cycle is tracked here by a composite index that is calculated by the Institute for Supply Management (ISM) in the US. The index monitors changes in employment, new orders, inventories and supplier deliveries.

In principle, an index level above 50 is going to be associated with an expansion in manufacturing, while an index level below 50 is likely to be associated with a contraction. The particular cycle beat being shown is that for January 1991 to October 2001. It is thus a relatively recent cycle and it covers a period when a revolution in information technology was providing a genuine low-inflation impulse to the economy.

Overlaid on the chart is the pattern deduced from Mr. Gurdjieff's book. There are short-term fluctuations in the ISM index that are not present in Mr. Gurdjieff's pattern, but the longer-term parallels are very clear. There are three waves (1-2-3) into a left-biased peak. This peak is then followed sequentially by: a sharp contraction (A), a three-wave recovery (a-b-c), and a final fall (C). The seven inner turning points occur more or less where they should and the amplitude of the wave b downswing within the a-b-c recovery is correctly predicted.

---

[11] Ouspensky, *In Search*.

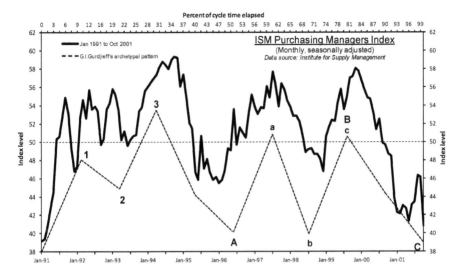

FIGURE 11-3: MR. GURDJIEFF'S PATTERN AND THE 10-YEAR CYCLE IN PRODUCER CONFIDENCE

In this example, only a single beat of the 10-year cycle has been used because the purpose is explicitly to confirm the potential presence of a deep wave b downswing. Had the average of a number of beats of the cycle been used, there would have been a tendency to iron out the fluctuations in individual cycles. One important inference is that Mr. Gurdjieff exaggerated the wave b downswing in order to emphasise its presence, not to insist that it was always likely to be severe.

A SECOND HIDDEN PATTERN

It might have been enough if Mr. Gurdjieff had left the pattern in this simple and straightforward form. However, he obviously had a point to make. In particular, there may have been a desire to ensure that such an important pattern was going to be found. So – as if to ensure that a researcher using other methodologies might find the pattern – Mr. Gurdjieff included the left-biased enneagram pulse a *second* time in *Beelzebub's Tales*. In this instance, though, it was reproduced *backwards* from the end of the book.

One of the sub-titles of the book is *An Objectively Impartial Criticism of the Life of Man* and one of Mr Gurdjieff's specific criticisms was that humankind perceives reality back to front: reality is seen as fantasy, and fantasy is perceived as reality.[12] So, it would not be surprising if Mr. Gurdjieff had built on this imagery.

---

[12] Gurdjieff, *Beelzebub's Tales*.

Beelzebub's Tales consists of 48 chapters and the first chapter – which, like the last chapter, has a different, more personal, content to the rest of the book – consists of 48 pages. This draws attention to the number 48 and could be a clue to the relevance of the 48th chapter. Hence, if Chapter 48 has to be taken as the *start* of a vibration, then we are almost certainly referencing a descending octave (because it cannot go any higher!). This suggests that the octave should end where the vibration halves. If we start at 48, the vibration accordingly ends at 24 – i.e. with the 24th chapter.

Details of the pages in all the chapters and the relevant percentage changes are shown in Appendix 5. Table 11-2 shows the data for the 24th to 48th chapters in reverse order. The results are plotted in Figure 11-4.

Reverse chapter	Changes (%)	Reverse chapter	Changes (%)
48	400.00	36	0.00
47	-8.33	35	-95.45
46	-25.00	34	450.00
45	-38.46	33	-42.86
44	-59.38	32	-38.24
43	-53.28	31	-54.67
42	191.49	30	108.33
41	-18.97	29	56.52
40	-15.94	28	-4.17
39	38.00	27	84.62
38	61.29	26	116.67
37	933.33	25	-81.25

TABLE 11-2: CHAPTERS 24-48 OF *BEELZEBUB'S TALES* IN REVERSE ORDER

The configuration is not just consistent with the first pattern derived from the whole of *Beelzebub's Tales* (Figure 11-2); its wave patterns are similar to that found in *Tunnel* (Figure 10-1). The pattern is that of a left-biased enneagram pulse. There are three waves (1-2-3) into a very marked peak. This is followed by an energy gap in the form of a sharp contraction (A), which ends halfway through the pattern. Then there is a volatile advance (B) that divides into three sub-waves (a-b-c). Within this advance, the first upswing (a) is particularly marked, which is what might be expected from a momentum measure following a significant fall. Finally, there is a fall (C), which brings the whole process to completion.

There are a number of features in this pattern. The first is that a significant momentum low is formed halfway through the pattern. Moreover, it is *lower* than either of those formed at the start and the end of the pattern. This unusual element also occurs in Mr. Gann's composition (Figure 10-1). Another feature is that, after the initial surge away from the mid-point low (wave a), momentum drops back sharply again (wave b). Again, Mr. Gann's pattern includes the same characteristic. Mr Gurdjieff's pattern reaches its peak 40% of the way through the pattern;[13] it then reaches its wave b low 70% of the way through the pattern. This means that the energy gap and its immediate after-shock last about 30% of the whole pattern. Mr. Gann's pattern reaches its peak 33% of the way through the pattern and reaches a wave b low 62% of the way through the pattern. Again, the elapse between the top of wave 3 and the low of wave b is not far off 30%.

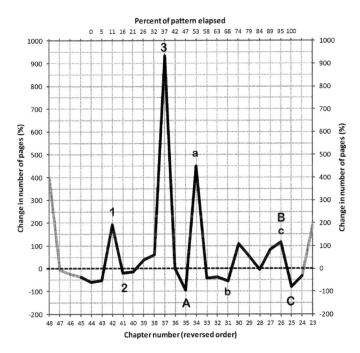

FIGURE 11-4: CHANGE IN PAGES PER CHAPTER IN REVERSE ORDER

An example of the second pattern

As with Mr. Gurdjieff's basic pattern, the pattern shown in Figure 11-4 can easily be found in the real world. Figure 11-5 shows the six-month momentum in the price of wheat during the inflationary disruption of 1973/74 and its aftermath. On the one hand, the economic and political causes of the inflation are relatively easy to enumerate. On the other hand, the whole process can be tracked in terms of a patterned oscillation.

The 1973/74 inflation was the natural response to monetary conditions that had been created between late-1969 and mid-1972. The ratcheting up of

---

[13] There is a hint here of the Golden Ratio, 38.2:61.8.

inflation expectations was then brought to a peak by the outbreak of war in the Middle East in October 1973 and the consequent oil embargo. Surging oil prices fed through to other commodity prices. By February 1974, wheat prices were almost five times higher than they had been in mid-1972.

Eventually, of course, the whole process went into reverse. The rise in prices obviously deflated real incomes and interest rates were raised dramatically to deal with rising inflation expectations. Economic weakness therefore developed in 1974 and 1975. And, as the US economy weakened, so did the momentum in commodity prices.

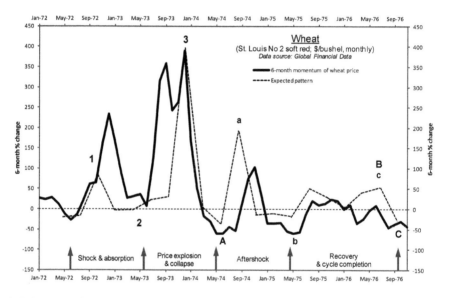

FIGURE 11-5: MOMENTUM IN THE PRICE OF WHEAT, 1972-76

Inner timings

Set against this 'fundamental' explanation – although not opposed to it – is Mr. Gurdjieff's pattern. Once the initial information shock has been registered, the pattern clearly anticipates subsequent movements. First, the pattern identifies the move in wheat prices between mid-1972 and early 1973 as being the information shock that eventually resulted in the 1973-74 explosion in wheat prices. Second, Figure 11-5 shows that the whole process can be divided into four phases:

1. Shock and absorption,

2. Price explosion and collapse,

3. Aftershock from the collapse, and

4. Recovery and cycle completion.

The time elapses of each of the first three phases are approximately equal to each other and the time elapse of the fourth phase is about one and a half times the length of each of its predecessors. To put the same thing another way: with Mr. Gurdjieff's diagram, the first three phases are equal in time; the second two phases last 1-1/4 times the length of the first two phases; and the fourth phase is half as long as the total time elapse of the first three phases.

Consequently, once the time elapse of the combined information shock and the absorption process had finished, it would have been possible to obtain a broad estimate both of the pattern of the subsequent price swings and of the associated timings. In Figure 11-5, the information shock and absorption process started in June 1972 and ended in June 1973 – i.e. 12 months. This meant that:

1. The price explosion and collapse would also last about 12 months;

2. The aftershock would last about 12 months; and

3. The recovery and completion would last about 18 months.

As of June 1973, the whole process was scheduled to end in late 1976 or early 1977. And this is exactly what happened.

CONCLUSION

Mr Gurdjieff's book, *All and Everything: An Objectively Impartial Criticism of the Life of Man*, or *Beelzebub's Tales to His Grandson*, thus transmits two patterns that are not only mutually consistent with one another, but are also similar to that conveyed by Mr. Gann in *The Tunnel Thru The Air*. These patterns seem to be a reflection of a fundamental *law of vibration*. If correct, there are two extraordinary corollaries.

First, a cycle can be identified, and its existence confirmed, by its adherence to the pattern of a left-biased enneagram-type pulse. Second, it means that collective human behaviours – including economic behaviour – are subject to hitherto unknown ordering principles. Both these conclusions have profound implications for economic theory and for economic policy.

The patterns need to be explored in more detail and this will be done in Chapter 15. First, however, we need to look at St. Matthew's original revelation.

CHAPTER 12

ST. MATTHEW'S GOSPEL AND THE LAW OF VIBRATION

"I believe there was a secret meaning…"

W. D. Gann

A MIRACULOUS SIGN

In *Tunnel Thru The Air*, Mr. Gann allows his alter ego Robert Gordon to register the importance of "the sign of the prophet Jonas" within the Gospel of St. Matthew, and to state that there is a "secret meaning" in the phrase "the Son of man be three days and three nights in the heart of the earth." It is, says Gann/Gordon, "the key to the interpretation of the future".[1]

The first point to make is that St. Matthew's text appears to contain at least two dimensions of interpretation, depending on whether the analysis uses the adjusted text citing the prophet Jonas (*Ιονας*) or the extant text referencing the prophet Jonah (*Ιονα*). Both contain information about the geometric contents of the text itself. As was shown in Chapters 4 and 5, when the Greek text is adjusted to include an apparently missing "ς", the "sign of the prophet Jonas" may be interpreted as containing a reference to an objective dimension to Time.

As I shall now show, if the text is left in its unadjusted form, "the sign of the prophet Jonah" reveals the same pattern of vibration that was found in *Tunnel* and *Beelzebub's Tales*.

---

[1] Gann, *Tunnel*.

Chapter 12 of St. Matthew's Gospel is basically divided into two parts: the first (verse 38) sets the scene, with the Pharisees "demanding a miraculous sign" from Jesus; the second part is Jesus' response. That response is itself split into two sections. The first section (verse 39) defines both the nature of those who are asking for a sign ("an evil and unfaithful generation") and the nature of the sign that was going to be given ("the sign of the prophet Jonah"). The second section (verse 40) then defines the contents of the sign ("For as Jonas was three days and three nights in the belly of the whale, so will the Son of man be three days and three nights in the heart of the earth").

THE LAW OF THREE

In the Greek text, Jesus' verbal response consists of just 48 words.[2] A closer inspection reveals that this response contains a number of allusions to the *Law of Three and to the Golden Ratio*. First, Jesus' response can be seen in three sections of almost equal length: verse 39 consists of 18 words; the first half of verse 40 (referencing Jonas in the belly of the whale) consists of 14 words; and the second half (referencing the Son of man in the heart of the earth) consists of 16 words. On the continuing assumption that Chapter 12 of St. Matthew's Gospel is the vehicle for genuine revelation,[3] even these numbers appear significant.

A starting point is the 18 words of verse 39. This 18 reduces to the number 9 (the "ennead") – that is, 1 + 8 = 9. This is the number of completion and initiation.[4] As shown in Chapter 3, however, the number 18 is the sum of the digits in the number 1746 (the number of fusion) and in the number 666 (the number of the active energy in creation). It is also a contraction of 1080 (the number of the receptive energy in creation). These three numbers are related to one another by the Golden Ratio, 0.618:1. The appearance of the number 18 is always going to presume a reference to the *Law of Three*, the Trinity and the Golden Ratio.

The number 14 – which is the number of words in the first half of verse 40 – reduces to the number 5 (the "pentad") – that is, 1 + 4 = 5. This particular number has obtained a degree of notoriety that is almost as great as that achieved by the number 666. The misuse of the five-sided star known as the pentagram has caused it to be associated with hedonism and power-seeking. However, in its original usage, the number 5 had two very important associations – with humankind and with the Golden Ratio. The former arises out of the parallel between a man standing with his legs apart and his arms outstretched, so that his 5 extremities – two legs, two arms and a head – are emphasised.[5] The latter

---

[2] Aland, *New Testament*.
[3] This was Mr. Gann's presumption.
[4] The number 9 is also the number that is most closely associated with Mr. Gurdjieff's enneagram.
[5] This was used by Leonardo Da Vinci in his drawing known as Vetruvian man.

arises from the fact that the Golden Ratio ($\phi = 0.618{:}1$) can be calculated from a simple equation that uses the number 5. That is:

$$\Phi = (1 + \sqrt{5}) / 2$$

The number 16 – which is the number of words in the second half of verse 40 – is the third number derived from Jesus' response to the Pharisees. The number 16 reduces to the number 7 (the "heptad") – that is, 1 + 6 = 7. The heptad is known as the *virgin* number because it cannot be multiplied by another whole number to produce a number between 1 and 10; nor can any two numbers between 1 and 10 be multiplied by one another to produce the number 7. Hence, the number 7 cannot generate and cannot be generated. This gave the number a sense of being somehow introduced into the world of phenomena from the world of the sacred.

In fact, the number 7 was traditionally associated with the measurement of time.[6] It therefore seems to be no accident that – as was shown in Chapter 5 – this specific verse within St. Matthew's Gospel contains an extraordinary insight into the objective nature of time. The number 7 is also a direct reference – via the seven tones in a musical octave – to the *Law of Seven*. And this, of course, is another name for the law of vibration.

THE GOLDEN RATIO

The Golden Ratio – and therefore the *Law of Three* – is also embedded in the number of words in Jesus' response to the Scribes and Pharisees. First, the ratio between the number of spoken words in verse 39 (i.e. 18 words) and the total number of words in verse 39 and 40 (i.e. 48) is 0.375:1. Second, the ratio of the difference between 48 and 18 (i.e. 30) to the total (i.e. 48) equals 0.625:1. The presence of these ratios may appear to be no more than an interesting by-product of meeting other objectives. Nevertheless, it is also true that the ratio 0.375:0.625 is very close to the Golden Ratio, 0.38:0.62. Indeed, 18 and 30 are the only numbers that can separate 48 into two parts that approximate the Golden Ratio.[7]

There are, however, three additional references to the Golden Ratio in verses 39 and 40 that are even more specific. First, the sum of the symbolic values of all the words in verse 39 is 10,063, while the sum of the values in verse 40 is 16,359. The ratio between the two numbers is therefore 62%. This means, of

---

[6] See Michell, *Dimensions of Paradise*. The number 28 also has an association with cycles, via its relationship to the number 7. The sum of the first seven numbers between 1 and 10 equals 28, and 28/4 = 7. The number 28 may have been important to Mr. Gurdjieff's book, *Beelzebub's Tales*. See Appendix 6.

[7] 18:48 = 0.375:1 and 30:48 = 0.625:1. Alternatively, 17:49 = 0.35:1 and (49-17):49 = 0.65:1; or 19:47 = 0.40:1 and (47-19):47 = 0.60:1.

course, that verse 39 has a symbolic value equal to 38% of the value of verse 39 plus verse 40.[8]

Second, and as shown in Table 5-1 in Chapter 5, the value by gematria of "the belly of the whale" is 2272, while the value of "Jonas in the belly of the whale three days and three nights" is 5919. Consequently, "the belly of the whale" is 38% of the whole phrase and, by deduction, the rest of the phrase (i.e. without "the belly of the whale") is 62% of the whole.

Third, and again as shown in Table 5-1, the symbolic value of "three days and three nights" is 2586, while the value of "the Son of man in the heart of the earth three days and three nights" is 6834. Hence, "three days and three nights" is 38% of the whole phrase and "the Son of man in the heart of the earth" is 62% of the whole phrase.

Each of these three calculations provides a direct reference to the Golden Ratio, 0.38:0.62 and, therefore, to the *Law of Three*. This is not only astonishing in its own right, but also suggests that the analysis is on the right track. Attention is undoubtedly being drawn to the relationships within verses 39 and 40 in general,[9] and to the relationships within Jesus' verbal response to the Scribes and Pharisees in particular. We therefore need to look more closely at the latter. Table 12-1 accordingly shows the numeric values, by gematria, of the relevant words.

Word number	Value	Word number	Value	Word number	Value	Word number	Value
1	64	13	48	25	114	37	770
2	309	14	370	26	770	38	1510
3	31	15	383	27	998	39	55
4	961	16	861	28	615	40	308
5	383	17	770	29	354	41	136
6	425	18	1528	30	31	42	508
7	31	18	1185	31	615	43	211
8	383	20	104	32	971	44	615
9	470	21	58	33	1770	45	354
10	607	22	1061	34	516	46	31
11	709	23	55	35	70	47	615
12	15	24	308	36	680	48	971

TABLE 12-1: GEMATRIAN VALUES OF JESUS' RESPONSE IN VERSES 39 & 40

[8] The accuracy of the Golden Ratio relationship between the gematrian values of verses 39 and 40 when the name of the prophet is left as "Jonah" suggests that the omission of the letter "ς" in the extant version of the text was purposeful. It doesn't mean that "Jonas" cannot then be used for a deeper search. In any case, the numbers involved are sufficiently large for the calculation to apply whether or not the name of the prophet is Jonah or Jonas. The extra value of 200 assigned to the letter "ς" does not make much difference: if the extant text is used, the ratio between the values is 62%; if adjusted text is used, the ratio is 63%. Both invoke the Golden Ratio, 0.62:1.
[9] It is worth noting again that William Gann, in *Tunnel*, makes what should be Chapter XXXIV into Chapter XXXIX.

THE SIGN OF THE PROPHET JONAH

The first point is that verses 39 and 40 taken together consist of 48 words, which parallels the 48 chapters in *Beelzebub's Tales*. This means that important information is likely to become apparent if 48 is divided by 12. This latter, it will be remembered, was traditionally associated with the zodiac and with the dimensions of heaven.[10] Furthermore, it is almost certainly not an accident – and is therefore a vital clue – that the whole structure of "the sign of the prophet" is made available in Chapter *12* of St. Matthew's Gospel.

Obviously, the result of dividing 48 by 12 is the number 4. This, in turn, references the square (in particular) and the rectangle, both of which were discussed in Chapter 4. The use of four dimensions gives stability to any structure; and Chapter 12 of St. Matthew's Gospel is no exception. Table 12-2 shows the profile of the gematrian value of the Greek words in verses 39 and 40 when successive batches of *four* words are consolidated.[11] Figure 12-1 shows the graphical results, with the sequence of word groupings measured against the absolute gematrian values of those groupings.

Word group	Gematrian value	Change in value
1-4	1365	
5-8	1222	-143
9-12	1801	579
13-16	1662	-139
17-20	3587	1925
21-24	1482	-2105
25-28	2497	1015
29-32	1971	-526
33-36	3036	1065
37-40	2643	-393
41-44	1470	-1173
45-48	1971	501

TABLE 12-2: WORD STRUCTURE OF VERSES 39 & 40

The results are – again – simply extraordinary. The emergent diagram is a left-biased enneagram pulse. There are three waves (1-2-3) into a very marked peak. This is followed by a sharp contraction (A), which would be an energy gap.

---

[10] It is relevant to the argument that the number 12 generates all the important numbers in music and in harmonic proportion. Hence, its *heavenly* properties. This contrasts with the number 10, which has unique properties in *terrestrial* mathematics. It is highly unlikely that the chapter numbers and verse numbers in St. Matthew's text are random. Chapter 12 makes direct reference to the number 12, which turns out to be very important for the calculations. The set-up for "the sign of the prophet" starts with verse 38. This may be a reference to – and therefore an instruction to search for – the Golden Ratio, 38:62::62:1.

[11] See Appendix 2.

Then there is a volatile advance (B) that divides into three sub-waves (a-b-c). And, finally, there is a sharp fall (C), which brings the whole process to completion. As calculated, the cycle runs over only 10 of the word groupings, thereby suggesting that the first grouping ends a previous cycle and the 12th grouping starts a new one.

The pattern is, undoubtedly, the *sign* of the prophet Jonah.

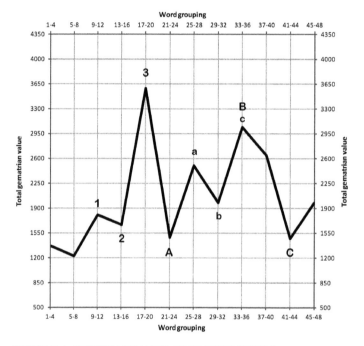

FIGURE 12-1: GEMATRIAN VALUES OF GROUPED WORDS

Importantly, the shape of the diagram changes only very marginally if the gematrian value for Jonah, in "the sign of the prophet Jonah" is replaced with the value of "Jonas". The extra value of 200 applied to the 16th word in Table 12-1 translates into a value of 1862 in the grouping of the 13th to 16th words in Table 12-2. The effect is only to eliminate the wave 2 fall in Figure 12-1. This is shown in Figure 12-2. In a practical sense, therefore, it doesn't seem to matter whether the name of the prophet is "Jonas" rather than "Jonah".

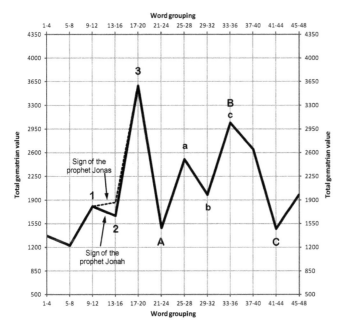

FIGURE 12-2: THE SIGN OF THE PROPHET

ST. MATTHEW'S PATTERN IN THE FINANCIAL MARKETS

The equity crash of 1987

As with the wave patterns produced by Mr. Gurdjieff and Mr. Gann, St. Matthew's esoteric pattern can only become meaningful if it actually exists in the exoteric world. There is no question that it does. Figure 12-3 shows the equity crash of 1987, as reflected in the UK's FTSE100 index and in a six-month percentage change in that index. Overlaid on the chart is St. Matthew's "sign of the prophet Jonah/Jonas". The pattern shows a three-wave rise (1-2-3) into a left-biased peak that is then followed by: a sharp contraction (A), a three-wave recovery (a-b-c) during a wave B advance, and an end-process fall (C).

There are three very significant points here. The first is that, while the timings are not absolutely precise, the overall match between the predictive pattern and the actual outcome is exceptionally good. This means that each stage of the pattern was a natural development from what went before: the wave A crash followed the 1986-87 bubble; the three-phase wave B followed the crash; and the process was not complete until some form of wave C correction had materialised. Just the simple knowledge of this process would have been immensely helpful once the shock of the crash had materialised.

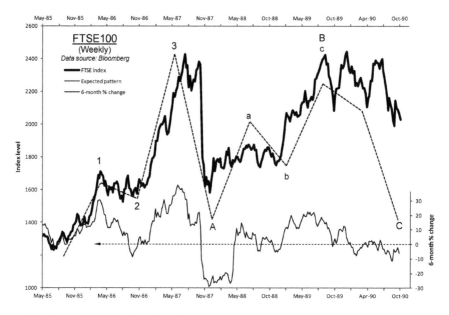

FIGURE 12-3: EQUITY CRASH OF 1987

The second point follows from this. A bubble and crash in any financial market is profoundly disruptive. St. Matthew's pattern therefore represents the insertion of a shock into a financial market. So it can be seen as a symbol of *new information* and the signature of change. In theory, the initial information shock itself is carried by waves 1, 2 and 3 of the pattern. However, the actual change process is only initiated when a collapse occurs. I shall be addressing this phenomenon in a little more detail in Chapter 13. In the meantime, we can conclude that wave A of the pattern confirms the validity of the original information and reflects the start of the process of necessary adjustment.

The third important point is that, once the pattern has emerged, a system will have been changed forever. Its deep-structure will have mutated into a different format, and it will be unable to return to the situation that existed prior to the impact of new information. In this sense, a bubble-and-crash episode is likely to represent the *start* of a whole new era, rather than just reflect the destruction of an old way of doing things. In December 1999, the FTSE100 was about 3.5 times higher than it was at the end of St. Matthew's change cycle in September 1990.

The bubble and crash in the Nikkei

These observations allow us to draw some important conclusions about one of the longest bubble-and-crash episodes in living memory – that of the Japanese stock market. Figure 12-4 shows the pattern of the Japanese Nikkei Stock Average, starting in 1973. There is obviously some slippage in the actual performance against the expected outcomes, and the sheer dynamism of the bubble suggests that it would be better represented by the pattern of "Jonas" from Figure 12-2 rather than the pattern of "Jonah".

Nevertheless, the formation underlying the whole movement between 1982 and 2003 is unmistakeable. In particular, there is a left-bias to the pattern, and the surge into the peak is followed by a long three-wave move down into the end of the process. There may, of course, be a larger version of the pattern operating, but the current inference is that the process of change that began in 1982 is actually over. This means, first, that a new era is already underway and that, second, the 2003-07 advance and subsequent collapse are properly part of the start of that new era.

FIGURE 12-4: JAPANESE NIKKEI, 1973 TO 2012

THE HUMAN HEARTBEAT

For completion, we can use the data in Table 12-2 to construct a chart based on *changes* in the gematrian values of verses 39 and 40 in St. Matthew's text. The results are shown in Figure 12-5. The vertical axis tracks the changes in the values when the text is grouped into batches of four words, and the horizontal axis shows the associated word groupings. Again, the pattern is that of a left-biased enneagram pulse, although the downswings are very much more pronounced compared with those in Figure 12-1. What is striking about this particular presentation is that it has parallels with the electrical activity of a human heart, as measured by a modern electrocardiogram (ECG). See Figure 12-6.

The notation used by medical professionals to identify specific phases of the heartbeat – P, Q, R, S, T and U – need not concern us here. But it is quite clear that: the rise to P and the fall to Q correspond to waves 1 and 2 of the enneagram pulse; the R-wave and the S-wave correspond to waves 3 and A; the rise to T matches the three-phase wave B; and the final downswing from T corresponds to wave C. The U-wave of the heartbeat is included for completion, but it is only occasionally present and is therefore usually assumed not to occur. The whole pattern is suitably left-biased, but the eye-catching element is the amplitude both of the R-wave (which is very dynamic) and of the subsequent S-wave (which makes a new low).

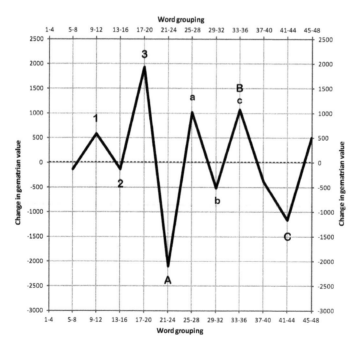

FIGURE 12-5: CHANGE IN GEMATRIAN VALUES OF GROUPED WORDS

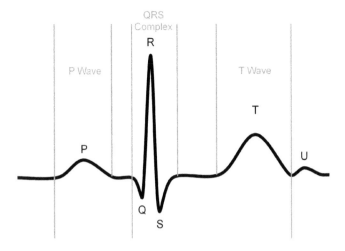

FIGURE 12-6: THE HUMAN HEARTBEAT

CONCLUSION

But what does this mean? The "sign of the prophet" was obviously considered to be so important that it had to be given in concise terms, but in a way that hid its true nature from the casual (and, indeed, not-so-casual) reader. But it seems valid to ask how the full implications of the text could possibly have been known at the time? How, for example, could a symbol hidden in an ancient text be applicable to a modern index of collective human behaviour? Or to the human heartbeat? In fact, would the *sign* even have been recognised as such, had its footprint been detected in the non-scientific milieu that existed when it was written?

St Matthew's Gospel was written sometime in the first century after the death of Jesus. There is a great deal of uncertainty about the exact dating of the Gospel, with estimates ranging from 38-45 CE to well into the second half of the first century.[12] However, even if we take a later date, the work is at least 1900 years old.

As mentioned in Chapter 4, we cannot know whether the Gospel's hidden contents have remained untainted since it was originally written. There is, for example, the issue about whether the sign given by Jesus is the "sign of the prophet Jonah" or the "sign of the prophet Jonas". On the one hand, the absence of the

---

[12] There is a split between Catholic and Protestant researchers. The former tend to favour earlier dates; the latter, later ones. Some German theologians go so far as to place the date in the early years of the second century CE. See Jacque Eugène Jacquier, 'Gospel of St. Matthew', in *The Catholic Encyclopedia* (Robert Appleton Company, New York, 1911). Part of the uncertainty derives from the possibility that the first version was written in St. Matthew's native tongue, Hebrew. However, the Greek version is regarded as being canonical – that is, belonging to the rules, laws and traditions of Christianity.

letter "ς" in the name of the prophet "Ιωνα" in canonical Greek texts allows that some changes could have been made – whether by accident or design – to the earliest versions. On the other hand, of course, the omission could have been a purposeful method of drawing attention to an important piece of information.

In either case, it is difficult to avoid the conclusion that a truly ancient work of literature, which is regarded as central to the beliefs of one of the world's great religions in its exoteric form, not only contains a significant body of esoteric knowledge but also is able to convey that knowledge in a small volume of Greek text.[13] This is an extraordinary conclusion, given that the vast majority of humanity at the time were uneducated and immersed in what might be called pre-rational consciousness.[14]

In just 48 words, St Matthew's Gospel references a series of geometric diagrams involving the *vesica piscis* (Chapter 4), the possible objective nature of time (Chapter 5), and a very specific wave pattern (this chapter). Centuries later, Mr. Gurdjieff suggested that the wave pattern represented some form of universal constant – the signature of the way in which change and evolution is transmitted through a living universe, from the higher reaches of the cosmos to the lower reaches of the micro-world.

The direct inference is that St. Matthew's Gospel contains a revelation that has remained hidden for the best part of two millennia. Moreover, if the findings of this book are correct, then that revelation includes a blueprint for the various natural behaviours of living organisms that – even with a cursory analysis – is consistent with modern evidence. The implications are truly staggering. Perhaps we can take a few small steps towards unravelling some of them.

---

[13] Perhaps there is more, very significant, information hidden in the text. It is also worth adding that, in contradistinction to modern beliefs, ancient wisdom – as reflected in the importance of the numbers 48, 12 and 4 – seems to have incorporated a belief in the relevance of the Zodiac.

[14] Pre-rational consciousness is prior to formal operational thinking and propositional, or hypothetico-deductive, reasoning. It is likely to be based on the pursuit of *archaic* physiological needs, a reliance on *magical* images, symbols and rudimentary concepts, and conformity with *mythical* tribal beliefs. See Ken Wilber, *Eye to Eye: The Quest for a New Paradigm* (Shambhala Publications, Boston (Ma), 1983).

CHAPTER 13

A UNIVERSAL PATTERN
OF VIBRATION

"The principle of the discontinuity of vibration means the definite and necessary characteristic of all vibrations in nature... to develop not uniformly but with periodical accelerations and retardations."

P. D. Ouspensky

SECRET KNOWLEDGE

The conclusion from the foregoing chapters is that three very different sources – George Gurdjieff's *Beelzebub's Tales*, William Gann's *Tunnel Thru The Air* and St. Matthew's *sign of the prophet Jonas* – contained, in a concealed form, specific patterns that had implications beyond the context in which they were presented. Moreover, it is already clear that the patterns look very similar to one another. In other words, all three authors were presenting their own versions of one particular construct.

So, why was it considered important to hide this pattern? Mr. Gurdjieff was very fond of, as he put it, "burying the dog" (and not just the bone)[1] so that people had to work for the knowledge that they received. Mr. Gann was probably right in believing that, in 1927 when he published *Tunnel*, the "general public [was] not yet ready for it and probably would not understand or believe it".[2] And the science of numbers and letters in the time of St. Matthew was

---

[1] John G. Bennett, *Gurdjieff: Making a New World* (Harper & Row, New York, 1976).
[2] Gann, *Tunnel*.

specifically reserved for a small intellectual elite who would seek out hidden meanings from holy scriptures in order to be able to confirm personal evolution and higher cosmic purposes.

Nevertheless, even these explanations – as valid as they are – do not fully address the inference that the pattern is in some way extraordinarily meaningful – and perhaps even dangerous. First, there is no obvious reason within the context of St. Matthew's text for the pattern to be presented at all. The pattern therefore emerges as a genuine revelation. Had people deduced its presence 1900 years ago, they could well have believed that they were dealing with something beyond the teachings of Christianity and therefore hazardous. Furthermore, I have always felt that Mr. Gann (who claimed that St. Matthew's text was his source) may have become concerned at some stage in his life about a potential misuse of the pattern, and therefore spent the latter years of his life trying to bury it.[3] His stock trading courses were certainly good enough to be effective, but they may also have helped to divert attention from the truth of what he'd found.

Perhaps we'll never know; but the most important possibility is that the hidden pattern is a universal constant – an archetypal pattern of vibration that somehow permeates the whole of the cosmos. This was Mr Gurdjieff's contention.

THE PATTERNS COMPARED

With these thoughts in mind, we can now look at the patterns of vibration provided by the three authors. In doing so, however, it needs to be emphasised that all interpretations should be regarded as being only work in progress. An attempt, after all, is being made to concretise something that Mr. Gurdjieff explicitly, and St. Matthew implicitly, regarded as being a fundamental principle behind what might be called "deep structure" processes within the universe. Any such attempt needs to be approached carefully, and in the certain knowledge that full answers will remain elusive.

As a start, the patterns can be shown together, so that they can be judged visually in relation to one another. Figure 13-1 therefore shows the patterns as they emerge directly from their respective texts. It includes *both* of Mr. Gurdjieff's patterns as well as those of St. Matthew and Mr. Gann.

---

[3] This is, of course, only an opinion. But it is relevant that Mr. Gann does not appear to have made a great deal of effort promoting *The Tunnel Thru The Air*.

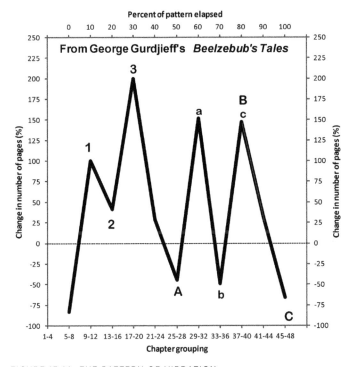

FIGURE 13-1A: THE PATTERN OF VIBRATION

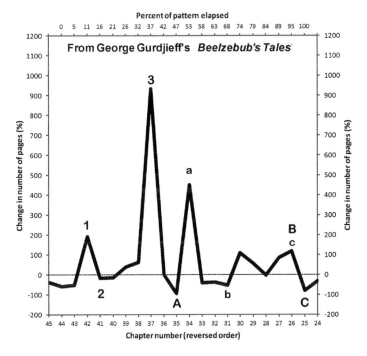

FIGURE 13-1B: THE PATTERN OF VIBRATION

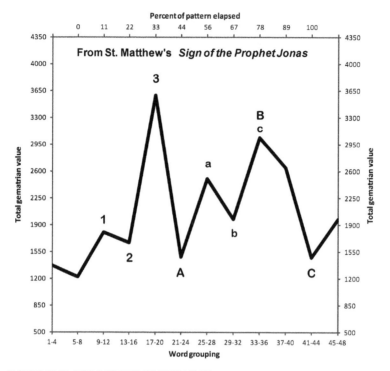

FIGURE 13-1C: THE PATTERN OF VIBRATION

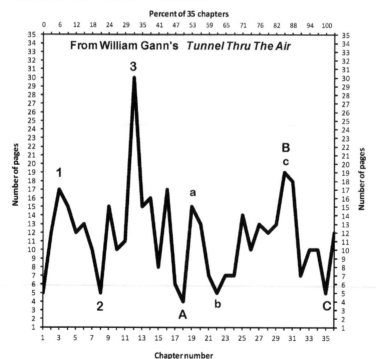

FIGURE 13-1D: THE PATTERN OF VIBRATION

Figure 13-2 shows St. Matthew's pattern compared with Mr. Gann's, and Figure 13-3 shows St. Matthew's pattern compared with Mr. Gurdjieff's primary pattern.

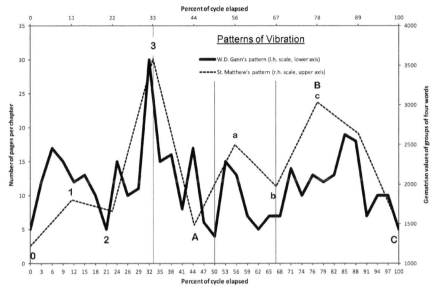

FIGURE 13-2: THE ARCHETYPAL PATTERNS OF VIBRATION: ST. MATTHEW AND W.D. GANN

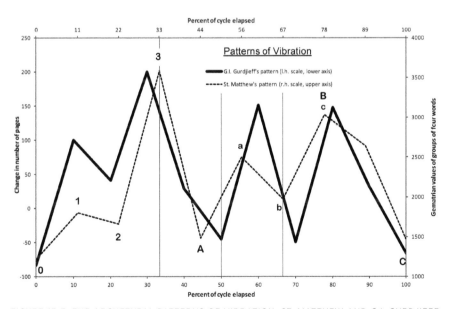

FIGURE 13-3: THE ARCHETYPAL PATTERNS OF VIBRATION: ST. MATTHEW AND G.I. GURDJIEFF

Figure 13-4 shows St. Matthew's pattern compared with the second of Mr. Gurdjieff's patterns – i.e. the one in Figure 13-1B. To help the comparisons, divisions of one-third, half and two-thirds of the horizontal width of the patterns are marked out. In addition, the established cycle notation (1-2-3/A-B-C) is applied just to St. Matthew's pattern, but on the understanding that it is applicable to all three patterns.

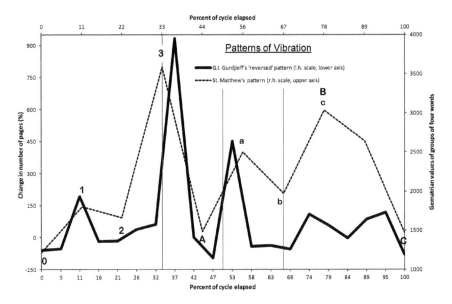

FIGURE 13-4: THE ARCHETYPAL PATTERNS OF VIBRATION: ST. MATTHEW AND G.I. GURDJIEFF

It is immediately apparent that the four patterns are essentially the same. There are differences in the extent of the swings and, at one extreme, St. Matthew's pattern is relatively simple while, at the other extreme, Mr. Gann's is complex. Nevertheless, all four patterns have a very specific locus at their core: there is a rising three-phase (1-2-3) pattern into a peak, followed by a three-phase (A-B-C) movement into a final low. The whole configuration has a left bias to it: the wave 3 peak occurs about a third of the way through the pattern; the wave A fall is very pronounced and occurs about halfway through the whole pattern; the wave B rally consists of three internal swings (a-b-c) and is relatively prolonged; and the final wave C fall is swift, but not as pronounced as the wave A collapse.

An anomaly

There is, however, an apparent anomaly that needs to be addressed. The patterns are certainly consistent with one another, but they diverge from the enneagram/price pulse patterns of Chapters 8 and 9 in one important sense: wave B within each of the patterns consists of three sub-waves (up-down-up) whereas the original enneagram pulse showed only one up-wave. *How can this difference be explained?*

One possible answer is that wave B of a pulse is modulated by the fluctuations of an *inner octave*. Figure 13-5 reproduces Figure 8-12 from Chapter 8. It shows how the corners of a triangle (representing the *Law of Three*) coincide with the notes Fa, La and Do[HI]. In the absence of an internal shock at Me – or an external shock at So – Fa and La act as barriers that keep the flow of energy trapped within the circuit. Consequently, after receiving the initial stimulus at Do the flow of energy starts at Re and proceeds in six waves around the enneagram. Within this flow, the move from Me to Ti corresponds to wave 3 of the vibrations in Figures 13-2 to 13-4, the drop from Ti to So corresponds to wave A, and the move from So to La matches wave B.

The important point here is that the notes Re, Me and So initiate inner octaves (see Table 6-4 of Chapter 6). Each of these inner octaves will therefore exhibit their own six-wave pattern; and, within each, there is going to be a drop from Ti to So. It is this drop that would produce the lower-level wave b within the a-b-c pattern that then constitutes the higher-level wave B. If the whole enneagram pulse is left-biased, such that the rising wave B evolves relatively slowly, then the drop might be very pronounced. This is reflected in Mr. Gurdjieff's pattern.

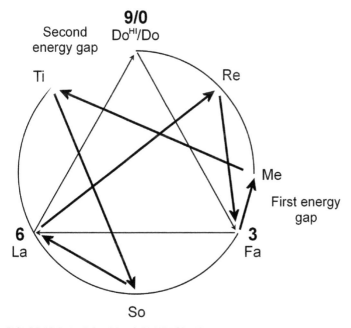

FIGURE 13-5: THE DIATONIC ENNEAGRAM

The left bias and the nature of learning

The idea that the pattern of vibration is intrinsically left-biased introduces some important considerations about the nature of learning. In Chapter 8, it was argued that the Mills-Hebb learning pattern was a three-wave process: there was an initial information shock (i.e. wave 1 of a 1-2-3 profile), a period of absorption (wave 2), and then a process of application (wave 3). The left-biased pulse now adds a potential qualification to this process because it suggests that there are two 'layers' of learning: the first (which corresponds to the Mills-Hebb pattern) is an inner adaptation; the second (which is the new insight) is deep structure change.[4] The point of difference is that the former involves taking an unchanged system to its limits, while the latter means actually changing the system.

Hence, an initial information shock will take a system to its inner limits, but if the environment continues to exert stress on that system, then the whole of the original three-wave movement becomes an information shock which changes the system itself. This is shown in Figure 13-6. The 1-2-3 advance in the first half of the diagram represents the initial quantitative behaviour within an unchanged system. The wave A contraction represents the *shudder* within the system as it finds itself no longer able to cope without structural change. Then the second half of the diagram represents the behaviour of the system after inner qualitative change has taken place.

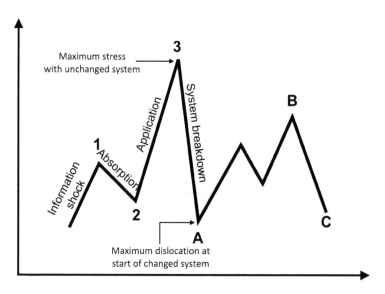

FIGURE 13-6: ADAPTIVE LEARNING AND SYSTEM CHANGE

---

[4] Bateson, *Mind and Nature*. Bateson also included a third adjustment – namely, genetic mutation in response to environmental change.

ANALYSING THE PATTERNS IN MORE DETAIL

We can now move ahead, and analyse the patterns in more detail. For simplicity, the second of Mr. Gurdjieff's patterns – i.e. the one derived from reversing the chapters and associated pages – will be put to one side. The following analysis therefore just concentrates on the patterns presented in Figures 13-2 and 13-3.

In what follows, I shall start with Mr. Gann's version of the pattern. There are two reasons for this. First, at a mundane level, Mr. Gann undoubtedly gave a great deal of thought to the subject. In fact, Mr. Gann basically devoted a whole book of 36 chapters and 418 pages just to expressing the pattern, albeit in a hidden form. This is in contrast to Mr. Gurdjieff, whose 48 chapters and 1238 pages were devoted to far more than just illustrating a pattern of vibration. Both are starkly in contrast to St. Matthew's pattern, which was defined in only two verses consisting in total of 48 words! It is possible therefore that Mr. Gann's pattern is a much more detailed version of those offered by Mr. Gurdjieff and St. Matthew.

The second reason for concentrating on Mr. Gann's pattern follows from this. His attention to detail hints at the possibility of additional information. That is, Mr. Gann's pattern might include information that was not provided by the other two. This does, indeed, turn out to be the case.

The Gann pattern

As discussed in Chapter 10, Mr. Gann's pattern is clearly divided into two equal phases: the falling wave A finishes 50% of the way through the pattern; the low of that wave is the lowest low of the pattern; and the low itself is formed by a distinctive data point. Moreover, the second phase recapitulates the first phase, although with significant differences in the velocities involved.

The second point is that waves 1 and 2 of Mr Gann's pattern are much more pronounced than the corresponding waves in the patterns imparted by Mr. Gurdjieff and St. Matthew. Without this emphasis, Mr. Gann's overall pattern would not divide into two equal phases. In Chapter 10 it was suggested that the structure of waves 1 and 2 indicated that they formed an initial information shock from which subsequent oscillations emerged. These subsequent oscillations consisted of two *beats*, or two sets of advances and contractions. In the diagrams of Mr. Gann's pattern (e.g. Figure 10-1), these two oscillations are waves 3 and A, followed by waves B and C. On this interpretation, the whole diagram consists of three oscillations, not just two; and this, in turn, implies the presence of the *Law of Three*. It can then be argued that each of the three beats might have a different function in relation to the whole: for example, the first beat initiates a process; the second beat fulfils the stimulus; and the third beat terminates the process.

The third point, in a sense, follows from the second. Once we start looking behind the apparent rigidity of Mr. Gann's dualistic pattern, a whole new set of relationships emerges, which involve the Golden Ratio. At a very simple level, and as was shown in Figure 10-2, Mr. Gann's pattern is not just divided into two equal parts, it is also divided into two unequal, but related, parts. Specifically, the ratio of the larger part of the vibration to the smaller part is defined by the Golden Ratio, 0.618:0.382. As described in Chapter 3, such expressions of the Ratio distinguish passive energies from active energies. The larger part is passive/receptive and the smaller part is active/generative.

The inference, therefore, is that the first part of the diagram in some way lays the foundation for the energy of the subsequent movement. This could mean that the apparently innocuous wave c of B is actually where the real strength of the pattern emerges. In financial markets, for example, this might be where sustained (and sustainable) action takes place. Where the resulting advance is highly speculative *learnt* behaviour, the subsequent wave C collapse can be dramatic.

Squaring price with time

This conclusion is borne out by another aspect of Mr. Gann's pattern that relates the Golden Ratio to the geometry of the square. Mr. Gann's name has become closely associated with the concept of *squaring price with time*, whereby movements in price along a vertical axis are matched with the evolution of time along a horizontal axis. According to the conventional interpretation, when price and time become equivalent along a geometric 45-degree line (i.e. when *squaring* takes place), a reversal of some degree can be expected. The big problem, however, is that there is no obvious way of making units of price comparable with units of time. It is like trying to match apples with potatoes.

One solution that is used by analysts is to note where a price low and a price high have occurred in the past, and calculate the associated relationship between the movement in price and the passage of time – i.e. the *speed* of the price movement. This relationship is then represented by a 45-degree line on a chart, with the axes adjusted to suit. The heroic assumption is that subsequent price inflexions will occur at points in the future that reflect the same speed as the original price-time relationship.

In practice, the technique works only erratically, if at all. The reason that analysts persist with it is an interesting comment on the belief that financial markets (and therefore collective behaviour) are organised by an unknown form of order, and the belief that Mr. Gann had access to the necessary knowledge. Both beliefs are undoubtedly correct, but the mistake has been to take Mr. Gann's extant teachings at face value. As I have already mentioned, these teachings may have helped to hide – rather than reveal – what he knew. A great deal of research still needs to be done on the subject, but we can now at least shed a little more light on it.

In Chapter 10, it was shown that Mr. Gann's 1-2-3/A-B-C pattern of vibration fitted precisely into a square of 35 units by 35 units. In Figure 10-1, the horizontal scale represented the number of chapters in the book and the vertical scale represented the number of pages per chapter. Mr. Gann's pattern ended when the number of chapters (35) equalled an equivalent potential number of pages per chapter (35). Since, geometrically, the top right-hand corner of a square coincides with a 45-degree line drawn from the lower left-hand corner of that square, this is where the two axes square off. Hence, if the vertical axis represents *price* and the horizontal axis represents *time*, then price squares with time in the top right-hand corner of the square. After such a point, quite obviously, a new vibration will begin.

The Golden Ratio and hidden energies

As it stands, this definition of *squaring* does not provide much genuine information. It is an outcome of the way that the diagram was conceived and then constructed, and so is as much an artifice as an indication of a genuine phenomenon. The specific problem for analysts is that none of the inflexion points within the vibration actually occur *on*, or along, the 45-degree line. However, there is a much more profound aspect to the diagram, which not only automatically deals with this problem, but also raises questions about the forces at work in collective human behaviour.

In Chapter 5 it was found that, if St Matthew's "sign of the prophet" was taken to belong to "Jonas" rather than "Jonah",[5] then it was possible to construct an extraordinary diagram that seemed to relate the measurable processes of life to some form of hidden energy represented by the Golden Ratio. Specifically, a process ended when the measured active and passive elements, each multiplied by 0.618, formed a square. This was shown in Figure 5-7.

Figure 13-7 shows Mr. Gann's original diagram adjusted so that the origin of both axes is zero.[6] This implicitly allows that the number of pages can start from zero. Next, the vertical heights of the vibrations in each of the two halves of the diagram (i.e. the heights of the two primary oscillations) are measured. Once this is done, it can be shown that the pattern of vibration finishes when the measured height of the *largest* of the two vibrations squares with the energies of *both* vibrations as represented by the Golden Ratio, 0.618:1. This outcome is a directly comparable to that shown in Figure 5-7 of Chapter 5. First, the maximum height of the vibration in the first half of the diagram is 30 units. When this is multiplied by 0.618, the equivalent horizontal value is 18.54 units. Second, the maximum height of the vibration in the second half of the diagram is 19 units. When this is multiplied by 0.618, the equivalent value on the horizontal axis is 11.74 units.

---

[5] This was Mr. Gann's own conclusion.
[6] This places it on an equal footing with Figure 5-7.

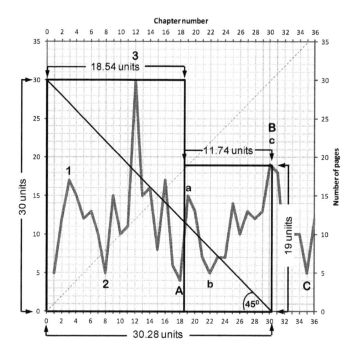

FIGURE 13-7: THE GOLDEN RATIO AND THE 45-DEGREE LINE IN MR. GANN'S DIAGRAM

Harmonising price with hidden energies

The result is that the highest point of the diagram measured on the vertical axis (30 units) is almost exactly equal to the sum of the two Golden Ratio defined widths on the horizontal axis (18.54 + 11.74 = 30.28 units). This outcome is directly comparable with that shown in Figure 5-7. There is obviously a small difference between the vertical and horizontal dimensions, amounting to 0.28 units;[7] but the fact remains that the active phases of the vibration terminate on a 30 x 30 square. This means that the peak of wave B coincides with the end of a 45-degree line[8] drawn from the top left-hand corner of the 30 x 30 square to the bottom right-hand corner. Once wave B has finished, the final wave C takes over.

In terms of the argument in Chapter 3, this means that the advance from 0 to the top of wave 3 is the *passive* element in the process and that the advance from the bottom of wave A to the top of wave B is the *active* element. Consequently, the first advance is likely to incorporate just quantitative changes, while the second advance is likely to embody quantitative changes *and* qualitative changes. More generally, this means that the first rectangle represents the total response

---

[7] In Figure 5-7 there is also a small difference between the vertical and horizontal distances.
[8] Given the variability, the actual line would be 45° 12'.

to the initial information shock of wave 1, and that the second rectangle reflects the resulting structural system changes. Again, this confirms that wave B takes place under the influence of deep structure changes.

If Figure 13-7 is translated into a financial market vibration, such that the vertical axis represents *price* and the horizontal axis represents *time*, the expansionary processes of the vibration will terminate when price squares with time. This may be why Mr. Gann makes Robert Gordon say in *Tunnel*: "In making my predictions I use geometry and mathematics… based on immutable laws".[9] Moreover, this conclusion holds true whatever units are measured on the horizontal axis.

Mr. Gann presented his pattern of vibration in the context of a square that is 35 units high and 35 units wide. But the use of a square to contain the vibration is not essential to the phenomenon of *squaring of price with time*. The Golden Ratio transforms the explicit energy being expressed on the vertical axis into an implicit energy on the horizontal axis, and thereby resolves the issue of making price *compatible* with time. The direct inference is that time itself has an objective element that is normally hidden from us. For simplicity, I am going to call this element *objective Time*.

The Jonas pattern

This obviously raises the question about the validity of such an approach in the context of St. Matthew's "sign of the prophet Jonas" and Mr. Gurdjieff's enneagram. Figure 13-8 shows St. Matthew's pattern of vibration. The first point to note is that, by construction, the whole pattern is contained within a square. As with Mr. Gann's pattern, this has the effect of ensuring that the whole pattern is completed in the context of a square.

The second point is that, because of this, the base of the diagram is not going to be zero, as with Mr. Gann's, but is going to be the actual start of the vibration at the second word grouping. The total increase in gematrian values from this point to the fifth word grouping is 2365. This number is almost exactly the product of the numbers 38.2 and 61.8. Since nothing within St. Matthew's text appears accidental, this could imply a direct reference to the Golden Ratio.[10] We can then construct a Golden Rectangle from this, with a height of 2365 and a width of 1461.6.

Next, we can construct a Golden Rectangle from the increase in gematrian values from the sixth word grouping to the ninth. This yields a rectangle with a height of 1554 and width of 960.4. If the two Golden Rectangles are placed contiguously, with a common base line, the horizontal width is 2421 units

---

[9] Gann, *Tunnel.*
[10] 38.2 x 61.8 = 2361.

against a maximum height of 2365 units. This is not quite a square, so a falling 45 degree line does not correspond precisely to the inflexion point at the end of wave B. But it *nearly* does. This suggests that there might be a zone, rather than a precise point, where an inversion takes place.

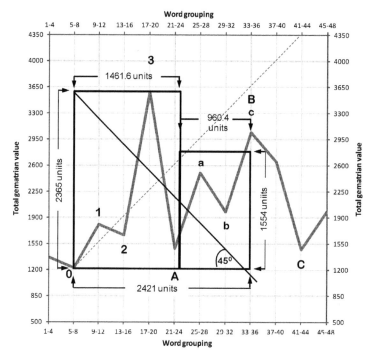

FIGURE 13-8: THE GOLDEN RATIO AND THE 45-DEGREE LINE IN ST. MATTHEW'S DIAGRAM

The Gurdjieff pattern

A similar conclusion applies to Mr. Gurdjieff's pattern of vibration. This is shown in Figure 13-9 where, again, the Golden Ratio transformation is applied to the maximum height of the first half of the vibration, and to the extent of the a-b-c rally in the second part. When the bottom edges of both Golden Rectangles are aligned in the chart, the total horizontal width is 294.3 units and the maximum vertical height is 283.6 units. Again, these dimensions do not quite replicate those of a square. But the point is that a square can come into existence *close* to the point of inflexion. The actual square is formed when the rally from A to B has become large enough to ensure that the sum of the Golden Ratio transformations on the horizontal axis equals the height of the initial three-wave impulse from 0 to 3.

There are three important points that emerge from a consideration of Mr. Gurdjieff's diagram. First, he may have emphasised the depth of the wave b downswing in order to focus on the fact that wave B can only finish when *three* sub-waves have evolved. In other words, the wave a advance cannot complete the process.

The second point follows from this. Once wave c of wave B has started, it is necessary continuously to calculate the height of the evolving wave B. This is because the larger Golden Rectangle has already been determined by the height of the initial three-wave advance, but the second, smaller, Golden Rectangle will grow as the wave B upswing progresses. When this second rectangle is large enough for its lower right-hand corner to intersect a 45-degree line drawn downwards from the top left-hand corner of the first rectangle, then the upswing will be reaching a terminal juncture.

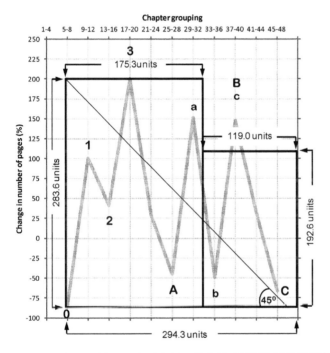

FIGURE 13-9: THE GOLDEN RATIO AND THE 45-DEGREE LINE IN MR. GURDJIEFF'S DIAGRAM

The third point, however, is probably the most significant – at least in theoretical terms. In Mr. Gann's diagram, *calendar (or cycle) time* and *objective Time* are visually correlated because they are both contained by a square. In Mr. Gurdjieff's diagram, however, the only way that cycle time and objective Time can be correlated is if the horizontal axis that tracks cycle time is adjusted. This has been done in Figure 13-10.

Specifically, the horizontal axis has been widened – and the squareness of the diagram gives way to a rectangle – so that the cycle pattern begins in the bottom left-hand corner of the first square and the last major peak occurs above the bottom right-hand corner. It does not really matter, however, where the contiguous Golden Rectangles are placed. Mr. Gurdjieff's diagram thus overtly separates the phenomenon of *time* as measured by the Earth's relation to the sun (or moon) and the phenomenon of *Time* as represented by the Golden Ratio. This separation draws attention directly to the importance of the latter.

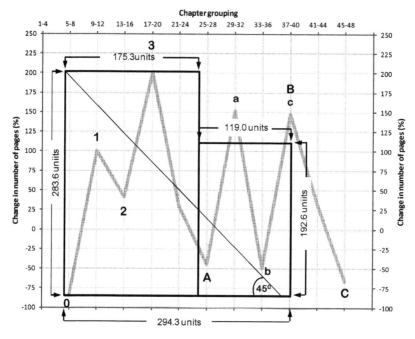

FIGURE 13-10: THE GOLDEN RATIO AND THE 45-DEGREE LINE WITH ADJUSTED CALENDAR TIME

SQUARING ACTIVITY WITH TIME

The obvious question, of course, is: does this idea of *squaring* explicit output with implicit input work in practice? In Chapter 11, I showed the performance of the ISM index of producer confidence between January 1991 and October 2001. The chart is reproduced in Figure 13-11. The initial three-wave recovery took the index from a low of 39.2 to a high of 59.4. This is a difference of 20.2 units. The recovery from the low of wave A to the high of wave B took the index from 45.5 to 58.1. This is a difference of 12.6 units. If the vertical heights are multiplied by 0.618, the results are 12.48 and 7.79 respectively. Added together, the result is 20.27, which is only marginally larger than the initial three-wave advance. It is not always this easy; but, in this case anyway, Mr. Gann's formula seems to have worked.

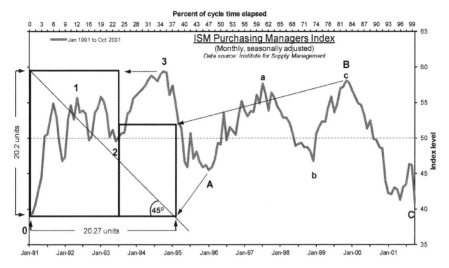

FIGURE 13-11: THE GOLDEN RATIO, THE 45-DEGREE LINE, AND THE ISM INDEX

As in Figures 13-7 to 13-9, the Golden Rectangles have been placed on the chart in a way that identifies the relationship between the first (i.e. largest) rectangle and the initial three-wave upswing. The second, smaller, Golden Rectangle will then expand as the wave B upswing evolves. When the resulting rectangle is large enough for its lower right-hand corner to intersect a 45-degree line drawn downwards from the top left-hand corner of the first rectangle, then the ISM upswing will be reaching a terminal juncture.

To repeat, however, the placement of the two Golden Rectangles on the chart in this way does not assume any specific relationship between calendar – or cycle – time and objective Time. The two phenomena can only be made to match visually if the cycle's horizontal axis is shortened (in this case, lengthened in other cases) to make sure that the start of the first upswing and end of the second upswing coincide with the boundaries of the two rectangles. For completion, this is done in Figure 13-12.

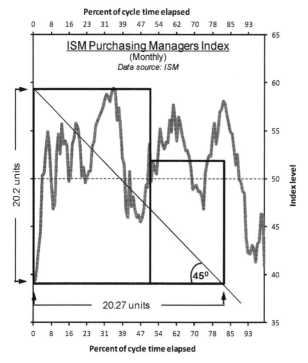

FIGURE 13-12: THE GOLDEN RATIO AND THE 45-DEGREE LINE WITH ADJUSTED CALENDAR TIME

CONCLUSION

The intersection of a 45-degree line with opposite corners of two contiguous Golden Rectangles may have been part of the phenomenon of vibration that Mr. Gann was trying to communicate through the page structure of *Tunnel*. But it is quite obvious that this version of squaring price with time bears very little relation to the formula that contemporary analysts attribute to Mr. Gann.

For a start, the 45-degree line slopes downwards from left to right. Second, there is no direct contact between the 45-degree line and the final turning point in absolute prices. What we are dealing with, instead, is something much more profound. The diagram appears to confirm the conclusion of Chapter 5 that the phenomenon that we call *time* is not just a method of dividing a continuous process into distinct and equal units; it is an energy in its own right that participates in that process. In other words, Time has an objective dimension: it is an energetic input that can be measured in relation to the associated output.

More subtly (and as argued in Chapter 3), this energetic input can be classified according to the relative sizes of the two rectangles: the larger one is *receptive* (or *passive*) and the smaller one is *generative* (or *active*). This means that the initial 1-2-3 upswing is essentially passive, while wave B (with its a-b-c oscillation) is active. One implication is that the initial upswing establishes the environment and sets the scene, while wave B is the one that creates the deep-structure changes.

In terms of economic activity and financial markets, this adds substance to the arguments in Chapter 8 concerning the nature of learning in the context of economic activity and financial market speculation: the whole of the initial upswing is the information shock; the wave A fall represents the absorption of the information; and wave B is where the learning is actively applied. Consequently, wave B is the location of persistent trends and permanent structural change.

This chapter has explored the shape of a universal pattern of change that was hidden in St. Matthew's Gospel, in Mr. Gurdjieff's *Beelzebub's Tales*, and in Mr. Gann's *Tunnel Thru The Air*. If the findings are correct, they have revolutionary implications for our understanding not just of collective human behaviour, but also of the evolutionary processes embedded in the worlds of the infinitesimally small and of the infinitely large. The processes of change may be much more organised than we thought.

CHAPTER 14

INNER OCTAVE CYCLES

"[I]t is necessary to have a clear idea of another property of vibrations, namely the so-called 'inner vibrations'."

P. D. Ouspensky, quoting G. I. Gurdjieff

THE CREATIVE SHOCK

The patterns that were explored in the previous chapter (Figures 13-1, 13-2 and 13-3) show a significant momentum low halfway through the complete cycle. This leaves the impression that the overall vibration consists of *two* sub-cycles – namely, 0-3-A and A-B-C.

Certainly, the second half of each diagram reproduces the first half, although in a compressed form: the a-b-c upwave mirrors the initial 1-2-3 upswing; and the final wave C fall recapitulates the wave A collapse. In practical terms, it can therefore often be appropriate to treat the vibration as a pair of cycles. Nevertheless, Mr. Gurdjieff was quite clear that any complete process should contain three distinct phases, or inner octaves (see Chapter 8). *So, where are these inner octaves in Mr. Gann's pattern?*

Figure 14-1 shows two data series: the upper one is Mr. Gann's pattern of vibration derived from the number of pages per chapter from *Tunnel*; the lower one is Mr. Gann's pattern converted to *momentum*, or changes in the number of pages between one chapter and the next. It is immediately clear that the vibrations *after* waves 1 and 2 consist of three sub-cycles, all of equal length.

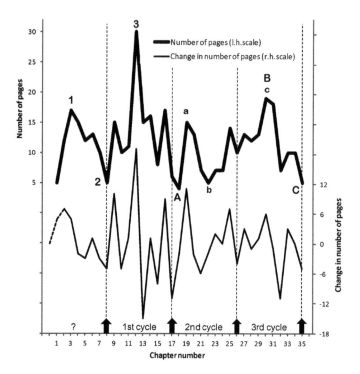

FIGURE 14-1: MR. GANN'S PATTERN CONVERTED TO MOMENTUM

These cycles are separated from one another and presented in Figure 14-2. All three have a basic signature: they start and end on a low, and are interrupted by a sharp contraction.[1] When they are averaged together (see Figure 14-2D), the unmistakable pattern is that of an enneagram-type pulse. The implication is that the oscillations are not random, and that the overall pattern references both the *Law of Three* and the *Law of Seven*.

However, this still leaves the problem of interpreting the first two waves of Mr. Gann's pattern. A possible clue can be found in the analysis of inner octaves in Chapter 6. A striking of the note Do triggers an ascending octave, with inner octaves being initiated sequentially by the notes Re, Me and So (Table 6-4). What is important here is that the initial Do occurs prior to, and independently of, what subsequently evolves as the *system*; and that that emergent system starts at Re. In other words, the initial Do is a *creative shock*.

If this logic is transferred on to Mr. Gann's momentum pattern, the first upswing can be viewed as the creative shock that corresponds to the initiating Do, and the subsequent downswing represents the removal of the shock. But the shock nevertheless creates three sub-cycles, which correspond to the three inner octaves.

---

[1] If cycles are naturally punctuated by sharp contractions, they are ill-represented by sine waves.

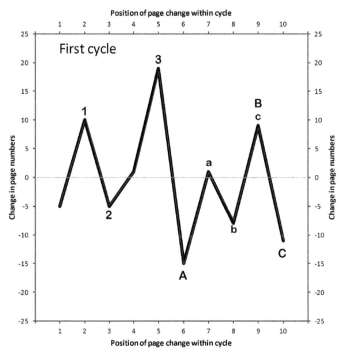

FIGURE 14-2A: CYCLES OF MOMENTUM

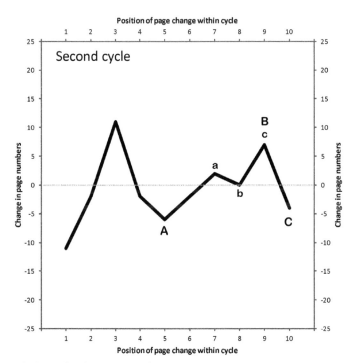

FIGURE 14-2B: CYCLES OF MOMENTUM

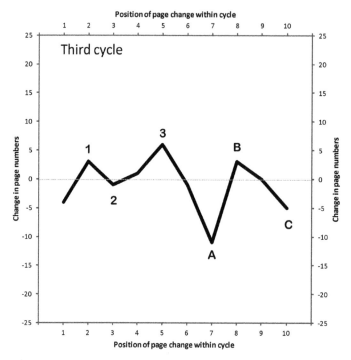

FIGURE 14-2C: CYCLES OF MOMENTUM

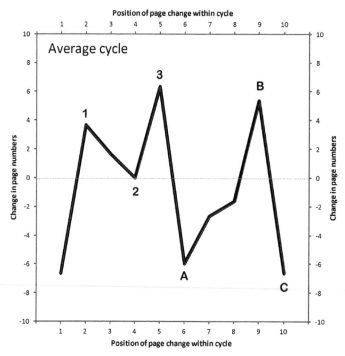

FIGURE 14-2D: CYCLES OF MOMENTUM

This pattern is shown in Figure 14-1. The shock embodied in the first rising wave (wave 1) in the upper part of the diagram will have an initial, once-off impact. But it will then either merge into the structure of the affected system or will simply fade away (wave 2). In the lower series in Figure 14-1, therefore, the initiating shock emerges from nothing (zero in the chart), has an impact and then fades away. But the system then vibrates.[2]

This still leaves open the question of the source of the shock: can it be created by the system itself or must it arise externally?[3] The question will be addressed in the next chapter. For the moment, it is sufficient to acknowledge that, whatever the source of the shock, the system has to respond to it. And it is this response that is reflected in the subsequent oscillations.

THE OSCILLATIONS

Each of the three sub-cycles that follow the shock exhibits a different pattern. The first cycle is balanced around a peak that is only slightly off-centre, and – most importantly – is very similar to the momentum pattern that was deduced from St. Matthew's text (see Figure 12-1). This is a strong indication of the importance of this particular pattern. Its emergence invariably signals the beginning of an adjustment. Its first three rising waves correspond to wave 3 of Mr. Gann's higher-level pattern, and its subsequent three falling waves correspond to wave A of the higher-level pattern. The rising phase takes the system as far as it can go without a change in the system and, consequently, the falling phase is an energy gap associated with a system failure of some sort. In this sense, the lower-level A-B-C pattern represents a genuine reversal of the preceding 1-2-3 advance.

The second cycle has two momentum peaks, rather than three. In particular, the initial recovery is dynamic and is followed by a sharp contraction. Then there is a prolonged advance to the final peak. The overall effect is to produce a simple left-biased pattern that reprises the more complex higher-level pattern.

Finally, the fluctuations in the third cycle match those in the first, except that wave A appears dramatic and the final wave B upswing is damped. Wave A often provides a shock that is so large that it effectively terminates the creative processes within the whole triad of cycles. Waves B and C then become aftershocks.

As Figure 14-2D then shows, the average of these three *inner* cycles looks very similar to a schematised version of the enneagram/price pulse discussed in

---

[2] It is an interesting fact that the idea of *change* is represented by the Greek letter delta – i.e. 'δ. The shape of the letter mirrors a shock that is followed by an advance that then fades. It is therefore also relevant that the capitalised version of 'δ' is 'Δ' with its implicit reference to the *Law of Three*.
[3] This is the difference between the endogenous and exogenous shocks of economic theory.

Chapter 9. Each cycle in a group of three will diverge from the average, and will play a different role in relation to the higher-level cycle of which it is a part. But the same basic dynamics are functioning all the time. These dynamics involve an initial *learning* pattern, an intra-cycle energy gap, a recovery and an end-cycle contraction. This is the archetypal pattern behind all cycles.

Outer and inner octaves

It is possible to explain the differences between each of the lower-level cycles in terms of the progress through an ascending octave, as described in Chapter 6. This progress is retarded at the intervals Me-Fa and Ti-Do so that the system fluctuates. As shown in Table 6-4 of Chapter 6, these particular intervals, or energy gaps, occur not just in the outer octave, but also in each of the three inner octaves. It is the interaction of the two levels that creates the differences between each of Mr. Gann's three sub-cycles. Table 14-1 reproduces Table 6-4, with the addition of extra columns showing the difference in each note's vibration when compared with the previous, lower, note. The points of slowdown are highlighted.

Whole phenomenon			Triple octave		
Tonic Sol-fa	Vibration	Difference	Tonic Sol-fa	Vibration	Difference
Do^{HI}	256	32	Do^4	256	16
			Ti^3	240	26.7
Ti	224	53.3			
			La^3	213.333	21.3
			So^3	192	21.3
La	170.666	42.7	Fa^3	170.666	10.7
			Me^3	160	16
			Re^3	144	16
So	128	42.7	Do^3	128	8
			Ti^2	120	13.3
			La^2	106.666	10.7
			So^2	96	10.7
Fa	85.333	21.3	Fa^2	85.333	5.3
			Me^2	80	8
			Re^2	72	8
Me	64	64	Do^2	64	4
			Ti^1	60	6.7
			La^1	53.333	5.3
			So^1	48	5.3
			Fa^1	42.666	2.7
			Me^1	40	4
			Re^1	36	4
Re	32	32	Do^1	32	
Do	0				

TABLE 14-1: THE HIGHER-LEVEL OCTAVE AND THE THREE INNER OCTAVES

In the first of Mr. Gann's momentum cycles, there are no points of retardation in the outer octave, which leaves the energy gaps at Me^1-Fa^1 and Ti^1-Do^1 to create the sharp falls in wave A and wave C respectively. In the second momentum cycle, the outer octave has a reversal point at Fa (see Chapter 8) and a gap at Me-Fa. These coincide with an inner octave gap at Me^2-Fa^2. This is why there is such a sharp fall so early within the cycle, and why a clear wave 3 is unable to develop. There is then the inner octave gap at Ti^2-Do^3 which draws the second cycle to a close.

In the third momentum cycle, there is a point of reversal at La in the outer octave (see Chapter 8) and an energy gap at Me^3-Fa^3 in the inner octave. These account for the sharpness of the cycle's wave A fall. But the subsequent recovery is limited by the outer octave's energy gap at Ti-Do. Specifically, the interval La^3-Ti^3 in the inner octave – which should be strong – is instead vulnerable to the Ti-Do^{HI} deceleration in the outer octave. This weakness is then compounded by the Ti^3-Do^4 interval in the inner octave. And then the cycle ends.

The triad of sub-cycles in practice

These ideas may appear to be somewhat abstruse. So, before proceeding further, it needs to be demonstrated that the ideas are not just theoretical niceties; they extend into practical realities. Figure 14-3 shows the annualised two-quarter percentage change in UK industrial production since the secular cycle low of 1980. Overlaid on the chart is the profile of Mr. Gann's pattern of vibration, expressed in terms of momentum. Inevitably there are divergences; but it is the similarities that are compelling. The 3-up/3-down pattern of the first cycle is very clear, as is the early peak and progressive advance of the second cycle. What really stands out, however, is the correlation between predictive theory and actual experience in the third cycle. The correspondences prior to, during and after the deep intra-cycle contraction are truly remarkable.

Mr Gann's pattern of vibration therefore presents an accurate picture of the forces operating on the momentum of UK industrial production: it is able to anticipate significant turning points, identify the direction of momentum and distinguish between different stages of change.[4] It means – among many other things – that the recessions of 1990-91 and 2001-02, and the collapse of 2008-09, were non-random and intrinsically forecastable. It also means that UK industrial production vibrates to the rhythm of a 10-year cycle, and three beats

---

[4] I have been using this very specific three-phase behavioural pattern in economic activity since the late 1990s (see, for example, Tony Plummer, *Forecasting Financial Markets (4th Ed.)* (Kogan Page, London, 2003)). The pattern was fully incorporated into my forecasting processes at Rhombus Research Ltd (2001-07), and is now central to my work at Helmsman Economics Ltd (2007 to date). What I did not know until 2011 was that the pattern was intrinsic to William Gann's methodologies. The point is that these *truths* could be deduced from the available data once it was accepted that non-random oscillating processes were at work.

of the cycle *chunk up* to form an overarching 30-year cycle. This has dramatic implications for the understanding of economic history and for the conduct of future economic policy.

These findings do not just apply to economic activity. Figure 14-4 shows the 12-month percentage change, between 1980 and 2002, in an index of US 10-year Treasury Note (or Bond) prices. As with the case of UK output, the 3-up/3-down pattern of the first cycle is very noticeable, as is the rightward bias of the second cycle, and the relatively mild contraction at the end of the third cycle. Most importantly, the intra-cycle retrenchments in 1983-84, 1990 and 1999 are very clear and coincide with the expected patterns.

One useful inference from the difference between the depth of the intra-cycle contraction in the third cycle and the subsequent end-of-cycle weakness is that the former marks the end of the dynamic processes of the cycle and the latter partly reflects the process of recovery. Again, the overriding point is that the evolution of the price vibration is non-random and basically forecastable. In the case of T-Notes, there appears to be a 7.3-year cycle, three beats of which form an overarching 22-year cycle. This also has important implications for the conduct of economic policy.

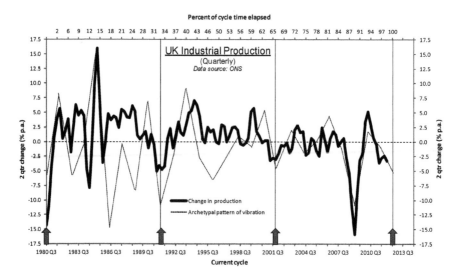

FIGURE 14-3: MR. GANN'S PATTERN OF 'INNER' VIBRATIONS; UK OUTPUT

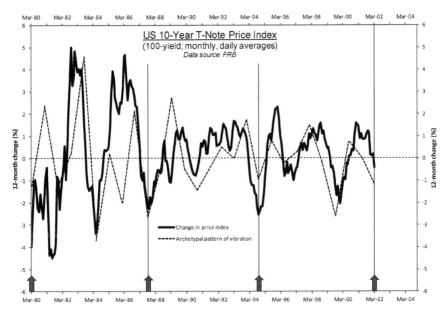

FIGURE 14-4: MR. GANN'S PATTERN OF 'INNER' VIBRATIONS; US 10-YEAR T-NOTES

The role of the sub-cycles

The combination of theory and reality shown in Figures 14-3 and 14-4 helps to confirm the idea that each of the sub-cycles plays a different role in the context of the higher-level process to which they contribute. The first cycle – which, to repeat, mirrors St. Matthew's pattern – is likely concerned with *separation* from the preceding higher-level cycle. Hence the 1980-91 cycle was very much involved with the shift away from a highly inflationary, heavily unionised, economy. It was therefore divisive and conflict-orientated, and ended in a deep recession.

The second cycle appears focused on the *implementation of change*. The 1991-2001 cycle oversaw the information revolution and the globalisation of markets. It was a low-inflation cycle that generated a sense of collective optimism. The third cycle then encompasses the *bedding down* or *incorporation* of new processes and structures. It is a cycle that has to deal with the fading of the processes of the preceding phase of innovation. It reflects structural limits on any further change. And it eventually involves an outright response to excesses. The cycle that started in 2001 has accordingly been characterised by stuttering economic activity, volatile crowd psychology and social unrest.

The three phases of separation, change and incorporation reflect the irreversible processes of evolution.[5] In terms of Figure 14-1, the information *shock* that triggers

---

[5] The terms *separation, change* and *incorporation* are different to the terms *transition, innovation* and *disruption* that I used in *Forecasting Financial Markets*. The meanings are the same, but the focus is different.

these three phases must occur prior to the first cycle in the series. If this idea is translated onto Figure 14-3, it implies that the relevant shock to the UK economy had to occur in the last stages of the higher-level cycle that ended in 1980. If we continue to assume the operation of a non-random process, then it is possible to hypothesise that the relevant information shock at the end of the preceding cycle was generated either by economic developments (such as surging inflation and/or economic recession) or by external social and political events (such as war).

It is a fact that the 1970-80 period, which preceded the period shown in Figure 14-3, was characterised by accelerating inflation and weak economic growth, and by the global impact of the Vietnam War. Such dislocations are always likely to emerge at the end of large cycles. They inevitably embody the sort of shocks that subsequently initiate a new evolutionary process.

The idea of a triadic hierarchy of cycles – with three cycles at one level combining to form a cycle at a higher level – can also be deduced from the structure of Mr. Gurdjieff's book, *Beelzebub's Tales*. As already mentioned, the first part of that book – the first sub-book within the book – consists of 28 chapters. The number 28 has its own heritage in relation to cycles. It is the product of 4 and 7, and is the sum of the numbers between 1 and 7. In the context of cycles and natural vibrations, the number 7 is always likely to be a reference to the *Law of Seven*. As a corollary, therefore, so is the number 28. This suggests that some of the same techniques that were applied to the whole of *Beelzebub's Tales* can be applied to the first 28 chapters. The details are shown in Appendix 6.

CONCLUSION

It hardly needs to be emphasised that all these findings are extraordinary. They imply that the swings in collective optimism and pessimism that are associated with oscillations in economic activity are going to proceed along broadly-defined, but nevertheless very specific, pathways. They also imply that, once a socio-economic vibration has been set in motion, policy-makers can only damp down, or add to, the oscillations; they cannot reverse them. This is consistent with the growing body of academic evidence that suggests that government activity is not an independent variable in relation to the economic system. It seems that the political conflicts and economic upheavals that are periodically experienced in our democracies are actually part of a broad process over which we have little or no control.

The presence of a common signature pattern in the different presentations made by Mr. Gann, Mr. Gurdjieff and St. Matthew is truly remarkable given the vast differences in the numbers of pages and words that are involved – 1238 pages for *Beelzebub's Tales*, 418 pages for *Tunnel* and only 68 words in St. Matthew's Gospel.

However, the achievement is more easily understood when it is recognised that the different authors were working with the same natural construct. That is, they were working with what Mr. Gurdjieff called the *Law of Three* and the *Law of Seven* (see Chapters 3 and 7), and with what Mr. Gann called the *law of vibration*, derived from St. Matthew's text (see Chapters 10 and 12).

The critical differences between Mr. Gann's pattern, and those of Mr. Gurdjieff and St. Matthew, are that, on the one hand, it was concealed in an appallingly trivial book and, on the other hand, it is very complex. It is this contrast that invites attention. It suggests that the book was constructed in order primarily to convey the pattern. Furthermore, since the pattern itself was given no attendant explanation, then it is highly likely that the pattern itself must hold additional information. This is exactly what this chapter has shown. Mr. Gann's pattern is a *carrier wave*: it holds three *inner octave* cycles that are generated by a preceding shock (Figure 14-1). Moreover, the average of these three cycles translates back into a basic pattern that is very similar to St. Matthew's (Figure 14-2).

There may be much more to Mr. Gann's configuration than has currently been identified. However, we can now draw three important conclusions. First, all natural cyclical processes can be represented by a left-biased enneagram-type pattern, which represents the *average* outcome. Second, a higher-level cycle consists of a sequence of three lower-level cycles, each of which has a slightly different profile. Third, cycles at all levels are likely to contain an *intra-cycle* contraction, as well as being separated from one another by *inter-cycle* contractions.

The next chaper will look more closely at how some of these ideas might work in practice.

CHAPTER 15

THE LAW OF VIBRATION
IN PRACTICE

"Cycle theory, or harmonic analysis, is the only thing that we can rely upon to ascertain the future."

W. D. Gann

A SUMMARY OF CONCLUSIONS

The preceding chapters have explored a specific pattern that was hidden in the structure of three very different texts: St. Matthew's Gospel; George I. Gurdjieff's *All and Everything: An Objectively Impartial Criticism of the Life of Man*, or *Beelzebub's Tales to His Grandson*; and William D. Gann's *The Tunnel Thru The Air*. The reasons why the pattern was included in St. Matthew's text cannot now be known. However, both Mr. Gurdjieff and Mr. Gann saw the pattern as being, in part, a symbol of perpetual motion within the living universe. But they also saw it as being a direct reflection of a real phenomenon. Mr. Gurdjieff called it the *Law of Seven*; Mr. Gann called it the *law of vibration*.

The two most important given aspects of this law are that the vibrations exist throughout the whole universe, without exception, and that the vibrations are discontinuous. Pyotr Ouspensky, quoting Mr. Gurdjieff, argued that "vibrations proceed in all kinds, aspects, and densities of matter... from the finest to the coarsest; they issue from various sources and proceed in various directions, crossing one another, colliding, strengthening, weakening, arresting one another..."[1]

---
[1] Ouspensky, *In Search*.

At the same time, these vibrations accelerate and decelerate. To quote Mr. Ouspensky again:

> "The force of the impulse acts without changing its nature and vibrations develop in a regular way only for a certain time which is determined by the nature of the impulse, the medium, the conditions, and so forth. But at a certain moment, a kind of change takes place in it and the vibrations, so to speak, cease to obey it and for a short time they slow down and to a certain extent change their nature or direction."[2]

This phenomenon was discussed in detail in Chapters 7, 8 and 9, and the different presentations from the three different authors were explored in Chapters 10, 11 and 12. It was found that the authors' patterns of vibration were basically identical to one another, and that the pattern could be found in collective human behaviour in economic activity and in financial markets. It is likely that the pattern can be found in many other arenas. In Chapter 8 it was argued that the pattern appeared to incorporate the distinctive archetypal pattern of the process of learning. In Chapter 14 it was further argued that the initial shock has its own pattern of vibration, that it is followed by an energy gap, and that the subsequent movement constitutes the application of learning. It is as if the information shock has to gain traction within a system before it can have an effect.

Mr. Gann appears to have taken this last argument a step further. The information shock can be seen either as a part of a whole, higher-level, pattern, or it can be seen as initiating three sub-cycles. In the first case, the shock is wave 1 of a 1-2-3 rising pattern. The shock is then absorbed in wave 2 and implemented in wave 3. In the second case, the shock occurs outside of the phenomenon being tracked, and therefore prior to three subsequent cycles. The first cycle is a volatile *response to a prior shock*; the second cycle incorporates a more sustained system response to the shock; and the third cycle reflects the limits to further change and exhibits fading energy.

US INDUSTRIAL PRODUCTION

It is not the purpose of this book to show in detail how the pattern of vibration can be used. This is for each individual to research. Nevertheless, some of the power of the pattern – and its potential to help with our understanding of the world – can be indicated by showing its presence in collective human behaviour in the context of economic activity. For the purposes of this exercise, I shall focus on US industrial production.

---

[2] *Ibid.*

The point of doing so is that the US – and therefore the West – is facing severe economic problems. These problems are not just temporary deviations from an ever-improving trend because the 2008 financial panic was an energy gap in the economic systems of most Western democracies. This *shock* has started a long process of deep structural change that will extend beyond the sphere of economic activity. The forces now at work will eventually alter the nature of social cohesion and collective attitudes to the role of government in a democracy.

Data is somewhat limited, but annual production data from 1790 is available from the National Bureau of Economic Research (NBER) and monthly data from 1919 is available from the Federal Reserve Board (FRB).[3] The former has the advantage of being a consistent series, but it has the disadvantage of not being constructed contemporaneously with the evolving US economy. It is likely to contain measurement errors. Nevertheless, it is likely that it shows the general direction of quantitative trends, even though it may not always accurately reflect the fluctuations around those trends. The FRB's data, on the other hand, are produced with a high degree of rigour.

Figure 15-1 shows 1-year rates of change in US industrial production from 1790 to 2011.

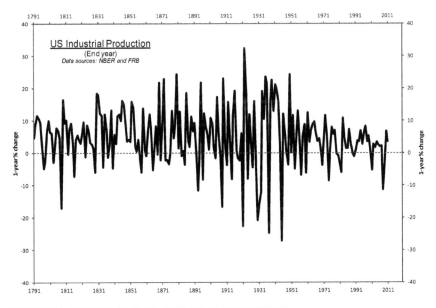

FIGURE 15-1: MOMENTUM OF US INDUSTRIAL PRODUCTION

---

[3] Volume data for US industrial production from 1790 to 1915 has been constructed by Joseph H. Davis (see, 'An Annual Index of US Production, 1790-1915', *Quarterly Journal of Economics* (November 2004)). Volume data for manufacturing production from 1863 to 1930 is available on the NBER's website. For the purposes of this exercise, the two data series have been merged and then concatenated with end-year data calculated by the Federal Reserve Board.

One of the characteristics of the US industrial production chart is the increase in the volatility of momentum between 1893 and 1945 (particularly on the downside). This is prima facie evidence of a system *responding* to one or more shocks. In fact, the first half of the 20th century incorporated some of the most destructive shocks in the 20th century. Moreover, the events followed each other sequentially, building shock upon shock. The financial crisis involving the Knickerbocker Trust collapse (1907-08) was followed progressively by the First World War (1914-18), a massive speculative boom and equity crash (1921-29), a prolonged depression (1930-39), and then the Second World War (1939-45). Not surprisingly, the whole period generated profound shifts in social attitudes, political opinions and economic policy.

Non-random fluctuations

The question, however, is: are the fluctuations random? A cursory examination would suggest that they are; but, once the idea of an archetypal pattern of vibration is applied to the data, a profound form of order emerges. The analytical process is somewhat lengthy. In the first place, it is iterative, involving a recurring comparison of Mr. Gann's three-phase *inner octave* pattern with the actual data. In addition, there are two complications.

The first is that each three-phase vibration is preceded by a build-up of the energy that will fuel the separation cycle. This transformational energy is reflected in the emergence of problems that are basically insoluble under the current paradigm and in a collective recognition that change is inevitable. This period has to be isolated and removed from the pattern-matching process. The second complication is that the evolution of the actual pattern through time will inevitably involve some degree of variation in the timings of each of the inner octave sub-cycles. This means that the sub-cycles have to be standardised graphically against each other. This standardisation is achieved by mathematically stretching the horizontal length of the shorter cycles so that they match the length of the longest cycle in any set.

Figures 15-2 to 15-5 accordingly show the patterns of change in US industrial output over four separate periods: 1801 to 1832; 1834 to 1870; 1875 to 1908; and 1911 to 1940. The time elapse of the four periods is, respectively, 31 years, 36 years, 33 years and 29 years; the average length of the four cycles is thus 32 years.

Each of the charts is overlaid with Mr. Gann's three *inner octave* sub-cycles. This splits the momentum patterns into three sections, reflecting the three-stage evolutionary process of separation, change and incorporation. Not surprisingly, there are differences between the actual patterns and those that would be expected from Mr. Gann's cycles. A great deal of allowance has to be made for potential errors in the original annual statistics. And even if the data is more or less correct, end-year data is simply not sensitive enough to pick up the precise timings of Mr. Gann's cycles. Nevertheless, the charts do show a good overall correlation between the expected direction of change (according to Mr. Gann's pattern) and actual changes.

What also emerges is that the gap between the ending of one cycle and the start of the next – that is, the period when transformational energy is being accumulated – is variable both in length and (therefore) in impact. The 1801-32 cycle was followed by a two-year interlude from 1832 to 1834; the 1834-1870 cycle was followed by a five-year interruption from 1870 to 1875; the 1875-1908 cycle was followed by a three-year gap from 1908 to 1911; and the 1911-1940 cycle was followed by a five-year interruption between 1940 and 1945. [4] Each such interruption – which invariably consists of some degree of recovery from an end-cycle low followed by a fall – can be called an *inter-cycle hiatus*.

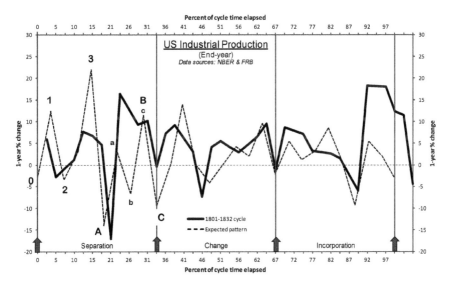

FIGURE 15-2: MOMENTUM OF US INDUSTRIAL PRODUCTION; 1801 TO 1832

---

[4] The pattern of this interruption is much clearer in the Federal Reserve's monthly data. See Appendix 7.

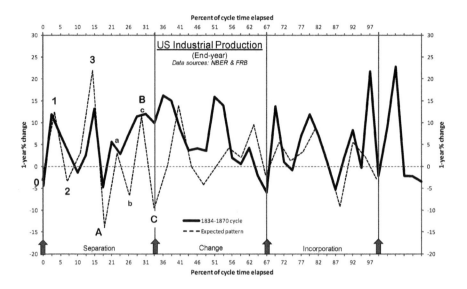

FIGURE 15-3: MOMENTUM OF US INDUSTRIAL PRODUCTION; 1834 TO 1870

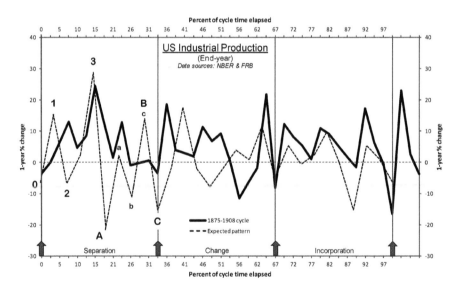

FIGURE 15-4: MOMENTUM OF US INDUSTRIAL PRODUCTION; 1875 TO 1908

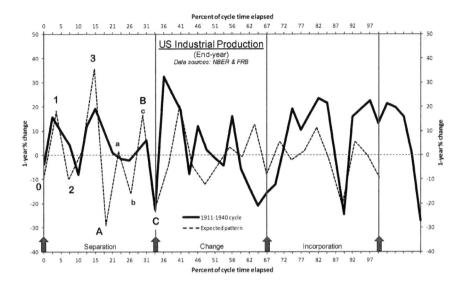

FIGURE 15-5: MOMENTUM OF INDUSTRIAL PRODUCTION; 1911 TO 1940

The inter-cycle hiatus

The gap between cycles seems to be very important to the law of vibration. On the one hand, the gap undoubtedly embodies unfinished business from the just-ended incorporation cycle. This latter almost invariably contains an intra-cycle recession (or slowdown), which will have impacted as a shock. The inter-cycle hiatus then allows the system to deal to some extent with remaining problems from this shock. But the important point is that this part of the process is likely to occur within the context of the existing environment. The environment itself doesn't necessarily change. Such a transformation only really starts to occur during the first (separation) cycle of the next era.

On the other hand, the inter-cycle hiatus does contain an essential forward-looking focus. In terms of the Table 14-1 of Chapter 14, it is part of the 'Do' that initiates the inner octaves of the subsequent overarching cycle.[5] The important point is that the interruptions are not new shocks as such; they are, instead, periods that are charged with creative energy. In the context of economic activity, they embrace all the forces that eventually generate a paradigm shift. These include – but are not confined to – political disquiet, labour unrest and policy ineffectiveness.

The central problem for analysis – at least in the context of Mr. Gann's pattern – is that the inter-cycle hiatus does contain a genuine degree of randomness: it

---

[5] Such inner octaves will start theoretically at 'Re', 'Me', and 'So' of the higher-level octave.

is not always easy to isolate in the historical data and its locus is not easy to forecast. It invariably consists of an advance and contraction, but the amplitude of each of the swings seems unpredictable. In practice, it may often be appropriate just to assign the experience of the inter-cycle hiatus to the cycle that is just ending.

Long-term order

If the inter-cycle hiatuses are nevertheless excluded from the behavioural patterns, it is possible to calculate an average of the patterns in Figures 15-2 to 15-5 and compare that average to the configuration produced from Mr. Gann's law of vibration. Figure 15-6 shows the results after each of the underlying inner octave cycles have been co-ordinated in length by mathematically stretching the shorter cycles to match the length of the longest cycle.

The correspondence between the patterns is very compelling. The average separation cycle incorporates the archetypal 1-2-3/A-B-C pattern, with wave B containing its own a-b-c pattern. The average change cycle exhibits two clear peaks, one early in the cycle and one late. And the average incorporation cycle contains the initial three-wave advance, a significant intra-cycle contraction, and an end-phase recovery and setback. Moreover, all three sub-cycles contain the expected inter-cycle contraction.

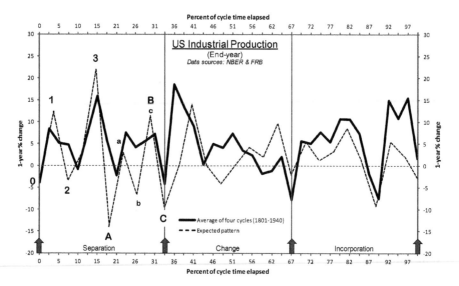

FIGURE 15-6: AVERAGE PATTERN OF US INDUSTRIAL PRODUCTION; 1801 TO 1940

There are three important conclusions that can be drawn from this analysis. The first is that there is a strong concurrence between the expected and actual shape of the first *inner octave* cycle that initiates each of the three big cycles. This agreement confirms the importance of the shape of the first (i.e. separation) cycle in a triad. Once an archetypal three-up/three-down (1-2-3/A-B-C) pattern has emerged, it means that a whole new process is well underway, and that the shape of the next two cycle beats are (to some extent) forecastable.

The second – and related – conclusion is that the time elapse of the initial separation cycle is going to provide a very good indication of the time elapse of the whole overarching cycle. This is because the second (change) and third (incorporation) cycles tend towards an equal length, both with the separation cycle and with one another. In practice, there is often some variability between the second and third cycles, but a lengthening in one seems to result in a contraction in the other.

In principle, the combined length of the change and incorporation cycles should be twice the length of the initial separation cycle. Hence, for example, the first sub-cycle in Figure 15-5 starts in 1911 and lasts for 10 years. This implies that the whole vibration will last for another two cycle beats of 10 years each, so that the overarching cycle should end in 1941. In the event it finished in 1940, which is encouragingly close.

The archetypal pattern

The third conclusion is based on the fact that there is a close theoretical match between the shape of the separation cycle within a triad and the *average* of all three *inner octave* cycles. This similarity was originally shown in Figure 14-2 of Chapter 14, and is shown more directly in Figure 15-7. The average cycle has a smaller amplitude than the separation cycle, because the oscillations tend to become damped as they evolve. But the parallels are unmistakeable.

The inference is that the shape either of the separation cycle or of the expected average can be used to estimate the evolution of all three cycles in a triad. As a corollary, if the process of averaging a series of fluctuations produces a pattern that is similar to either of those shown in Figure 15-7, then it is likely that the fluctuations are tracking a genuine cycle. In effect, this is what happened in Figures 9-4 and 9-5 of Chapter 9. The process of averaging a series of 3.5-year cycle beats in the Dow Jones Industrial Average produced a basic three-up/three-down pattern.

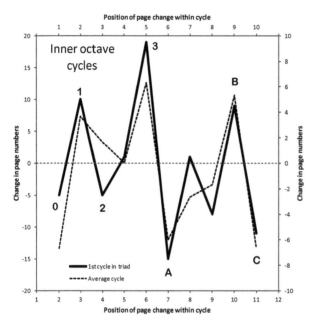

FIGURE 15-7: THE ARCHETYPAL PATTERN

Figure 15-8 therefore shows the average of all of the nine *inner octave* cycles that were used in Figure 15-6. The pattern is a very close match for the average expected pattern. This means that, once the periodicity of the vibrations have been established by the separation cycle, the average pattern can be used to track the two subsequent cycles in the triad. It is, of course, important to remember that the patterns constructed by St. Matthew, Mr. Gurdjieff and Mr. Gann all conform to this same archetype.

These comments confirm that the law of vibration is not just confined to the observable overall pattern and its three inner sub-cycles. It also involves three specific features: the distinctive shape of the first cycle, which mirrors the shape of the whole cycle; the importance of the periodicity of the first cycle in determining the length of the whole overarching cycle; and the relatively unstructured inter-cycle hiatus at the end of a set of three inner octave cycles. There may well be other aspects that are, as yet, undiscovered.

THE POST-WAR PERIOD

We now have enough information to move on to an analysis of the post-war period. On annual data, the final war-induced momentum low occurred in 1945; but, on monthly data, it occurred in February 1946. Figure 15-9 shows the 12-month momentum of US output from November 1940, and therefore also shows the inter-cycle hiatus that ran from November 1940 to February 1946. In effect, the hiatus coincides with the Second World War. Overlaid on the momentum is Mr. Gann's expected three-phase pattern of vibration.

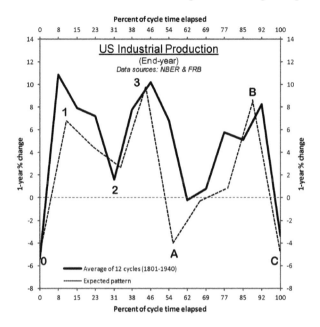

FIGURE 15-8: THE AVERAGE EXPECTED PATTERN AND ACTUAL BEHAVIOUR; 1801-1940

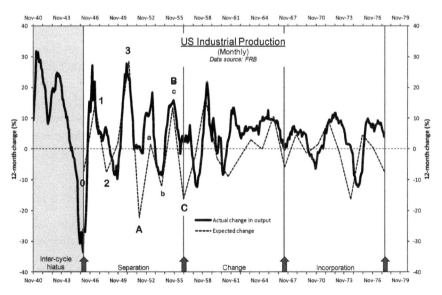

FIGURE 15-9: MOMENTUM OF US INDUSTRIAL PRODUCTION, 1946-78

The results are quite remarkable. The first (separation) cycle exhibits the pattern that is associated with a new phase of development: a very clear 1-2-3 advance is followed by a pronounced A-B-C contraction; and, within this latter, wave B subdivides into three (a-b-c) waves of its own. The wave C downswing ends in 1956, which means that the length of the initiating separation cycle is about 10.5 years.

This timing can be confirmed by two calculations. The first is that the end-date coincides with the expected date, once the actual highs and lows of the separation cycle are matched with the expected pattern. Second, when subsequent oscillations in the change and incorporation cycles are matched to the expected pattern, the overall cycle ends in 1978 and is therefore 32 years long. In other words the length of the whole cycle is three times the length of the initial separation cycle. Nevertheless, this interpretation does not include the deep recession of 1957-58, which would therefore have been difficult to anticipate in real time.

The second (change) cycle then shows a sharp recovery and a pronounced fall, followed by a more prolonged advance. It ends with a late, but relatively sharp, drop. The whole cycle therefore starts in 1956 and ends in 1967. It is just over 10.5 years long.

Finally, the third cycle shows an initial three-phase recovery, followed by a very sharp drop. There is then a muted recovery, followed by a short contraction that ended the whole cycle. As theory predicts, however, there was then an inter-cycle hiatus that initially involved a short recovery, but was subsequently dominated by another prolonged contraction.

This pattern is relevant to understanding the events of the 1970s. The period was highly inflationary as a result of the method that was used to finance the Vietnam War. Too much money was borrowed from the banks rather than from savers, and monetary growth exploded. There was, eventually, a financial crisis: government bond yields soared during 1974 and, not surprisingly, the private sector dropped into a deep recession. But this event did not end the cycle. It was an *intra*-cycle shock that had to be absorbed by markets, by businesses and (most importantly) by policy makers.

Resistance to change

The truth is that politicians will only put aside – or more often, adjust – favoured policies when they are actually faced with a crisis. In this case, the devastation that was being wreaked by the combination of government spending and inflation was placed in temporary abeyance when the Vietnam War drew to a close. However, proper measures to deal with the problem were too slow in materialising. As always with government spending, there was resistance from the electorate. President Gerald Ford made some half-hearted attempts and President Jimmy Carter was unable to gain a second term in the White House because of his more aggressive proposals. Consequently, inflation advanced again in the late 1970s,[6] monetary policy was reluctantly tightened and the private sector slumped back into recession.

The period from late 1978 to mid-1980 involved resistance to change rather than actual change. But, underneath, there was a massive build-up of pressure in the desire to deal with inflation. The electorate eventually recognised the seriousness of the problem after being confronted with rising oil prices, widespread and disruptive strikes, soaring interest rates and high unemployment. This strengthening of unreleased tension is the central characteristic of an inter-cycle hiatus. The appointment (by President Carter) of Paul Volcker to the post of Chairman of the Federal Reserve was probably the most important reflection of the changed attitudes to inflation. Mr. Volcker quickly moved to tighten monetary policy at the expense of higher unemployment.

THE 1980-2012 CYCLE

The idea of a mid-cycle contraction in the incorporation cycle and of a relatively unstructured interlude – or inter-cycle hiatus – between that cycle and the next separation cycle helps to explain the five-year gap between the 1974-75 crisis and the start of the next big cycle in 1980. Figure 15-10 shows the 12-month momentum in US output between 1978 and 2012. The hiatus that occurred between 1978 and 1980 is shown as the shaded area. The momentum pattern is then overlaid with a schematic of Mr. Gann's ideal three-phase pattern.

Again, the parallels between actual and expected momentum are compelling. First, the chart confirms the presence, sequentially, of a separation cycle in 1980-91, a change cycle in 1991-2001, and an incorporation cycle that started in 2001 and is due to end in 2012 or soon thereafter. The patterning clearly picks out the three-wave recovery after the 1980 low, the strong advance after the mid-1990s and the much weaker performance in the first half of the 2000s. It also clearly identifies the deep end-cycle recession of 1990-91 and the sudden end-cycle recession of 2001-02.

Second, the separation cycle lasts for just over 10.5 years, ending in March 1991. This suggests that the change and incorporation cycles, when combined, should last for just over 21 years, finishing in mid to late-2012. The whole pattern from 1980 should therefore last for about 32 years. Importantly, this is the same

---

[6] One of the factors was a surge in oil prices in 1979, caused initially by the overthrow of the Shah of Iran and subsequently by the interruption of oil supplies during the Iran-Iraq War. It is arguable, however, that oil prices would not have had the same impact if inflationary expectations had not already been hyper-activated.

duration as the 1946-1978 cycle, and the same as the average of the four cycles that evolved between 1801 and 1940. The chart therefore confirms the idea that, in general, the US economy has been driven by an oscillation that lasts for more than three decades and that sub-divides into three lower-level cycles each of which lasts 10 to 11 years.

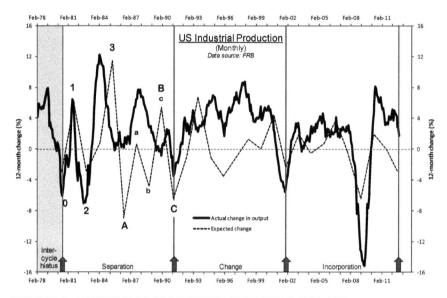

FIGURE 15-10: MOMENTUM OF US INDUSTRIAL PRODUCTION, 1980-2012

Third, the pattern picks out *intra*-cycle weakness in 1984-85, 1995-96 and (most noticeably) 2007-09. These particular episodes were just over 11 years apart, which resonates with the periodicity of the lower-level cycles and with the overarching higher-level cycle.

The 2007-09 shock and its aftermath

Presented in this way, Mr. Gann's pattern reveals the intrinsic purpose of the 2007-09 economic contraction. It was a profound shock that has started a process of adjustment. This adjustment will consist of two parts. First, it will consist of the recovery and setback that terminates the natural evolution both of the incorporation cycle that began in 2001 and of the overarching cycle that began in 1980. Second, the adjustment will then consist of an inter-cycle hiatus that will build-up the energy for a subsequent separation cycle.

At the time of writing (2012), the first (recovery and setback) stage of the process is all but over. This can be confirmed from Figure 15-11, which shows the evolution of the 2001-12 incorporation cycle, compared with the expected change. The US economy should have completed its initial response to the 2007-09 collapse by the end of 2012 and thereby set the stage for the second (hiatus) stage of adjustment. In quantitative terms, this second stage should – on the basis of previous cycles – last for three to four years and consist of an initial short recovery followed by a bout of pronounced weakness.

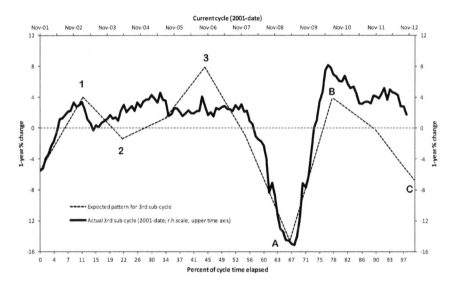

FIGURE 15-11: THE 2001-2012 INCORPORATION CYCLE IN US INDUSTRIAL PRODUCTION

This implies that there will be some form of an economic recovery between late-2012 and (possibly) mid-2014, followed by a period of weakness. At the moment, we can expect this weakness to be relatively pronounced, but we cannot know precisely how long it will last. On the basis of historical precedent, an end-date target of somewhere between mid-2015 and mid-2016 seems appropriate. The central point is that the period will almost certainly be characterised by: a progressive build-up of economic tensions; deepening uncertainty about financial market trends; and rising anger towards ineffective politicians. Public rhetoric will increasingly focus on whatever it is that needs to be changed. When sufficient political momentum for deep change has developed, then – and only then – a whole new pattern of vibration will begin.

CONCLUSION

In the 1920s, William Gann constructed a book in order specifically to convey what he considered to be secret or sacred information. *The Tunnel Thru The Air* visually and integrally resonated with the Golden Ratio and the *Law of Three*, and carried within its architecture a very specific pattern of vibration derived from the *Law of Seven*. At a basic level, the pattern was virtually identical to the configurations associated with George Gurdjieff and St. Matthew. As such it can therefore be regarded both as a symbol of transformation and as a pattern that is likely to appear in indices of collective human activity when a change is actively underway.

However, Mr. Gann's pattern was much more complex than either Mr. Gurdjieff's or St. Matthew's. When deconstructed, it reveals a three-phase oscillation, with each phase displaying a marked inter-cycle contraction. Significantly, the three-phase pattern is circumscribed by an undefined shock at its start and by an unforecastable inter-cycle hiatus at its close.

In order to assess the practicability of Mr. Gann's ideas, his three-phase pattern was applied to a data series on US industrial production. To an untrained eye, that data series looked random. Moreover, it almost certainly contained measurement errors. Nevertheless, the results were remarkable. Even though individual periods showed significant divergences from Mr. Gann's *ideal* pattern, the average of all periods clearly converged on that pattern. This is consistent with the idea that collective behaviour contains a strong deterministic element. Hence, it is possible to confirm our location within the big economic and financial market trends – and anticipate the future trajectory of those trends – in a way that does not yet seem available to conventional economic analysis.

In truth, however, the analysis has only scratched the surface of a subject that has huge implications for our understanding both of the nature of cosmic forces and of the behaviour of humanity. For this reason alone, the comments in this chapter must not be regarded as the final word on the accuracy, or otherwise, either of the law of vibration itself or of its application to economic indices. Other researchers may well come up with other timings and other interpretations. Furthermore, there are additional layers of meaning and influence that have not been addressed. Nevertheless, what emerges is evidence of an ordered process over which humankind *en masse* has very little independent influence. This process is the law of vibration.

The law of vibration, and the energy pattern behind it, shows us something very specific about the way that energy oscillates within living systems. Insofar as human beings merge together into collective wholes in search of a sense of safety and feeling of well-being, they are subject to these oscillations. Perhaps we would do better to recognise this and, in so doing, facilitate a new social attitude to politics and economic policy. The alternative is to allow unconscious mass behaviour – both in the private and public sectors of the economy – to create destabilising excesses.

CHAPTER 16

THE FINAL WORD

"There are more things in heaven and earth, Horatio, than are dreamt of in your philosophy."

William Shakespeare (*Hamlet*: Act 1, Scene V)

SECRET LAWS

There can be little doubt that a very specific pattern was hidden in the structure of three texts: in St. Matthew's Gospel, in George Gurdjieff's *Beelzebub's Tales to His Grandson* and in William Gann's *The Tunnel Thru The Air*. There can also be little doubt that the pattern somehow relates to the processes of change in living systems, including systems involving collective human behaviour. But what is less certain is why the authors considered this particular pattern to be so important – and, in a sense, so sacred – that it had to be hidden.

On the face of it, the pattern is very simple. It is divided into two distinct sections, both of which involve a three-wave advance followed by a fall. Importantly, the advance-and-contraction in the first half of the pattern is significantly more dynamic and potentially destructive than the advance-and-contraction in the second half. Consequently, the whole pattern has a pronounced leftward bias. At the very least, the pattern is strongly suggestive of the way that living systems adjust dynamically to the input of new information and energy.

More generally, however, and given the context within which Mr. Gann presented his version of the pattern, the design supposedly represents a law of vibration that pervades the known universe. Its dynamics reflect what Mr. Gurdjieff called the *Law of Seven* and its existence would necessarily affirm the accompanying presence of a creative *Law of Three*. According to Mr. Gurdjieff, these two great cosmic laws are vital both to the evolution of the universe and to life on this planet.

According to modern scientific enquiry, however, such *laws* cannot exist independently of the narrow context within which they arise. This means either that science is blind to the presence of certain primordial laws that predate life on Earth, or that the teachings of St. Matthew and Mr. Gurdjieff are simply incorrect. Yet even an unsophisticated – and cursory – analysis of some of the potential applications for the law of vibration reveals at least a hint of its ubiquity. Hence, there is a strong case for further research on the subject.

Only research by open-minded analysts, working within their own fields of investigation, can provide the necessary evidence for the reality of a law of vibration. If it is shown to exist, it will have implications far beyond anything that has been discussed in this book. It could be relevant to new ideas in disciplines stretching from quantum physics to astrophysics, from social sciences to earth sciences, and from biological evolution to genetic mutation.

A LONG HISTORY

But what, then, is its history? What was its original source? Who had access to it and why? And for what reason has it been so deeply hidden? The answers – insofar as they can be found – seem to arise more in the form of an ever-deepening mystery than as a precise solution. The alleged pattern of vibration presents itself as – to use Mr. Gurdjieff's terminology – a left-biased "enneagram"-type pulse. But, as far as is known, Mr. Gurdjieff himself did not actually reference such a bias in his enneagram teachings. In hiding it, therefore, in *Beelzebub's Tales*, he was implicitly signalling its importance and preserving it for some future purpose.

He was also taking the same path that St Matthew had done almost 2000 years earlier. Indeed, the fact that the left-biased enneagram pulse was so deeply buried in a tiny piece of text in one of the Christian Gospels, and then left there without any further comment, compounds its mysterious nature and adds credibility to its potential importance within the flow of history. It seems highly unlikely that anyone would have been able to recognise its implications in the first century C.E. because there would have been no way of applying it directly to the then-known world. If anything, it is likely that it would have been regarded as being an important, but unintelligible, symbolic representation of God. But are we any better placed now? Even if it is found to be widely applicable to processes within living organisms and systems, would science be able to accept its implications about the nature of the universe?

WILLIAM GANN'S LEGACY

Mr. Gann undoubtedly had more than just an inkling about what the pattern meant. He considered it to have been sufficiently important to construct a version that carried a remarkable volume of extra information. His pattern contains a reference to a three-phase structure to evolution, it suggests that there is an objective element to the energy of time, and it intimates that the oscillation of living systems can be tracked through time using geometry. His construction undoubtedly took a lot of thought, effort and skill.

As it happens, it has long been rumoured that Mr. Gann *knew something* that was unusual – which is why his extant work remains so popular even though it is largely unfathomable. But the precise details of his concept of a law of vibration have never been made available in the sort of detail that is being presented here. Mr. Gann hid the information in the complex structure of a largely irrelevant book. Why did he do so? One answer, of course, is that it added to his sense of importance. But this seems misplaced, given his attitude to spirituality that was evidenced in the most obscure of his books, *The Magic Word*.[1] In fact, as shown in Appendix 8, Mr. Gann applied the same techniques to *The Magic Word* as he did to *Tunnel*.

It seems likely that – for some reason – Mr. Gann felt that the pattern behind the law of vibration couldn't be revealed during his lifetime, but nevertheless had to be made available for future use. This resonates with Mr. Gurdjieff's treatment of the pattern.

Perhaps the most important fact, however, is the one that is the simplest: the intellectual environment in the first half of the 20th century still wasn't sufficiently receptive to the idea of unknown *laws* embedded in the cosmos. In the 300 years since the dawning of the Age of Enlightenment, scientific research has progressively shifted the focus of attention away from inner truths and eternal verities to external events and quantifiable realities.

More recently, it is true, the evidence from quantum physics and from consciousness research has started to blur the distinctions between inner and outer, and between the infinitesimally small and the infinitely large. Nevertheless, there is still a vacuum in scientific research caused by the exclusion of purpose, meaning and overarching self-organisation. Consequently, science cannot yet explicitly recognise the existence – let alone the validity – of a *Law of Seven* or of a *Law of Three*. So it literally cannot see the specific pattern that these laws are supposed to generate.

---

[1] Gann, *The Magic Word*.

CONCLUSION

Perhaps, therefore, when St. Matthew's version of the pattern was originally conceived, it was destined to be found only when sufficient supportive information was generally available, and when the research environment was receptive to new ideas and new approaches. In other words, St. Matthew's pattern could be the harbinger of – or even the catalyst for – one or more paradigm shifts within the scientific community. Indeed, it may be that Mr. Gann and Mr. Gurdjieff are links in a chain of understanding that connects the modern era all the way back – at least – to St. Matthew.

And this raises two intriguing possibilities. The first is that the pattern is in some way an archetypal symbol for the *presence* of information within the deep-structure of the universe. The pattern does not manifest in a quantifiable manner until it is somehow triggered; but the fact that the same basic pattern is always observable under conditions of change suggests that it may be a genuine outward sign of the inner coherence within what David Bohm has called the "implicate order".[2] Perhaps it was even embedded within the dynamics of the so-called "Big Bang".

The second possibility relates to the message that St. Matthew might have been trying to convey. The preliminary layer of interpretation of his Greek text reveals the symbol for the astrological Age of Pisces that was gestating 2000 years ago. A subsequent layer of analysis then reveals the left-biased enneagram-type pattern, but only when account is taken of the 12-fold structure of the Zodiac. It is therefore possible that St. Matthew's pattern is a valid symbol for the new astrological Age into which we are stumbling – the Age of Aquarius. The pattern is, after all, wave-focused in its dynamics. But, more strikingly, it is also wave-like in its appearance. A comparison of the pattern with the traditional representation of the symbol of Aquarius not only reveals the parallels between the two, but it also shows a particular difference: St. Matthew's version has a conspicuous *tsunami*-like shape.

If this conjecture is correct, there would be two implications: first, St. Matthew's text unquestionably transcends Time; and, second, the new Age will involve profound changes to – among other things – humankind's social, political and economic structures.

It is my opinion that the pattern that St. Matthew hid in his Gospel, that George Gurdjieff concealed in *Beelzebub's Tales to His Grandson* and that William Gann buried in *The Tunnel Thru The Air*, is profoundly meaningful. It is not just a symbolic representation of an implausible law relating to oscillations within the Earth's biosphere, but is instead a container of fundamental truths about the deep-structure of the cosmos. We can ignore it. Or we can accept it for what it may well be: the final statement of a revelation that was initiated in St. Matthew's Gospel almost 2000 years ago.

---

[2] See David Bohm, *Coherence and the Implicate Order* (Routledge & Kegan Paul, London, 1980).

Appendices

APPENDIX 1

NUMERICAL EQUIVALENTS OF NEW TESTAMENT GREEK LETTERS

Lower case	α	β	γ	δ	ε	ζ	η	θ
Upper case	A	B	Γ	Δ	E	Z	H	Θ
Number	1	2	3	4	5	7	8	9

Lower case	ι	κ	λ	μ	ν	ξ	o	π
Upper case	I	K	Λ	M	N	Ξ	O	Π
Number	10	20	30	40	50	60	70	80

Lower case	ρ	σ, ς	τ	υ	ϕ	χ	ψ	ω
Upper case	P	Σ	T	Y	Φ	X	Ψ	Ω
Number	100	200	300	400	500	600	700	800

In addition, the value of the combined letters $\sigma\tau$ could be either 6 or 500.

APPENDIX 2

ST. MATTHEW'S GOSPEL, CHAPTER 12, VERSES 38-40. GREEK TEXT

Τ	ο	τ	ε		α	π	ε	κ	ρ	ι	θ	η	σ	α	ν		α	υ	τ	ω		τ	ι	ν	ε	ς
300	70	300	5		1	80	5	20	100	10	9	8	200	1	50		1	400	300	800		300	10	50	5	200
675					484												1501					565				
Then					said												to him					some				

Τ	ω	ν		γ	ρ	α	μ	μ	α	τ	ε	ω	ν		κ	α	ι		φ	α	ρ	ι	σ	α	ι	ω	ν
300	800	50		3	100	1	40	40	1	300	5	800	50		20	1	10		500	1	100	10	200	1	10	800	50
1150				1340											31				1672								
of the				scribes											and				pharisees								

λ	ε	γ	ο	ν	τ	ε	ς		δ	ι	δ	α	σ	κ	α	λ	ε		θ	ε	λ	ο	μ	ε	ν
30	5	3	70	50	300	5	200		4	10	4	1	200	20	1	30	5		9	5	30	70	40	5	50
663									275										209						
demanded									rabbi										we wish						

α	π	ο		σ	ο	ν		σ	η	μ	ε	ι	ο	ν		ι	δ	ε	ι	ν
1	80	70		200	70	50		200	8	40	5	10	70	50		10	4	5	10	50
151				320				383								79				
from				you				miraculous sign								personal				

VERSE 38

Ο		δ	ε		α	π	ο	κ	ρ	ι	θ	ε	ι	ς		ε	ι	π	ε	ν		α	υ	τ	ο	ι	ς
70		4	5		1	80	70	20	100	10	9	5	10	200		5	10	80	5	50		1	400	300	70	10	200
70		9			505											150						981					
he		but			answered											saying						himself					

γ	ε	ν	ε	α		π	ο	ν	η	ρ	α		κ	α	ι		μ	ο	ι	χ	α	λ	ι	ς
3	5	50	5	1		80	70	50	8	100	1		20	1	10		40	70	10	600	1	30	10	200
64						309							31				961							
generation						evil							and				unfaithful							

σ	η	μ	ε	ι	ο	ν		ε	π	ι	ζ	η	τ	ε	ι		κ	α	ι		σ	η	μ	ε	ι	ο	ν
200	8	40	5	10	70	50		5	80	10	7	8	300	5	10		20	1	10		200	8	40	5	10	70	50
383								425									31				383						
miraculous sign								seeks									but				miraculous sign						

ο	υ		δ	ο	θ	η	σ	ε	τ	α	ι		α	υ	τ	η		ε	ι		μ	η		τ	ο
70	400		4	70	9	8	200	5	300	1	10		1	400	300	8		5	10		40	8		300	70
470			607										709					15			48			370	
no			shall be given										it					if only			not			the	

σ	η	μ	ε	ι	ο	ν		Ι	ω	ν	α		τ	ο	υ		π	ρ	ο	φ	η	τ	ο	υ
200	8	40	5	10	70	50		10	800	50	1		300	70	400		80	100	70	500	8	300	70	400
383								861					770				1528							
sign								Jona					(of) the				prophet							

VERSE 39

ω	σ	π	ε	ρ		γ	α	ρ		η	ν		ι	ω	ν	α	ς		ε	ν		τ	η
800	200	80	5	100		3	1	100		8	50		10	800	50	1	200		5	50		300	8
1185						104				58			1061						55			308	
as						indeed				was			Jonas						in			the	

κ	ο	ι	γ	ι	α		τ	ο	υ		κ	η	τ	ο	υ	ς
20	70	10	3	10	1		300	70	400		20	8	300	70	400	200
114							770				998					
belly							of the				whale					

τ	ρ	ε	ι	ς		η	μ	ε	ρ	α	ς		κ	α	ι		τ	ρ	ε	ι	ς		ν	υ	κ	τ	α	ς
300	100	5	10	200		8	40	5	100	1	200		20	1	10		300	100	5	10	200		50	400	20	300	1	200
615						354							31				615						971					
three						days							and				three						nights					

ο	υ	τ	ω	ς		ε	σ	τ	α	ι		ο		υ	ι	ο	ς		τ	ο	υ
70	400	300	800	200		5	200	300	1	10		70		400	10	70	200		300	70	400
1770						516						70		680					770		
in the same way						will be						the		son					of the		

α	ν	θ	ρ	ω	π	ο	υ		ε	ν		τ	η		κ	α	ρ	δ	ι	α		τ	η	ς		γ	η	ς
1	50	9	100	800	80	70	400		5	50		300	8		20	1	100	4	10	1		300	8	200		3	8	200
1510									55			308			136							508				211		
man									in			the			heart							of the				earth		

τ	ρ	ε	ι	ς		η	μ	ε	ρ	α	ς		κ	α	ι		τ	ρ	ε	ι	ς		ν	υ	κ	τ	α	ς
300	100	5	10	200		8	40	5	100	1	200		20	1	10		300	100	5	10	200		50	400	20	300	1	200
615						354							31				615						971					
three						days							and				three						nights					

VERSE 40

Source: Nestle-Aland Greek-English New Testament, *Deutsche Bibelgesellschaft, Stuttgart, 1990.*

APPENDIX 3

THE *VESICA PISCIS* AND TIME

It can be shown that the element of time is *implicitly* present in the *vesica piscis*. St. Matthew's version relates the circle of Jonas to the square of the Son of man, and measures 1061 units in width and 1592 units in height. First, the numeric value of the Greek word ημερασ, meaning "days" is **354**; and the width of the diagram (i.e. 1061 or 1062 units) is *three* times the number 354. That is:

354 x 3 = 1062

The *width* of the diagram is therefore symbolically equivalent to 3 "days". See Figure A3-1 (page 184).

Second, the total height of the diagram is measured as the radius of the Jonas's circle plus the height of the Son's square. That is:

1061 + 531 = 1592

The number **1592** is virtually equivalent to the numeric value of "three nights" (i.e. 1586). The *height* of the diagram therefore corresponds to "three nights". See Figure A3-1 again.

Hence, the two phrases "Jonas in the belly of the whale" and "the Son of man in the heart of the earth" can be taken to refer to a diagram involving a circle and a square (or, two circles and two squares encapsulating a *vesica piscis*) whose total boundary is described by the term "three days and three nights". Furthermore, if the width is divided by the height, the result is a number that has already been discussed. It is the number of the active creative power in the universe, namely **666**. That is:

1061 / 1592 = 0.666

In other words, any construction of the *vesica piscis* references not just the active energy of creation but also the passage of time.

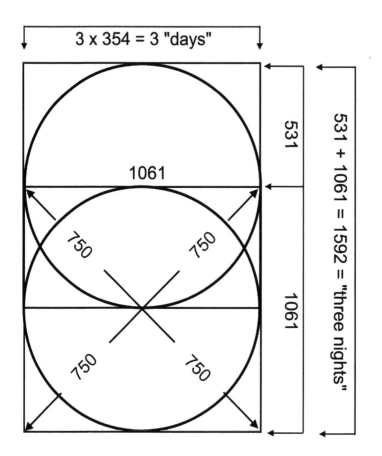

FIGURE A3-1: 3 "DAYS" AND "THREE NIGHTS"

APPENDIX 4

THE STRUCTURE OF WILLIAM GANN'S *TUNNEL THRU THE AIR*

Chapter number	Chapter pages		Number of pages	Proportion of total (%)
	Start	End		
1	1	5	5	3
2	6	17	12	6
3	18	34	17	8
4	35	49	15	11
5	50	61	12	14
6	62	74	13	17
7	75	84	10	19
8	85	89	5	22
9	90	104	15	25
10	105	114	10	28
11	115	125	11	31
12	126	155	30	33
13	156	170	15	36
14	171	186	16	39
15	187	194	8	42
16	195	211	17	44
17	212	217	6	47
18	218	221	4	50
19	222	236	15	53
20	237	249	13	56
21	250	256	7	58
22	257	261	5	61
23	262	268	7	64
24	269	275	7	67
25	276	289	14	69
26	290	299	10	72
27	300	312	13	75
28	313	324	12	78
29	325	337	13	81
30	338	356	19	83

Chapter number	Chapter pages		Number of pages	Proportion of total (%)
	Start	End		
31	357	374	18	86
32	375	381	7	89
33	382	391	10	92
34 ·	392	401	10	94
35	402	406	5	97
36	407	418	12	100

Source: Financial Guardian Publishing, New York, 1927. Reprinted Lambert-Gann Publishing, Washington, USA, 1990.

APPENDIX 5

THE STRUCTURE OF GEORGE GURDJIEFF'S *BEELZEBUB'S TALES*

Chapter	Start	Finish	Pages	Changes (%)	Reverse chapter	Changes (%)
1	3	50	48		48	400.00
2	51	55	5	-89.58	47	-8.33
3	56	65	10	100.00	46	-25.00
4	66	69	4	-60.00	45	-38.46
5	70	72	3	-25.00	44	-59.38
6	73	75	3	0.00	43	-53.28
7	76	78	3	0.00	42	191.49
8	79	80	2	-33.33	41	-18.97
9	81	86	6	200.00	40	-15.94
10	87	93	7	16.67	39	38.00
11	94	97	4	-42.86	38	61.29
12	98	102	5	25.00	37	933.33
13	103	105	3	-40.00	36	0.00
14	106	108	3	0.00	35	-95.45
15	109	120	12	300.00	34	450.00
16	121	133	13	8.33	33	-42.86
17	134	148	15	15.38	32	-38.24
18	149	176	28	86.67	31	-54.67
19	177	206	30	7.14	30	108.33
20	207	226	20	-33.33	29	56.52
21	227	251	25	25.00	28	-4.17
22	252	267	16	-36.00	27	84.62
23	268	314	47	193.75	26	116.67
24	315	346	32	-31.91	25	-81.25
25	347	352	6	-81.25	24	-31.91
26	353	365	13	116.67		
27	366	389	24	84.62		
28	390	412	23	-4.17		
29	413	448	36	56.52		
30	449	523	75	108.33		
31	524	557	34	-54.67		
32	558	578	21	-38.24		

Chapter	Start	Finish	Pages	Changes (%)	Reverse chapter	Changes (%)
33	579	590	12	-42.86		
34	591	656	66	450.00		
35	657	659	3	-95.45		
36	660	662	3	0.00		
37	663	693	31	933.33		
38	694	743	50	61.29		
39	744	812	69	38.00		
40	813	870	58	-15.94		
41	871	917	47	-18.97		
42	918	1054	137	191.49		
43	1055	1118	64	-53.28		
44	1119	1144	26	-59.38		
45	1145	1160	16	-38.46		
46	1161	1172	12	-25.00		
47	1173	1183	11	-8.33		
48	1184	1238	55	400.00		

Source: Fifth Impression, Routledge & Kegan Paul, London, 1967.

APPENDIX 6

THE STRUCTURE OF THE FIRST 28 CHAPTERS IN *BEELZEBUB'S TALES*

The number of pages in each of the first 28 chapters can be found in Appendix 5. Figure A6-1 plots the chapter number against both the number of pages (lower section) and the percentage change in the number of pages (upper section). At first glance the pattern appears somewhat random, but the underlying order comes into focus both when the lower part of the diagram is compared with Figure 10-1 of Chapter 10, and when the upper part of the diagram is split into three equal sections.

The lower part of the diagram shows that, from the eighth chapter onwards, there is a rising five-wave pattern, with the fourth wave consisting of three sections, denoted a-b-c. The pattern is essentially similar to one derived from the whole of *Beelzebub's Tales* and shown in Figure 10-1. They both show a rising pattern, including a three-phase fourth wave. If we continue to assume that the page and chapter structure of the book was carefully designed, then the similarities are not accidental.

More importantly, however, is the fact that the upper part of the diagram can be seen as showing a sequence of three enneagram-type cycles: the first pattern is a left-biased cycle, whose wave b makes a new high; the second pattern is a centred cycle with an impulsive wave 3; and the third cycle is slightly left-biased, but has a muted finish.

If we put these two features together, it is possible that Mr. Gurdjieff was pointing to extra dimensions to the enneagram and the associated law of vibration. An impulsive movement in any system is not only modulated by cycles, but the latter also appear in batches of three.[1] From one perspective, this is a natural deduction from the presence of three inner octaves in a complete outer octave. From another perspective, it implies that each sub-cycle will be influenced by developments in the higher-level cycle (or trend) of which it is a part; and that activity arising within each lower level cycle will, in turn, contribute to the evolution of the higher-level cycle.

---

[1] We thus have a situation where an apparent five-phase impulse movement is actually the result of three contiguous enneagram-type fluctuations placed around a rising trend. This may help to reconcile Ralph Elliott's five-phase Wave Principle with the idea of triadic cycles.

Just as with Mr. Gann's pattern, Mr. Gurdjieff's triadic pattern can be found in data series of collective human behaviour. Figure A6-2 shows the locus of producer confidence in Germany. Such confidence is here represented by a business climate index that is calculated by the German *Ifo Institute* from monthly survey data. The broad oscillations are tracked by the percentage deviation from a 10-year moving average of the data. Again, the parallels are compelling. Mr. Gurdjieff's pattern predicts three cycle beats with a common periodicity, and this is exactly what emerges in Germany after 1982. Three beats of a 10-year cycle – i.e. 1982-93, 1993-2003 and 2003-12(?) – constitute an overarching 30-year cycle. What is particularly noticeable in Germany's case is the first cycle's surge in optimism just prior to, and then immediately after, the fall of the Berlin Wall in 1989; the second cycle's *three waveness* after the recession of 1991-92; and, eventually, the third cycle's surge in optimism in 2003-07, followed by the panic of 2008.

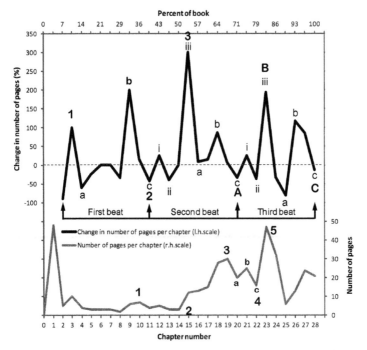

FIGURE A6-1: THREE PHASES IN A COMPLETED CYCLE

There would, of course, be some difficulties in using Mr. Gurdjieff's pattern as a blueprint for all cycles. For example, Mr. Gurdjieff's pattern seems to have reversed the first and second cycles of Mr. Gann's pattern. It may be that Life itself indicates which of the two patterns has to be used. In addition, some of the short-term fluctuations have different amplitudes to what might have been expected. Even so, the timings of the important moves are very precise.

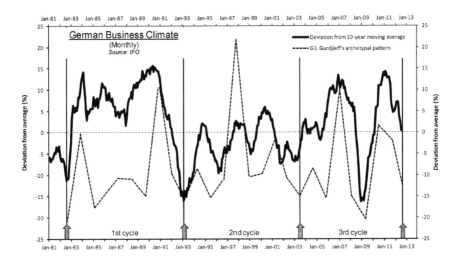

FIGURE A6-2: MR. GURDJIEFF'S PATTERN OF VIBRATION; GERMAN BUSINESS CLIMATE

APPENDIX 7

THE 1940-45/46 INTER-CYCLE HIATUS

Figure A7-1 shows the momentum of US industrial production between 1921 and 1946. Data is monthly and momentum is shown as a 12-month rate of change. As already mentioned, monthly data is only available from 1919, but it is nevertheless placed on a chart that starts from 1911. In this way, it is possible to show momentum in the same context as that shown in Figure 15-5 of Chapter 15.

As presented, output momentum follows the general pattern indicated by Mr. Gann's inner octave blueprint. However, momentum is much more dynamic than the blueprint in 1921-22, and is much weaker for longer in 1930-32. It is important to note that the process ends in 1940. It is followed by a brief rise into 1941 and then by a very sharp fall into early 1946. On this analysis, the evolution of the inner octave pattern does appear to end on time, but the environment created by the exigencies of war meant that another big fall was still needed during the inter-cycle interruption.

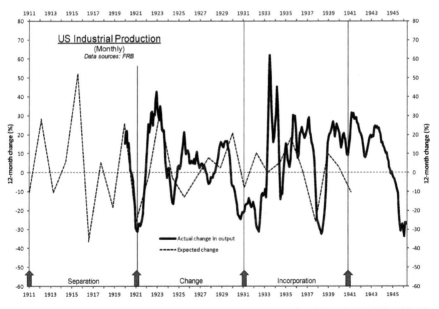

FIGURE A7-1: MOMENTUM OF US INDUSTRIAL PRODUCTION; 12-MONTH CHANGES, 1911-46

APPENDIX 8

A NOTE ON WILLIAM GANN'S *THE MAGIC WORD*

In 1950, Mr Gann published a paperback entitled *The Magic Word*. The parallels with *Tunnel* are unmistakeable: *The Magic Word* includes the instruction that it is to be read "at least three times over a period of three weeks"; and is embellished with biblical quotations, aphorisms and blank pages. The similarities suggest that we can apply the same analytic techniques to *The Magic Word* as were applied to *Tunnel*. Even so, given the subject matter of the book, any conclusions can only be regarded as conjecture.

At a straightforward level, the book is an instruction manual for meditation. It advocates a mantra using the seven-letter/three-syllable word "Jehovah"; it recommends visualisation techniques; and it encourages attention to breathing. The full-page diagrams, which are constructed from triangles, circles and words, can be used for contemplation. Such techniques didn't really enter popular consciousness until the 1980s. Mr. Gann's ideas were therefore significantly ahead of their time.

At a more subtle level – and in its original format[2] – the book contains much more information than might initially be apparent. The first clue comes in the shape and size of the book. It is 8-11/16 inches wide and 11-1/8 inches high, which makes it strangely large for a metaphysical text. Even the ratio between the width and the height (0.78:1) seems not to have any specific meaning. However, when account is taken of the size of the back as well as the front, and an allowance is made for the width of the spine, the whole cover forms a Golden Rectangle, 0.62:1. It looks ordinary, but open it up and something else appears!

When the book *is* opened, what immediately becomes apparent is that it includes a number of pages that contain only diagrams, a significant number of blank pages and a very large number of biblical quotations. The second clue to additional information, therefore, is that – like *Tunnel* – *The Magic Word* has been padded out. The book is actually divided into two parts. The first part contains 16 unnumbered pages: eight pages from the start to the last blank page

---

[2] Revisions that have been made to *The Magic Word* for recent publication have involved not just a change to the structure of the book but also considerable alterations to the text. This completely eradicates the hidden message(s) that Mr. Gann was trying to convey and – in my opinion – dishonours his work.

before the introduction; and eight pages covering the introduction, the index and the blank pages after the index. In fact, there are eight blank pages in the first 16 pages. In effect, the first section therefore contains a threefold reference to the completed octave, with two being explicit and one – the blank pages – being implicit.

One interpretation is that the explicit double octave implies the completion of a whole Gann pattern in its dyadic form, and that the implicit octave references the influence of other, unseen, forces. This, in turn, suggests that something – i.e. psychological work or stage of life – has to be complete before the processes alluded to in *The Magic Word* can be activated.

These processes are referenced in the second – or main – part of the book, which consists of 12 chapters. Moreover – and unlike in the first part of the book – each page is numbered. This means that the number of pages in each chapter can be plotted against the chapter number. When this is done, a very specific pattern emerges (see Figure A8-1). The first half of the pattern shows a rise and fall that obviously resonates with the first half of the pattern found in *Tunnel*. It is actually much simpler than the version in *Tunnel*, but it contains a clear three-wave advance followed by a dramatic collapse. Like the original, the third wave reaches a peak one-third of the way into the pattern and the low occurs about half way into the pattern.

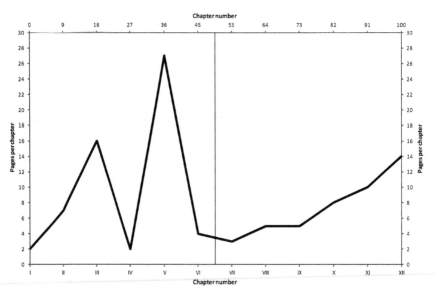

FIGURE A8-1: PAGES PER CHAPTER IN *THE MAGIC WORD*

These similarities not only support the methodologies used in *Tunnel*, but also suggest that presence of the pattern in *The Magic Word* was intentional and meaningful. This, in turn, suggests that the three-wave advance and single-wave contraction may reference a learning process that involves an initial move to the limits of an unchanged system, followed by a collapse as the system has to adjust itself to irreversibly changed circumstances.

What is significantly different about the overall pattern in *The Magic Word*, however, is that the second half of the configuration shows a persistent rise, rather than a three-wave rise followed by a fall. In other words, the pattern doesn't have an explicit termination point. This may well be an allusion to the results of meditation – at least as experienced by Mr. Gann. The fact, therefore, that the pattern leaves Chapter 12 (with its implicit reference to the heavens) on a rising trend hints either at the success of his personal spiritual endeavours or at least at his expectations regarding those endeavours. This interpretation is consistent with the fact that the last three pages of the book are left blank. This could be a reference to *The Void* of ancient wisdom or to the *quantum vacuum* of modern science.

Hence, the pattern in *The Magic Word* could be interpreted as a process of development that:

1. Starts when the person is ready (the double octave in the first part of the book);

2. Involves a period of intense effort, followed by a collapse of internal psychological structures (the first half of the diagram); and

3. Proceeds steadily into some sense of the numinous (the second half of the diagram).

These ideas may seem very idealistic. But there are three points that suggest they may have been part of the intended message: in 1950, the ideas were completely new; they were being referenced at a time when general religious opinion would have been overtly hostile; and they are absolutely consistent with Mr. Gann's belief in the influence of a Power greater than himself.

The Magic Word almost certainly reflects Mr. Gann's experience of some form of *hidden* Christianity. And the diagram buried within it is consistent with – and therefore validates the idea of – the behavioural pattern concealed in *The Tunnel Thru The Air*.

Bibliography

The Holy Bible (Authorised (King James), English Revised Version, 1881)

The Ticker and Investment Digest (December 1909)

Akerlof, George A. and Shiller, Robert J., *Animal Spirits: How Human Psychology Drives the Economy, and Why it Matters for Global Capitalism* (Princeton University Press, 2009)

Aland, Kurt, et al., *Greek-English New Testament* (Deutsche Bibelgesellschaft, Stuttgart, 1981)

Bandura, Albert, *Social Learning Theory* (General Learning Press, New York, 1977)

Bateson, Gregory, *Mind and Nature – An Essential Unity* (Wildwood House, London, 1979)

Bennett, John G., *Enneagram Studies* (Coombe Springs Press, Masham, 1974)

Bennett, John G., *Gurdjieff: Making a New World* (Harper & Row, New York, 1976)

Bentov, Itzhak, *Stalking the Wild Pendulum* (Wildwood House, London, 1978)

Bohm, David, *Coherence and the Implicate Order* (Routledge & Kegan Paul, London, 1980)

Bond, Bligh and Lea, Simcox. *Gematria* (Basil Blackwell, Oxford, 1917)

le Bon, Gustave, *Psychologie des Foules*. Reprinted as *The Crowd* (Macmillan, New York, 1922)

Campbell, Robert, *Fisherman's Guide: A Systems Approach to Creativity and Organization* (Shambhala, Boston (Ma.), 1985)

Coveney Peter and Highfield, Roger, *The Arrow of Time* (W.H. Allen, London, 1990)

Cowan, Bradley F., *Pentagonal Time Cycle Theory* (Private publication, USA, 2009)

Davis, Joseph H., 'An Annual Index of US Production, 1790-1915', *Quarterly Journal of Economics* (November 2004)

Dyer, John, et al, 'Consensus decision making in human crowds', *Animal Behaviour* 75:2 (February 2008)

Easton, Alexander (Ed.) and Emery, Nathan (Ed.), *The Cognitive Neuroscience of Social Behaviour* (Psychology Press, London, 2005)

Elliott, Ralph Nelson, *The Wave Principle* (Elliott, New York, 1938)

Fama, Eugene, 'Random Walks in Stock Prices', *Financial Analysts Journal* (September/October, 1965)

Fideler, David, *Jesus Christ, Sun of God: Ancient Cosmology and Early Christian Symbolism* (Quest, Wheaton (Il.), 1993)

Gann, William D., *The Tunnel Thru The Air* (Financial Guardian Publishing, New York, 1927)

Gann, William D., *Supply and Demand Letter: 1929 Annual Stock Forecast* (W. D. Gann Scientific Service Inc, New York, 23 November 1928)

Gann, William D., *45 Years in Wall Street* (Library of Gann Publishing Co., Pomeroy (Wa.), 1949)

Gann, William D., *The Magic Word* (Library of Gann Publishing Co, Pomeroy (Wa.), 1950)

Gimbel, Theo, *Form, Sound, Colour and Healing* (C.W. Daniel Company Ltd, Saffron Walden (Essex), 1987)

Gurdjieff, George I., *All and Everything: An Objectively Impartial Criticism of the Life of Man,* or *Beelzebub's Tales to His Grandson* (Routledge & Kegan Paul, London, 1950)

Hayes, Michael, *The Infinite Harmony: Musical Structures in Science and Theology* (Weidenfeld and Nicolson, London, 1994)

Hebb, Donald, *The Organisation of Behaviour* (John Wiley, New York, 1949)

Jordan, D.W. and Smith, P., *Nonlinear Ordinary Differential Equations* (Oxford University Press, Oxford, UK, 1977)

Keynes, John M., 'The General Theory of Employment', *Quarterly Journal of Economics* (February 1937)

Keller, David, (Ed.), *Breakthroughs in Technical Analysis* (Bloomberg Press, New York, 2007)

Koestler, Arthur, *Janus: A Summing Up* (Hutchinson, London, 1978)

Kuhn, Thomas, *The Theory of Scientific Revolutions* (University of Chicago Press, Chicago (Il.), 1962)

Laszlo, Ervin, *Science and the Re-enchantment of the Cosmos: The Rise of the Integral Vision of Reality* (Inner Traditions, Rochester (Vt.), USA, 2006)

Lawlor, Robert, *Sacred Geometry: Philosophy and Practice* (Thames and Hudson, London, 1982)

Lebergott, Stanley, 'Wages and Working Conditions', *The Concise Encyclopedia of Economics* (Library of Economics and Liberty, Indianapolis (In.), 1993)

Levarie, Sigmund and Levy, Ernst, *Tone: A Study in Musical Acoustics* (Kent State University Press (Kent), 1980)

Livio, Mario, *The Golden Ratio* (Review, London, 2002)

Lucas, Robert, *Models of Business Cycles* (Basil Blackwell, Oxford, 1987)

Mandelbrot, Benoit, *The Fractal Geometry of Nature* (Freeman, New York, 1977)

Malkiel, Burton G., *A Random Walk Down Wall Street* (W.W.Norton & Co., New York, 1973)

Michell, John *City of Revelation: On the Proportions and Symbolic Numbers of the Cosmic Temple* (Garnstone Press Ltd., London, 1972)

Michell, John, *The New View Over Atlantis* (Thames and Hudson, London, 1983)

Michell, John, *The Dimensions of Paradise* (Thames and Hudson, London, 1988)

Mills, Henry, *Teaching and Training* (Macmillan, London, 1967)

Moran, Jim, *The Wonders of Magic Squares* (Vintage Books, New York, 1982)

Mouravieff, Boris, *Gnosis* (Praxis Institute Press, Newbury (Ma.), 1992)

Murchie, Guy, *Music of the Spheres* (Dover Publications, New York, 1961)

Muth, John F., 'Rational Expectations and the Theory of Price Movements', *Econometrica* (July 1961)

Naranjo, Claudio, *Ennea-Type Structures* (Gateways/IDHHB inc, Nevada City (Ca.), 1990)

Neumann, Erich, *Depth Psychology and a New Ethic* (Shambhala, Boston (Ma.), 1990)

Nott, Charles S., *Journey Through This World* (Routledge & Kegan Paul, London, 1969)

Ouspensky, Pyotr D., *In Search of the Miraculous: Fragments of an Unknown Teaching* (Harcourt, Brace & World, New York, 1949)

Plummer, Tony, *Forecasting Financial Markets (4th Ed.)* (Kogan Page, London, 2003)

Plummer, Tony, *Forecasting Financial Markets (6th Ed.)* (Kogan Page, London, 2010)

Prechter, Robert R., (Ed.), *The Major Works of R.N. Elliott* (New Classics Library, New York, 1980)

De Santillana, Giorgio and von Dechend, Hertha, *Hamlet's Mill: An Essay on Myth and the Frame of Time* (Gambit, Boston, 1969)

Shakespeare, William, *Hamlet*

Schonfield, Hugh, *The Essene Odyssey* (Element, Shaftesbury (Dorset), 1984)

Schonfield, Hugh, *The Original New Testament: A Radical Reinterpretation and New Translation* (Waterstone & Co, London, 1985)

Skidelsky, Robert, 'The Relevance of Keynes', *Cambridge Journal of Economics* (January 2011)

Smith, Russell A., *Gurdjieff: Cosmic Secrets* (The Dog, Sanger (Tx.), 1993)

Tarnas, Richard, *Cosmos and Psyche: Intimations of a New World View* (Plume, New York, 2007)

Ulansey, David, *The Origins of the Mithraic Mysteries* (Oxford University Press, London, 1989)

Walker, Kenneth, *A Study of Gurdjieff's Teaching* (Jonathan Cape, London, 1957)

Wellbeloved, Sophia, *Gurdjieff, Astrology & Beelzebub's Tales* (Abintra Books, Aurora (Or.), 2002)

Whitehead, Alfred North, *Process and Reality* (Free Press, New York, 1969)

Wilber, Ken, *Eye to Eye: The Quest for a New Paradigm* (Shambhala Publications, Boston (Ma), 1983)

Wilber, Ken, *Up from Eden: A Transpersonal View of Human Evolution* (Routledge & Kegan Paul, London, 1983)

Wilber, Ken, (Ed.), *The Holographic Paradigm* (Shambhala, Boston (Ma.), 1985)

Wilber, Ken, *The Atman Project* (Quest Books, Wheaton (Ill.), 1989)

Wilson, Colin, *G. I. Gurdjieff: The War Against Sleep* (The Aquarian Press, Wellingborough, 1986)

Wilson, Louise L., *Catalogue of Cycles* (Foundation for the Study of Cycles, Pittsburgh (Pa.), 1964)

Yau, Shing-Tung and Nadis, Steve, *The Shape of Inner Space: String Theory and the Geometry of the Universe's Hidden Dimensions* (Basic Books, New York, 2010)

Zukav, Gary, *The Dancing Wu Li Masters: An Overview of the New Physics* (William Morrow, New York, 1979)

Index